Worship as Community Drama

Worship as Community Drama

Introduction to Liturgy Evaluation

Pierre Hegy

FOREWORD BY
Bruce T. Morrill

WIPF *&* STOCK · Eugene, Oregon

Contents

Foreword

CHRISTIAN LITURGY, SUCH AS the mass of the Roman Rite, only exists in practice. However much theology about the Eucharist hierarchs, academicians, catechists, or others of the faithful may generate, the fact is that such theories—scholarly or popular, historically informed or ideologically synchronic—must return to the symbolic act. For liturgy, being derived from the Greek *leitourgia*, is an *ergon*, a work (*-ourgia*), a ritual action. Written, taught, or preached theologies about liturgy both depend upon and influence, for better or worse, actual celebrations of the rites. This anthropological, and thus ecclesiological, fact has increasingly come to influence academic theology about the sacraments, for which the overwhelmingly predominant subject in Roman Catholicism is the Eucharist or mass. The pace, nonetheless, has been slow due to a lack of theoretically sound, field-based studies of the mass in motion.

The Second Vatican Council's Constitution on the Sacred Liturgy, bringing to official fruition a century's worth of ecumenical liturgical scholarship and experimental pastoral practice, decreed that "all the faithful should be led to that fully conscious and active participation in liturgical celebrations which is demanded by the very nature of the liturgy." In order that bishops and priests might foster the "full and active participation by all the people," and thereby serve the council's priority for the liturgical reform and renewal, the Constitution also mandated that seminary education not only include compulsory courses on the history, theology, and pastoral practice of liturgy, but also that instruction in all subjects (e.g. sacred Scripture, theology, ethics, etc.) include treatment of their connections to the liturgy. How that has worked out over the ensuing half century has largely been a matter of the particular ideology of the priesthood driving the mission of any given seminary, forming clerics' concepts of sacramental symbols and power in the classroom and chapel. To my observation, moreover, a primary source of liturgical formation for the most recent generation or two of clerics has been video footage or direct experience of papal masses, especially those at the Vatican. Images, not historical information and theological arguments, have shaped the liturgical postures, gestures, emphases, and, indeed, policies of the current bishops and their priests.

Meanwhile, at least in the North Atlantic church-world, serious historical scholarship and the enlistment of modern philosophical resources has generated on university faculties, in scholarly journals, and through youth and adult educational programs a far less clerically dominated theology of sacraments, especially baptism and Eucharist. The degree of sustained success along those lines and in those sectors is a topic whose analysis exceeds what can be considered in a brief foreword to a book. What I wish, however, to note is how nearly all of the theological textbooks function on the basis of *ideas* about what the sacraments *mean* and how, from any particular author or publisher's philosophical, theological, or pedagogical perspective, their celebrations instill such meaning in the faithful-participants. Here is where theology *about* liturgy and sacraments meets formidable (if not, at times, seemingly insuperable) limits. In addition to the clash of cultures between Roman Catholic clerics and the majority of people in their charge (whether the latter be consumerist individualism or centuries-old ethnic customs), the very practical nature of liturgical performance itself resists the theologies of liturgy and sacraments that scholars largely generate.

The great challenge for sacramental-liturgical theology seeking to serve the reform and renewal of the church is to find adequate methods for engaging theory and practice, history and theology, context and text, such that people—clergy and laity—can get a better sense of what has been, is, and might yet become the real, physically and socially embodied encounter with Christ in the celebration of the church's rites. Pierre Hégy, drawing on an impressive span of participant-observations of sacramental celebrations across multiple contemporary social, ethnic, and ecclesial contexts, has enlisted one apt sociological theory to guide a rich comparison and contrast of real-life liturgical worship. Along this journey, through such varied socio-political-liturgical sites as various US parishes, the Cathedral of Notre Dame in Paris, the Vatican, and communities in sub-Saharan Africa, Professor Hégy enlists an array of auxiliary social-scientific and ecclesiological theories, while also regularly tipping his hand to show his own agenda for church-liturgical reform. Readers eager with eyes to see and ears to hear such rich descriptions and analyses of the actual workings of worship—theology in practice—may find themselves, like me, regretful in having to put the book down along the way or in the

end. They can expect, nonetheless, to end up equipped with new insights
and information for contributing to the advancement of liturgical, and
thus church, renewal.

Bruce T. Morrill, SJ

Edward A. Malloy Professor of Roman Catholic Studies
Vanderbilt University, Nashville, Tennessee

Introduction

And Acknowledgements

BRITISH ROYAL WEDDINGS—OF PRINCE Charles and Diana, Prince Williams and Kate, and more recently Prince Harry and Meghan—present to the world a microcosmic view of the British society and its religion. More generally, weddings and funerals are community dramas expressing the faith, emotions, and social roles of the participants, and so are bar mitzvahs, first communions, quinceañeras, and all Sunday services. Even when worship is performed by a minister acting alone in front of an assembly, there may be at work the drama of the passive silence of the people in the pews. Any worship service reflects the collaboration and tensions between the clergy and the assembly, the joys and sufferings of the community, and the common quest for divine blessings.

The title *Worship as Community Drama* paraphrases Durkheim's view that religion is essentially social: "Religious representations are collective representations which express collective realities,"[1] and these "collective presentations" express a people's "collective consciousness." In short, religion is a social creation rather than a psychic projection as claimed by Durkheim's contemporaries Herbert Spencer and James Frazer, or more recently by Sigmund Freud. It is true that ritual scripts are usually the creations of liturgical committees in centralized churches, but in liturgical productions, whether Catholic, Protestant, Jewish, or Muslim, the ritual performances express the common beliefs and practices, and the emotions and moral values of the participants. This is why, according to Durkheim, religious rituals—the performed rituals, not the ritual scripts—are collective manifestations. To accept Durkheim's view of religion as social representation does not imply that one accepts his reductionist view of religion as nothing but a social production. Nor do we accept today the extreme opposition between religion as

---

1. Durkheim, *Elementary Forms*, 10.

social production and religion as individual psychological quest; religion is social-psychological, being both institutional and psychic.

By studying local collective representations, that is, the particular beliefs, practices, and values of a given community, are we not turning away from the scientific search for universal laws and patterns? Not necessarily. The study of local forms of worship should lead the researcher to move from the local to the universal; this is what anthropology and participant observation have been doing for ages. The last chapter of this book is on vision and mystagogy. What local research about worship should lead to, according to this research, is the discovery of sociological visions and mystagogical insights—far more than what most sociological research is often able to achieve. Thus the study of local worship should lead to specific patterns of universal collective representations, and this is what I found in each of the local worship studies presented here.

Worship is an essential part of all major religions, yet there is little research about it. Social scientists (mainly anthropologists) have investigated many non-Christian rituals but seldom Christian ones. This work on liturgical practices hopes to reverse this trend.

I define rituals as interactions between participants and also between participants and God (the "sacred" in the Judeo-Christian tradition). This view is similar to defining church services as encounters with God, or as a personal relationship with Jesus Christ. "Interaction" is a common term in the social sciences, while "encounter" and "relationship with God" are more common terms in religious parlance.

Although there are various approaches to ritual analysis, I have selected the interaction model of Randall Collins, who included in his model the basic Durkheimian dimensions of sacredness, emotions, moral values, and community organization, but Collins himself never applied it to religion. The model consists of eight variables applicable to all types of interaction, for instance a date, a job interview, or a Sunday service. These variables are, in the form of questions, (1) what can I learn in advance about my date or about a given Sunday service? (2) What did actually happen during the date, the interview, or during that service? (3) Did I feel emotionally moved, positively or negatively? (4) How close did I feel during the date, or how close to neighbors and God during the ritual? When the interaction is over, one should interview the pastor and staff members in order to further ask, in the case of worship, (5) what did I learn from them about leadership and church growth? (6) What values do people have in common and how much do they agree? (7) What type of relationship is likely to prevail in future dates, or what is the prevailing ecclesiology in the church just visited? And (8), as a general conclusion to the previous questions: do I want to continue this relationship? Or, will I go back to this church or not? This model will be explained in chapter 1.

The eight Sunday services discussed in chapters 2 to 9 are examples presented for the sake of worship analysis. Two are quite ordinary and two are rather exceptional; they are examples rather than ritual models to emulate.

Worship analysis should lead to sociological and theological insights by going through the eight steps of Collins's empirical investigation. Each chapter will focus on a different theoretical issue, but each issue could be applied to all other chapters. Thus the relationship between faith and culture (in chapter 3), and segmentation in liturgies (in chapter 4) can be applied to all worship services.

Chapter 2 looks at TV masses, which involve, besides a priest, a token altar server and no assembly. Chapter 3 discusses the relationship between faith and culture displayed during pontifical masses in the cathedral of Notre Dame in the city of Paris. Chapter 4 gets into worship segmentation, which happens when various participants in a worship activity perform independently of one another. Such tends to be the case in papal masses where the choir, the body of prelates, the assembly, and the officiating pontiff tend to perform independently.

Chapter 5 introduces the evaluation of worship using the research findings of the Willow Creek Church. In light of this research, I describe three parishes, two that are ordinary (chapter 5) and one that is dynamic (chapter 6.) Chapter 7 moves beyond corporate growth to deal with individual development as presented by James Fowler in his classic work, *Stages of Faith*. His analysis is applied to an evangelical/Pentecostal church in which it is commonly believed that individual salvation will automatically lead to social transformation. In chapter 8, I investigate liturgical creativity at the St. Sabina church and conclude that, even within the confines of rigid Catholic regulations, there are really few limits to worship creativity. Chapter 9, on the Zairean Rite of the Democratic Republic of Congo, brings together various themes developed in the book, using the thesis of *lex orandi lex credendi* discussed by Aidan Kavanagh in his treatise, *On Liturgical Theology*. In the concluding chapter I emphasize the need for a rigorous methodology, insightful theory, and mystagogy.

This book will hopefully be the first step in a long series of empirical studies of worship. By all accounts, Sunday worship is the most important expression of Western religiosity. Empirical research could be greatly instrumental in its improvement.

This book would not have been possible without the help of many contributors. First of all, many thanks to the pastors and staff members of the various churches presented in this work. They all welcomed me as if I were one of their own. I wish I could give their names and recognize them publicly. I also owe a special debt to colleagues who have read one or several chapters of this book. They were very kind for what were mostly rough drafts, which, in several instances, had to be discarded. My special thanks to Rev. James Bretzke, SJ, now at Fordham University; Anton Jacobs, teaching at the Divine Word College; Nathan Kollar from St. John Fisher College; Michael Lawler from Creighton University; Michael McCallion from the Sacred Heart Major Seminary; Anthony Pogorelc from St. Mary's University in San Antonio; Rev. Thomas Splain, SJ, parish pastor, and Joseph Weiss from Boston College.

Summary Presentation
of Worship Analysis

IN THE NEXT FEW pages I want to give a summary of the steps followed in my worship analysis. These steps will be further explained in chapter 1 and followed in each of the following chapters. For the sake of clarity in this project I want to begin with a short summary.

Worship is understood here as a communitarian interaction with God rather than just an individual ritual. There is a long tradition of interaction analysis, applied to all kinds of social situations but seldom to religion. I have selected the interaction model of Randall Collins, which posits that any interaction is part of a chain that over time leads to an increase or a decrease in the relationship. The process can be analyzed in eight steps, the first four being merely descriptive, and the following four analytical. Here is his model as I use it:

Interaction processes: description	Interaction outcomes: analysis
1. Basic information and description	5. What we learned: leadership and growth
2. Description of the ritual process	6. Patterns of relationship
3. Emotions and attitudes	7. Moral consensus
4. Closeness to others and to God	8. Spiritual and emotional energy

What follows are practical indications about what to do at each step.

1. **Basic Information and Description.** Before attending a service at a new church, it is desirable to collect as much information as possible. The church's web page may have pictures of church services, give the name of the pastor and staff members, and list the main services and ministries. The church bulletin gives information about the main activities and sometimes

about the church finances. With this information, one has an idea about what to expect at a given church before attending for the first time.

2. Description of the Ritual Process. This description must contain all the information necessary for the analysis. The processional entrance is of great symbolic importance because it often suggests the atmosphere of the whole service. How clear are the readings? What is the performance of the minister? Is the assembly singing or merely humming along? What is the behavior of small children during the celebration? When the observer is sitting in the back of the church, he or she can observe the level of participation of the assembly. According to Gallup research, in all US denominations about 30 percent are "engaged" in their church, 50 percent are "not-engaged," and 20 percent are "actively disengaged."[1] Is this the case in the church under observation? What percent of the faithful open their hymnal or missalette in the front pews and in the back? What percent of the assembly arrives late and what percent leaves early?

The music is an essential aspect of most liturgies. Is the singing a solo performance, a concert, or an inspiration fostering the participation of the assembly? How is communion (if any): mechanical, row after row, or pious? Is the exit procession a rush to the door or a joyful leaving in peace?

It is important to take notes at all times, especially during the homily. It may be useful to record the whole service on a digital recorder. After attending for a few weeks at the same church, one will have in memory a film of the Sunday worship; hence video recording is not necessary and may be disturbing to the assembly.

3. Emotions and Attitudes. There seems to be no special emotions at most Sunday services. Gallup would confirm this view since about 50 percent of the people are "not-engaged," emotionally or otherwise. There are also two categories of explicit emotions and attitudes, those of the "engaged" and those of the "actively disengaged." Emotions are not measured but observed. Some observations may be ambiguous yet we must at least raise questions. Does the pastor's piety seem real or role-played? Does non-participation mean non-engagement or personal reflection? On some Sundays the emotions and attitudes may be easy to observe; thus when the church is 80 percent empty, non-participation is often obvious. But there are also exceptional celebrations with a variety of emotional expressions in music, singing, ritual performances, and collective enthusiasm.

1. Winseman, "Congregational Engagement Ascends."

4. Closeness to Others and to God. Emotion and closeness are two dimensions of any interaction, secular and religious, and both can only be observed, not necessarily measured. Closeness to others and to God is important for our understanding of liturgical practices.

Closeness to others can be observed in church seating. Do the first arrivals sit at the end of the pews, as far as possible from one another like in a public library? When the pews fill up, do people greet one another or ignore one another? Is there informal communication between families at the end of the service, or do people rush to their cars to beat the traffic?

Closeness to God is more difficult to observe. Faces may betray a spiritual dimension, and the quality of the singing may suggest inner conviction. In the course of the liturgy there often emerges a sense of piety that may be difficult to describe; it may be weak but it seems undeniable.

The Interviews. Besides observing the liturgical processes, one must become familiar with the life of the parish. The activities of the week are usually announced at the end of the service and printed in the bulletin; they need to be explored and documented.

From the pastor one may learn the size of the parish and its attendance rate. He may give information about the ethnic groups of the parish and their socio-economic status. He or she can provide an overview of the various departments, ministries, and devotional group, and facilitate getting in contact with them. Finally, it is important to learn about the pastor's own spiritual and theological orientations, what he hopes to accomplish, and what his priorities are. Most pastors and staff members agree to be recorded; a digital copy may be emailed to them as a thank-you gesture.

Here is a chart indicating the various steps of the interaction analysis.

Description of interactions		Analysis of outcomes
2. Description of ritual process	▸	5. What we learned: leadership and growth
3. Attitudes and emotions	▸	6. Patterns of relationship
4. Closeness to others and to God	▸	7. Moral consensus

The ritual processes observed in step 2 are analyzed in light of the homilies and the interviews; this analysis is done in step 5, "what we learned." The emotions and attitudes of step 3 form the basis of the patterns of relationship in step 6, and the observed closeness to others (in step 4) is indicative of the moral consensus (in step 7). Let us look at the various steps.

5. What We Learned: Leadership and Growth. Before beginning the analysis, one must have transcribed all the homilies and interviews, and now is the time to analyze them critically. A homily should convey a central idea; without it, the pastor cannot transmit a clear vision to his church. Since in many churches homilies are supposed to explain the Sunday readings, the pastor should have a good understanding of Scripture, which is usually suggested by biblical quotations and references. Finally the quality of the homilist's rapport with his audience is likely to reflect his or her rapport with the faithful throughout the week.

In reference to the content of the homilies, we may consider the theological level and quality of the homilies, and ask whether they promote prayer and devotional practices and encourage good deeds besides financial giving at the Sunday collection.

Interviews are most useful in order to understand the functioning of the church ministries. In some churches there is segmentation, in others tension, in others harmony and dedication. How and why were the staff members hired? How many people volunteer in church services? What fosters or inhibits volunteer participation and church attendance in general? Is the church in a state of growth, maintenance, or decline? Interviews about leadership and growth help understand the dynamics of the liturgical practices.

6. Patterns of Relationship. For social scientists, social cohesion and survival depend on the quality of social relations. The first basic question is whether a parish is a community in the sociological sense of face-to-face interactions, or whether it is an aggregate of people like moviegoers, library patrons, or sports spectators. Granted, all the faithful share the same faith, but sports fans also share the same passion for sports. Many churches, especially the larger ones, do not seem to be communities in the strict sense but aggregates.

Ecclesiology is the field of theology that deals with social relations. Avery Dulles in *Models of the Church* has outlined six basic church images: the church as institution, as worshiping community, as sacrament, as herald of the good news, as servant to the world, and as school of discipleship. Each of these models implies a certain pattern of relationship, ranging from submission and blind obedience to active participation in the liturgy and church life. A Sunday service is likely to be inspired by one of these models. What is the church model and what are the social relations that prevail in the church under study?

7. **Moral Consensus.** There can be no society without common values, and without consensus society disintegrates. The level of consensus is suggested by the closeness that church members show towards each other. In many churches there exists a tacit consensus of noninterference: Anglos and Latinos may worship in the same church at different times but may have no contact with one another, and the Sunday church attenders at different services may similarly ignore one another. Consensus as lack of conflict is not sufficient; social consensus must be moral, that is, related to common values.

Common ethnicity, similarity in social class, education, and sociopolitical ideology may foster a sense of common values, but these may fade easily in a pluralistic society. Hence in a church it is the love of God that should be the basic foundation for common values. In any parish or congregation this love manifests itself in specific forms of faith, hope, and good deeds, which inspire the various ministries and devotional groups. Liturgical practices usually reflect the life of a given church throughout the week and cannot be understood without them.

The common values of one generation may be rejected by the next one, and then the church will decline. One constructive solution for the pastor is to encourage enthusiastic attitudes and strong consensus at least among the staff members, if not in the whole parish. The worst situation is disagreement between the pastor, his staff, and his parish, in which case the church may need a change of leadership. What is the situation of the church under study? What are the common values and how strong is the consensus about them?

8. **Spiritual and Emotional Energy.** In Collins's model, the emotional energy produced in a given interaction (or liturgy) is the sum of all positive outcomes in emotions, attitudes, closeness to others and God, patterns of relationship, and moral consensus, in which case the relationship will grow, and parishioners will continue coming to church. The outcome of one interaction affects the next one and all others, and all interactions form a chain. This model is most appropriate for the study of liturgical practices over time, showing either growth, stagnation, or decline.

I would add to this model a question about spirituality. Each church has its own brand of spirituality that may range from traditional to postmodern. Moreover, one church may emphasize devotions, another social justice, another evangelization, and another Bible studies. What spirituality prevails in your church? How strong or weak, how popular or elitist is it? The emotional energy of a church is strongly increased by its spirituality of whatever kind.

This general presentation only gives the outline followed in this book. It is not a "recipe" that stands by itself; on the contrary it should be supplemented by theological, spiritual, and sociological considerations. It is these theoretical considerations that constitute the substance of this book, from the first chapter on methods to the conclusion on general principles of worship analysis.

1

Ritual Theory

Collins's Model for
Worship Analysis

THIS BOOK HOPES TO create a framework of analysis easy to follow. It consists of eight variables usable in any kind of worship, whether Catholic, Protestant, Jewish or Muslim. Four of these variables involve the observation of worship services and four a reflection about these observations and interviews with the pastor and staff. In the best of circumstances this can be done in a few weekends.

The purpose of this research is to identify strategies for change by assessing the strengths and weaknesses in a given parish, after observations of worship, leadership, ecclesiology, and moral consensus. We will also raise basic sociological and theological questions, like sacramentalism and ritualism, faith and culture, spiritual growth, segmentation versus integration, and creativity versus submissive obedience. This book consists of nine chapters describing worship issues in a given church with corresponding strategies for change.

There is very little empirical research about Jewish, Christian, or Muslim worship. There are numerous articles on cults, hero and idol worships, a few ethnographic studies about local, mostly foreign, worship practices, but practically none about worship across Christian parishes or congregations. There has been, however, a long tradition of empirical research in the areas of symbolic interactionism and ritual interaction. These studies observed interactions in the secular sphere but not religion; yet their tools are ready for use in worship analysis. The original contribution of this work, therefore, consists of applying well-established sociological tools to religious services.

This chapter is divided into three parts. First it presents a brief review of the literature on ritual interaction; next I briefly introduce other fields of research applicable to worship analysis, and lastly I introduce three liturgical theologies with different emphases in the liturgy: encounter with God, symbolic exchange, and transcendent enchantment.

I. Ritual Interaction Analysis

I will not introduce Durkheim mentioned in the introduction. His conception of religion as social creation is central in sociology. He also emphasized that social phenomena must be studied as "facts," that is, in their observable manifestations; he did not put much emphasis on interpretation, which is the main contribution of Max Weber. Let us come directly to the contemporary scene.

The study of congregations and parishes can be seen as a distant introduction to worship analysis. Since the publication of Joseph Fichter's *Southern Parish* in 1951, there have been numerous studies of church participation, satisfaction, contributions, leadership, ethnicity, etc. A great source of information about congregational life is the US Congregational Life Survey in which over 2,000 congregations participated. A major study of American parish life is *The Emerging Parish: The Notre Dame Study of Catholic Life Since Vatican II* by Jim Castelli and Joseph Gremillion (1987); it was to answer the question, "Where have the last twenty years of Vatican II reform taken the American Catholic parish?"[1] A recent replication of this extensive study has been published under the name of *Catholic Parishes of the 21st Century.*[2] I will return to the Notre Dame study later in my analysis.

Ritual studies are closer to our topic of worship analysis. The pioneer in this field was Ronald Grimes who founded the *Journal of Ritual Studies*. Grimes defined basic concepts like ritualization, decorum, ceremony, liturgy, magic, and celebration,[3] but these concepts do not clearly identify a field of study. Since one can see rituals in a great variety of contexts, cultures, and historical settings—rituals not being clearly defined—the field of ritual studies tends to be too broad to be of much help for worship analysis.

At this point, let me say a few words about the ancestors and direct creators of ritual analysis, namely Alfred Schutz, George H. Mead, Erving Goffman, and especially Randall Collins.

Alfred Schutz fled the Nazi invasion and came to the US in 1939. In his teaching at the New School of Social Research of New York, he promoted phenomenology in the tradition of Husserl and Max Weber, that is, an emphasis

---

1. Castelli and Gremillion, *Emerging Parish,* 3.
2. Zech, *Catholic Parishes of the 21st Century.*
3. Bradshaw and Melloh, *Foundations in Ritual Studies,* 131–165.

on intersubjectivity and interpretation. One of his major contributions is the notion of life-world.[4] According to phenomenological theory, each individual constructs his or her own world out of experiences about events, persons, and objects in everyday life, including the interactions within one's family, ethnic group, and social class. Schutz calls these subjective worlds the life-worlds. These constructed worlds are also psychological prisons that make social interaction difficult. Thus the clergy and the laity often live in different life-worlds and may talk past one another unless there is mutual listening. The Sunday worship is usually determined by priests, who do most of the talking and praying during the liturgy. If worship is to be an encounter or a symbolic interaction, there has to be mutual listening between the different life-worlds; without it there is segmentation.

Symbolic Interactionism is a type of social analysis that became popular in America around the middle of the twentieth century. Its main source of inspiration was George H. Mead (1863–1931), but there is great variation in the symbolic interactionist camp that he inspired. Herbert Blumer, a student of Mead, systematized the basic ideas of the movement. His two major insights are that social worlds are created by finding meaning in things, events, and processes, and that meaning is found through interaction.[5] What differentiates symbolic interactionism from Schutz's approach is the assumption that meaning is found in symbolic interpretation and social interaction rather than individual reflections. These views have become widely accepted in many fields.

A special contribution of George H. Mead for our study of ritual analysis is his notion of inner dialogue between the "I" and the "me" because this inner dialogue can be seen as a model for prayer. According to Mead, we are in a constant "conversation" with ourselves.[6] The self can somewhat split itself into two, the social self or "me," and the transcendent self or "I."

This distinction is best understood introspectively. When we look at some past memories, these mental images constitute the "me" while the self that is looking at these mental images is the "I." Then the self is "an object to itself," reflecting on itself by looking at its images like in a mirror. We are our past and our social images, but we can also transcend the social persona of the "me." This type of reflection makes possible a constant conversation

4. Schutz, *On Phenomenology*.
5. Blumer, *Symbolic Interactionism*.
6. Mead, *Mind, Self, and Society*, 140.

between the "I" (the creative self and center of moral judgment) and the "me"(the social self).[7]

When a person prays, there is similarly a tension between the social and the personal dimensions. No prayer can exclusively involve the "I" with no relation to anything outside itself. Conversely, a ritual prayer that does not engage the subjective self is only a prayer of the lips, not of the heart. To the extent that liturgical prayers are performed from a script they may leave little room for the spiritual "I." Instead of being uplifting they can be deadening by fostering mechanical performance and audience passivity. Other psychologists have further characterized our inner conversations as self-talk or intrapersonal communication. A prayer that is only self-talk is not interaction with the divine.

Erving Goffman (1922–1982) developed further the interactionist perspective by viewing interactions as dramaturgical performances. This perspective is well suited for the study of liturgical worship—the performance of a liturgical script. Three basic concepts of dramaturgical analysis are onstage performance, backstage performance, and idealization. These distinctions are relevant to cultic performances when onstage performance do not always reflect private conviction. Idealization occurs when actors try "to show the world a better or idealized aspect of [them]."[8]

In his 1961 book, *Asylums,* Goffman analyzed the interaction of mental patients in what he called "total institutions" in which individuals "lead an enclosed, formally administered round of life."[9] Prisons and mental hospitals are obvious examples of restrictive institutions that foster submission. On the other hand, elite boarding schools, military academies, and institutes of religious formation often foster empowerment rather than submission. Some churches tend to be total institutions because they endeavor to guide all aspects of their members' religious lives. The balance of power between the clergy and the congregation determines whether a particular institution is restrictive or empowering. The empowerment of the worshiping assembly will be part of our analysis of ritual interactions, especially in chapters 6 and the following ones.

Goffman analyzed everyday encounters as ritual interactions but gave no systematic outline of such rituals. Randall Collins was more ambitious: he theorized that interactions create links that over time will grow into stronger or weaker interactions. His theory proposed specific variables that can be

7. Mead, *Mind, Self, and Society,* 174–175.

8. Goffman, *Presentation of Self,* 35.

9. Goffman, *Asylums,* xiii.

applied to various interactions so that their effects can be compared with one another. He outlined a systematic program for interaction analysis.

Before turning to ritual analysis, a word should be said about the abundant research in the field of the history of liturgies and rituals. It is important to note that these studies rely on texts, never on empirical observations. Most prominent is the *Oxford History of Christian Worship*[10] in which 34 specialized chapters review most of the literature on the subject throughout the ages, with special emphasis on the Reformation. A more recent work is *Introduction to the Study of Liturgy* by Albert Gerhards and Benedikt Kranemann;[11] this book, too, relies on text and not on empirical observations.

Most Protestant seminaries and divinity schools have courses on worship. Catholics often do not, but they have courses on the sacraments, the mass being only one of the seven. Catholic research on the liturgy tends to focus on the theology and history of the sacraments. The Society for Catholic Liturgy promotes and publishes research, with an emphasis on historical forms of worship and traditional practices. A cursory introduction to this field is James White's *Roman Catholic Worship since Trent*.[12] There is Stringer's *Sociological History of Christian Worship*, which shows that the various forms of worship over the last two thousand years are expressions of power or the lack of it—a somewhat limited perspective.

Randall Collins and Interaction Rituals

Collins is a theorist with a strong background in Durkheimian theory and in Goffman's dramaturgical analysis. To a certain extent his theory of interaction rituals is the culmination of his life as a theorist. After a brief presentation of his model, we will look at its limitations and begin to see how it can be applied to worship.

In *Interaction Ritual Chains*, Collins summarizes his model in one graph which is followed by a page of explanations and a few more pages of comments. There are two parts in this model, the ritual process itself and the outcome. The four variables of the ritual process are (1) bodily co-presence, (2) barriers to outsiders, (3) mutual focus of attention, and (4) shared moods. I will re-phrase these in my implementation of Collins's model. The four outcome variables are (1) group solidarity, (2) symbols that represent the group, (3) feelings of morality, and (4) emotional energy. When applied to worship, my own terminology will be different.

---

10. Wainwright and Tucker, *Oxford History of Christian Worship*.

11. Gerhards and Kranemann, *Introduction to the Study of Liturgy*.

12. White, *Roman Catholic Worship*.

All variables form feedback loops, which Collins calls rhythmic entrainment, each being affected by all others. Moreover, interactions form a chain leading to increase or decrease in the interaction process. Applied to worship, this implies that the singing, the readings, the sermon, and so on influence each other and form a chain of interactions that will affect worship activities in the future.

> Interactions produce emotional chains that link participants together; they also link liturgical interactions over time in a continuous chain of worship experiences.

Interactions produce emotional chains that bind the participants because they "contribute to the core process of inter-subjectivity and shared emotions."[13] According to Durkheim, the glue of society is solidarity. For Collins it is emotions because solidarity is achieved "by focusing, intensifying and transforming emotions."[14] The end result of an interaction is the increase (or decrease) of emotional energy. There are short-term emotions that occur during the interaction process and also long-term emotions that pertain to the interaction outcome. The latter are important because they create emotional energy. Positive energy implies satisfaction and happiness ("joy, elation, enthusiasm, effervescence") while negative energy is linked to dissatisfaction and sadness ("disappointment, dreariness, and depression"). In Collins's words, happiness and sadness "are related to . . . [w]hat I am calling high and low emotional energy."[15]

In Collins's book, the theoretical part is relatively short (only one chapter), and the rest is dedicated to examples. Collins illustrates his theory in sports and competitions, among firefighters, and in conflict situations.[16] Whole chapters are dedicated to interaction in the market place (chapter 4), to social processes (chapter 5), sexual interaction (chapter 6), and tobacco rituals (chapter 8), but there is nothing on religion.

In the published studies involving Collins's analysis of ritual interaction, there are mainly impressionistic uses of his model. In an address to the Society for the Scientific Study of Religion, Stephen Warner argued that singing creates solidarity. More specifically, he claimed that "*making this music together*, not *listening to it*, creates solidarity." As he put it, "Music comes before language," and music through "rhythmic entrainment" creates solidarity.[17] Another study found that face-to-face interactions between consumers

13. Collins, *Interaction Ritual Chains*, 49.

14. Collins, *Interaction Ritual Chains*, 102.

15. Collins, *Interaction Ritual Chains*, 107.

16. Collins, *Interaction Ritual Chains*, 58, 88–95, 121–25.

17. Warner, "2007 Presidential Address," 180 and 187.

and producers leads to solidarity and motivates support for the Fair Trade movement.[18] In "Interaction Ritual Chains and Religious Participation" Jason Wollschleger reports that church attendance is higher in denominations where people jump, shout, or speak in tongues.[19] In "Effervescence and Solidarity in Religious Organizations," Scott Draper explained how he tested whether ritual density, ritual length in time, organizational attendance, and barriers to outsiders (e.g., no drinking, dancing, and gambling) produce solidarity in congregations.[20] None of these variables could easily be applied to other settings such as a church service or a Catholic mass. Collins's theory is not just about effervescence and solidarity; it outlines eight variables that can be operationalized and applied to all kinds of interactions, both secular and religious. Rebecca Erickson sensed the problem when she reviewed the book, noting that the success of interaction ritual chains will depend on whether sociologists can devise rigorous methodological applications. "Herein lays the theory's greatest challenge."[21]

The Eight Variables of Interaction Ritual Chains in the Present Study

Following Collins I will distinguish between the interaction processes and the outcomes. For each variable I will give examples from everyday life and also from worship. Let me present the variables in the table introduced previously.

Interaction processes: description	Interaction outcomes: analysis
1. Basic information and description	5. What we learned: leadership and growth
2. Description of the ritual process	6. Patterns of relationship
3. Emotions and attitudes	7. Moral consensus
4. Closeness to others and to God	8. Spiritual and emotional energy

1. Basic Information and Description

Before any interaction, whether a date, a job interview, or a visit to a new church, one begins by seeking basic information. From publicly available information about a given church one may be able to guess what type of

18. Brown, "Interaction Ritual Chains and the Mobilization of Conscientious Consumers," 121–41.

19. Wollschleger, "Interaction Ritual Chains and Religious Participation," 896–12.

20. Draper, "Effervescence and Solidarity," 220–48.

21. Erickson, "Review Essays," 209–11.

worship will be found there. Basically, there are two extremes in Christian worship. Traditional worship is clergy-centered, pietistic, and introverted. The emphasis is on sin and salvation. Non-traditional worship is charismatic, evangelical, and extroverted. Here the emphasis may be on inclusiveness and pluralism. Of course, between these extremes there can be a full range of worship styles.

2. Description of the Ritual Process

Worship services from entrance to exit must be described in details, more particularly the performances of the ministers and the choir, the responses of the audience, the homily or sermon, the use of props and symbols, the high point of the service, and the use of screens.

There is an obvious opposition between an aesthetic of parsimony and one of profusion. A ritual is parsimonious when it tries to achieve the greatest effect with the minimum number of images and words. Such a ritual uses plainchant, simple decorations and lights, and usually takes place in a building with few or no religious symbols. Most evangelical churches are of this type, and so also are Catholic masses using Gregorian chant. The aesthetic of profusion, on the other hand, uses a concatenation of sounds and lights; this aesthetic prevails in baroque Catholic churches, in Renaissance polyphony, and in Eastern Orthodox worship.

These two aesthetics are linked to two forms of spirituality: the apophatic, which tends to exclude images of the divine (as in Islam and Judaism), and the kataphatic, which seeks the divine through things that are visible (as in Hinduism and traditional Catholicism). There are limitations and dangers in both. The apophatic aesthetic of parsimony can be so restricted in words and sounds (e.g., through long periods of silence) that attendees become disengaged. Similarly, the kataphatic aesthetic of profusion can be so rich in details that the mind gets lost in its profusion. In the next chapter we will see that the masses seen on TV can be so simple in structure that they become monotonous, while in chapter 4 we will see that papal masses in Rome may be so sumptuous that they come across as performances.

The choir may similarly be simple and prayerful or profuse and theatrical. We can distinguish three basic functions of the choir: to be supportive of the singing of those in attendance, to be inspirational for meditation, or to be festive so as to enhance celebrations. These three functions are clearly noticeable in the Notre Dame of Paris masses

Three basic functions of the choir are to support the assembly in its singing, to inspire people in their meditation, and to bring joy to festive celebrations.

described in chapter 3, but they are only inchoate and rudimentary in the parishes presented in chapter 5.

3. Attitudes and Emotions

Any interaction involves emotions. Dull and unpleasant interactions are likely not to be repeated, while interactions that arouse positive emotions can lead to long-lasting relationships. Worship services involve emotions through the use of songs, symbols, Scripture texts, banners, and exhortations. The theological virtues of faith, hope, and love also involve emotions. These attitudes and emotions in turn facilitate closeness to one another, cooperation between the faithful and the clergy, and closeness to God.

According to Gallup research based on thousands of questionnaires in US congregations, about 30 percent of church attenders are "engaged," about 50 percent are "not engaged," and less than 20 percent are "actively disengaged."[22] The "engaged" are the backbone of the churches since they support the church activities besides attending worship services. The "not-engaged" church members attend Sunday services but nothing else; their connection to the church is mainly habit and custom. The "actively disengaged" may attend church but they are apathetic or negative about their church. Among Catholics, fewer than 20 percent are "engaged," and more than 30 percent are "actively disengaged"; thus more Catholics are "disengaged" than "engaged." Gallup did not disclose how these three categories were constructed. Yet they are quite suggestive about what is happening during church services.

The three basic attitudes of Gallup's research—engagement, non-engagement, and disengagement—can be broadly applied to worship services; it is often easy to notice whether the main attitude of the faithful is engagement, disengagement, or passive participation.

4. Closeness to Others and to God

The purpose of any interaction is to achieve closeness through words and gestures. In worship services, closeness to one another may be symbolic of closeness to God. Mutual closeness is suggested by the physical closeness to others in the pews, by mutual greetings, by ritual gestures such as the sharing of peace, and by the relationship between worship leaders and those in attendance. Implicit in this inquiry about human and divine closeness is whether the church service leads to greater participation in religious activities. In chapters 2 and 5, we will observe that parishioners make little or no

22. Winseman, "Congregational Engagement Ascends."

contact by sitting as far as possible from one another. It is only in chapters 6 through 9 that social cohesion will become an important factor.

Closeness to God is subjective, but it can be observed in facial expressions and inferred from the intensity of common prayers. Moreover, it is possible to distinguish between various attitudes towards the divine. There can be respect and awe, and an attitude of distance that prohibits excessive casualness like coming to church in improper dress. There can also be an attitude of piety, emphasizing deference to clergy or obedience to authority. There may be formalism and ritualism that require proper behavior and the exact execution of rules. Finally, there may be enthusiasm and religious emotionalism. This evaluation is intuitive yet quite reliable. We easily guess, when we see two people on screen or in real life, whether they are close and a couple, or distant and unrelated. It makes little sense then to ask for scientific and objective criteria—a positivistic bias.

> Closeness to God cannot be measured objectively, but often it can be observed in its manifestations, especially in the apparent lack of it in cases of active non-participation.

So far we have considered the four variables of interaction processes. Now we will turn to the outcome variables that assess the effect of the interactions and their lasting emotional energy in the chain of future interactions.

5. What We Learned: Leadership and Growth

After a date, a job interview, or a casual meeting, it is common to think about how it went. The same is true when, on the way home after a worship service, one reflects on what happened. According to Collins's model, one can reflect on the intellectual content of the interaction, on the pattern of relationship, on the moral consensus, and finally on the spiritual and moral energy gained in the process. Sermons and homilies are a prime source of information. The church activities announced at the end of the service are another important source. In most cases it is useful to interview the pastor and staff members for a better understanding of church dynamics.

When reviewing the interaction processes, one should reflect on the preaching and its contribution to the spirituality of the members. Homilies and sermons should foster the transformation of beliefs into theological faith. They should also encourage, at least indirectly and implicitly, a life of prayer and other religious practices. Finally, preaching should encourage good deeds ranging from financial contributions to social justice in the neighborhood and the larger society.

In order to decrease lay passivity, power should be shared with the whole congregation or parish. This can be done through the diffusion of theological and scriptural knowledge, the access to ritual functions, and the increased responsibility in church management. Democratic participation can be a powerful tool to reduce lay powerlessness.

Church activities are often announced at the end of the church service and they are printed in the church bulletin. Some of these activities may be sporadic or involve only a few members. Hence it is important to learn from the pastor and staff about the actual performance of activities that are announced or listed in the bulletin.

6. Patterns of Relationship

Any interaction tends to establish a specific pattern of relationship, for instance between friends or among employees. Before we meet a person a second time, we can often guess what the interaction pattern will be. The same holds for churches.

Every church has an implicit or explicit ecclesiology; for instance, a church may see itself as a hierarchical structure or as an egalitarian society of disciples. This ecclesiology is most obvious in the relationships between ministers and the laity. We should also inquire about the role of the assembly in the liturgical process. Does the worship service reinforce lay empowerment or lay submission? After the Scripture readings, is there a sharing of experiences and insights, or is the teaching from the top down? To answer some of these questions, interviewing the pastor may be very helpful.

7. Moral Consensus

The notion of moral community is basic in the Durkheimian tradition. It assumes that any association is based on common moral values that bind members together. Sunday teachings usually include exhortations for moral standards in at least three areas: controversial issues (e.g., abortion, divorce, and same-sex marriage), spiritual practices, and financial contributions. Common standards on controversial issues, devotional matters, and financial contributions create stronger moral communities.

The closeness to others and to God observed during the interaction process is usually indicative of the moral consensus of a given church. Similarities in education, wealth, and ethnic identity are also positive factors of social integration. These social factors are at work in any organization or club but may not be sufficient to hold a congregation together in changing times. Ultimately it is the closeness to God that binds people in worship. It is this supernatural faith that may attract newcomers and prevent defections among marginal members.

> A church is a moral community not because it follows moral precepts but because it enforces its moral values.

In Durkheim's works, there are two basic forms of integration. Mechanical solidarity exists when people relate like cogs in a machine in undifferentiated societies. This type of integration is based on uniformity, obedience, and discipline. This type of solidarity was found in Catholicism prior to Vatican II and will be described in chapter 2. By contrast, in differentiated societies, the mutual dependency of specialized individuals in the collective division of labor creates organic solidarity. This type of integration is found in churches that emphasize inclusiveness and democratic participation. This type of integration will be described in chapters 6 through 9.

8. Spiritual and Emotional Energy

In Collins's perspective, each interaction has immediate as well as long-term effects. Each of the seven variables described so far contributes some emotional energy that moves the relationship forward, upwards or downwards. The emotional energy created by a given interaction (e.g., a church service) is the total score on the seven variables after assigning a positive or a negative score to each of them. This total score, however, is more symbolic than mathematical.

There is one more dimension of emotional energy that needs to be taken into account, namely spirituality that animates the whole process and each of the seven variables. The various forms of Catholic spirituality can be placed on a continuum from pre-Vatican II to post-Vatican II theologies. Each local parish has its own version of spirituality within this spectrum.

The spiritual dimension of a given parish of congregation is found in the theological tradition of its wider church or denomination. To analyze the worship practices of different churches—for instance Lutheran, Baptist, Orthodox and Catholic—would require theological fluency in each of these churches, and this is practically impossible. Hence one has to limit one's research to a given tradition, with only one or two adventures into other traditions. For practical reasons I will limit myself to the Catholic tradition, with one chapter on an Evangelical church.

II. What is Missing: Art, Music, Visual Effects, and Prayer

There is more to worship than interaction. There are sounds and sights that condition any interaction. In churches there are images, statues, furniture, and decorations. There is music and singing. In some churches there is choreography and dance. And, of course, there is individual and collective prayer. Collins's interaction model has no room for these aspects. Finally there are the sociological characteristics of race, class, education, ethnicity, age, and gender, all of which obviously affect worship. If all these dimensions were included in the study of worship, it would be quite cumbersome and probably beyond the competency of one single researcher. I will briefly touch upon them here.

Academic research in art, music, and prayer is of little help in the study of local worship. Most churches do not have art pieces but commercial art. What is needed is pastoral research about how worshipers relate to the images and stat-

> There is a need for pastoral research about the spiritual importance and effect of church statues, decorations, and ritual pomp. There can be no guidelines for pastors without such research.

ues of their churches, the kind of hymns they prefer to sing, and the effect of the choir and orchestra performances. Such pastoral studies should be undertaken at the level of dioceses, denominations, and parishes, but none is available so far.

The interior decoration of a church creates a visual setting for the worship. The studio decorations of the masses on the CatholicTV channel (chapter 2) are stereotypical and unimaginative, although they could be changed overnight since they are studio decorations. At the Notre Dame Cathedral in Paris, its pastor called for greater beautification through music rather than just the enjoyment of its splendidly restored beauty (see chapter 3). By contrast, the settings of St. Peter's Basilica in Rome seem immutable in their papal pomp (chapter 4). Of all the churches surveyed in this book, it is St. Sabina of Chicago that has been most transformed from an all-white average house of worship to an all-black church in taste and sensitivity (chapter 8). The importance of church decoration is easily experienced when a pastor removes traditional plaster statues or introduces new ones of his own taste, because then many parishioners may be upset.

Worship usually includes music and singing. Of greatest importance is the choir director. In nearly all the churches surveyed, the director was turned towards the choir at all times, never to the audience, like at a concert. The two extreme cases are the TV masses where we hear a female singing off screen (there is no audience and of course no choir), and the papal masses in Rome where the choir director functions as court musician, performing pieces mostly in Latin that are incomprehensible to the faithful. In many parishes there is also a song director to lead people into singing. Yet the four churches in this book with the greatest participation in the singing had no song director: a lay-run parish (chapter 6), an evangelical church (chapter 7), the black church of St. Sabina (chapter 8), and the churches of Kinshasa in the Republic of Congo (chapter 9). In these churches singing was spontaneous, as an expression of faith rather than the mandated participation in the collective ritual.

The traditional organ, which is still common in Catholic parishes, usually only produces unimaginative music, as in the case of the TV masses in this study. By contrast the evangelical church of 3,000 members (chapter 7) has an orchestra of 20 to 30 musicians, the lay-run parish and St. Sabina have hired the best music directors in town, and the churches in Congo use drums to great effect. Generally speaking, the more limited the number of instruments, the more limited the participation in the singing. Most churches use choreography in the form of an entrance and an exit procession of the clergy and ministers. Dance and choreography also have a place in worship when they are part of the local culture, as in the case at St. Sabina and the churches in the Congo. There is also some limited choreography at the evangelical church. Dance is likely to have little place in rigidly controlled rituals and introverted services calling for inner reflection.

> The presence of an orchestra and a large choir, and the use of visual effects are often the expression of—and sometimes the cause of—active participation of the whole community.

More and more churches use visual effects, mostly by projecting texts and images on a screen. This was the case in the evangelical church. In four chapters of this book the services were analyzed from videos downloaded from television programs. Increasingly people can see religious programs on television and the Internet, hence the TV photography director plays an important role in what the public will and will not see. A recording can be quite unimaginative when the camera is placed in front of the ministers with few camera movements; this was the case at the TV masses. There is a great difference between the recordings of the pontifical masses in Paris and in Rome. In the first case, the camera expressed theological concepts through the use of general shots or close up; in the second case the camera zoomed in to show human interest images like a cuddling baby, the ring of a cardinal, or exotic female headdresses. We live in an image-saturated society, and an inspiring religious image may be worth a thousand words in a sermon.

The most important aspect of worship is prayer, not art, music, or special effects. Because I followed Collins's model, the description of the interaction processes was limited to ritual performances at the exclusion of personal prayer. While at the TV masses there was only ritual prayers with no praying audience, in the services with most singing participation a great deal of time was dedicated to prayer, because there the singing was prayer and prayer was singing. At Notre Dame of Paris (see chapter 3), at the end of the pontifical masses the celebrant usually walked to the statue of the Mother of God to sing the *Salve Regina*. In the Congo (see chapter 9), after a three-hour Zairean mass, the faithful often recite the rosary in front of a statue of the Virgin Mary. At St. Benedict (see chapter 5) there is great piety in the form of numerous moments of silence during mass and brief devotional prayers in front of the statue of a saint after mass.

Art, music, and prayer will be described in passing in the course of the interaction processes presented in the coming chapters.

III. Three Theological Insights

Sacramental theology is the area of theology that deals with worship. Because it is beyond my competency to give an overview of the theology of worship, I will just present three major insights that should help our understanding of Catholic liturgies, namely the insights of Edward Schillebeeckx, Louis-Marie Chauvet, and David Brown.

Schillebeeckx: Sacraments as Encounters

In his classic *Christ the Sacrament of the Encounter with God* (1960, 1963), Edward Schillebeeckx introduced two themes that were amplified during and after Vatican II. First, revelation is the self-revelation of God in an encounter rather than a set of doctrines, and second, the church is a sacrament rather than an institution. Both were and still are revolutionary as they are at the heart of Catholic worship.

A decade earlier, Henri de Lubac had already written, "The Church is for us the sacrament of Christ,"[23] meaning that for believers the church functions as a symbol rather than an institution. Two decades later, Avery Dulles analyzed the church *as* sacrament.[24] For Schillebeeckx, Lubac, and Dulles, the church functions as a sacrament, a sign, or a transcendent symbol. In other words, "Sacraments *are not things but encounters* of men and women on earth with the glorified man Jesus by way of a visible form."[25]

For Schillebeeckx, worship "is essentially a personal relation of man to God, of person to person; a personal encounter of a personal communion with God."[26] Such

> For Schillebeeckx, Lubac and Vatican II, sacraments are encounters with God, not just sacred rituals.

a statement was prophetic in the pre-Vatican II days when sermons dealt mainly with morality, mortal sins, the Last Judgment, and heaven and hell.

23. Lubac, *Catholicism*, 29.
24. Dulles, *Models of the Church*, ch. 4.
25. Schillebeeckx, *Christ the Sacrament*, 44 (emphasis added).
26. Schillebeeckx, *Christ the Sacrament*, 4.

At that time (and often today) sacraments were regarded as "things." This insight is important because rituals are commonly seen as things, as practices that are supposed to have an automatic effect. How can ritual be more than a thing? Three generations later, Chauvet provided an answer: rituals are linguistic and symbolic constructs, not things.

Chauvet: Ritual as Symbolic Exchange

For Louis-Marie Chauvet, language is symbolic and we only know reality through language. We become humans through language by learning to decipher reality as symbolic. It is through symbolic development that we find our individuality. "It is precisely *by* constructing reality as 'world' that the subject constructs *itself* as subject."[27] There are multiple constructions of reality because the symbolic medium of language leads to pluralism and interaction.

The use of language implies exchange between a sender and a receiver. In the *instrumental use of language*, the exchange consists of two monologues with little mutual reception. According to Chauvet, sacraments (indeed all rituals) should be symbolic exchanges and not unilateral monologues. In a market exchange, there is only the mutual transfer of goods and money, while in a *symbolic exchange*, there is first of all the reception of a message seen as symbolic gift, and next a return gift of appropriate symbolic value. In a market transaction there is only the exchange of goods of equivalent value while in a symbolic exchange there is a ternary structure of gift—reception—and return-gift.[28] Schillebeeckx wrote of "encounters," Chauvet of "exchange," and the social sciences of "ritual interactions," but all three point to the same symbolic dimension at work in worship.

Chauvet outlined briefly two models of sacramentality: the objectivist model which emphasizes cause and effect relationships inherited from scholasticism, and the Vatican II model which gives "priority [to] the ecclesial 'We'." In the first model, it is the priest who "makes" the Eucharist; in the second model, it is Christ himself who is the mediator in the exchange between the faithful and God. "Consequently, the more one stresses that the liturgical action is that of Christ himself the more one is led to emphasize that the assembly, which is his present body of humanity, is the active sacramental mediation of his action, in particular of his praise to the Father."[29] In

> According to Chauvet, worship must be understood as symbolic, not as instrumental communication.

27. Chauvet, *Sacraments*, 8.

28. Chauvet, *Sacraments*, 121.

29. Chauvet, *Sacrament*, 33.

the first model the laity is the passive recipients of the sacraments; in the second model, the laity is the "active sacramental mediation" in the worship exchange.

How can an encounter with God be an exchange when we recognize that humans have little to offer? In the anthropological perspective adopted by Chauvet, the first step of the exchange is "the *reception* of the gift *as* gifts and not as anything else."[30] In this perspective the reception of the Word as gift is the first step, the "first sacrament." This reception implies a time of praise and worship for all the gifts received, the physical as well as the spiritual ones. For believers, the greatest gift is Jesus Christ as "bread of life." Through the eucharistic celebration this "bread of life" is recognized as gift in words of thanks, and is offered to God the Father as a return-gift by the whole body of Christ. This view stands in sharp contrast to the common understanding of rituals as mechanical performances having a quasi-automatic effect. Here again, sacramental theology helps understand ritual worship.

David Brown on Imagination and Enchantment

As an Anglican theologian, David Brown has the liberty to take a perspective broader than that of many Catholic thinkers. In the Catholic tradition, the discussion of faith and reason is often limited to the relationship between revelation, the magisterium, and tradition. For Brown, such a discussion should also include experience and the power of the imagination that shape traditions. "One of the principal ways in which God speaks to humanity is through the imagination."[31] For Brown, the imagination refers to the human creative powers, not to fictions and fairy tales. This continuous development can be seen in religious art, Christian piety, biblical exegesis, and the development of non-Christian religions.

Tradition itself has never been a fixed deposit. "The imagination is absolutely integral to the flourishing of any religion, Christianity included."[32] In Scripture we often find a "moving text" rather than a "fixed text" when over the centuries the same text has acquired new meanings. The story of Abraham as recorded a millennium after the event is understood differently in Judaism, Christianity, and Islam. The meaning of some Jewish prophecies changed when it was applied to Jesus. The pseudo-Pauline letters added new insights to Paul's words. Revelation has been continuous throughout history at the local level and not just at the top.

---

30. Chauvet, *Sacrament*, 123.

31. Brown, *Tradition and Imagination*, 6–7.

32. Brown, *Tradition and Imagination*, 366.

Brown opened a space for non-dogmatic creativity—that of the arts, the liturgy, and popular piety. He concluded that today more than ever Christianity needs "an imaginative structure that can speak meaningfully to the life of our contemporary believers."[33] Similar views have been expressed by Bernard Lonergan in *Insights* (1957), David Tracy in *The Analogical Imagination* (1981), and sociologist Andrew Greeley in *The Catholic Imagination* (2000).

With *God and Enchantment of Place: Reclaiming Human Experience* (2004), Brown responds to Max Weber's claim that in the "iron cage" of the modern world, religious enchantment has given way to instrumental rationality and the pursuit of economic productivity.[34] In response, Brown surveys the importance of transcendence and immanence in art, architecture, sports, and everyday life. There are chapters on Orthodox icons, Western Renaissance paintings, and on the numinosity in landscape paintings and modern abstract art. Everywhere there are implicit myths, symbolic animals, and a cosmic order leading to transcendent awe and mystical immanence.

> In works of art, landscapes, houses, and churches are more than things, and so it is about rituals.

There is no need to follow Brown in his encyclopedic exploration because implicit in his theology of enchantment is the power of the imagination seeking God in all things. Without such imaginative seeking, icons, landscapes, houses, and churches as well as sacraments are just things. But with spiritual imagination, all things become symbolic and numinous.

Conclusion: Rituals are Imaginative Traditions, Not Things

From Schillebeeckx and Chauvet, we learned that sacramentality refers to interactional processes, not mechanical rituals with automatic effects—although the study of rituals as things is a valid field of research, but is not the one followed here. Brown broadened the perspective: revelation itself is not a thing or "deposit" to be safeguarded by religious authorities but a continuous process of growth. Because revelation is continuous in the hearts and minds of believers, there will always be periods of renewal and development. Hence the empirical analysis of worship must reveal this continuous process of imaginative growth, accompanied by the simultaneous trend towards ritual reification.

Enlightened by these theological insights we are ready to investigate their implementation with the use of sociological tools.

33. Brown, *Tradition and Imagination*, 367.

34. Brown, *God and Enchantment*, 17.

Outline of Chapters

The chapters are presented in a progressive order, beginning with the simplest form of ritual interaction, the TV mass, continuing with a synthesis between faith and culture, then a chapter on segmentation, and ending with chapters showing creative integration. Here is a summary of the chapters.

1. Ritual Theory: Collins's Model for Worship Analysis. The theory and practice of ritual interaction analysis. The insights of Schillebeeckx, Chauvet, and David Brown.

2. The American TV Masses: Sacramentalism and Ritualism. Discussion of the studio masses celebrated in front of a camera but without anyone in attendance. There is no entrance song, no offertory, no communion, and no exit song. The homily is three and a half minutes long on average. These masses tend to foster sacramentalism and ritualism.

3. Pontifical Masses at Notre Dame of Paris: Faith and Culture. The issue of the relationship between faith and culture was brought up by the Cardinal Archbishop of Paris in the first of the recorded masses. In these pontifical celebrations, there is high professionalism. The choir supports the singing of the assembly, and the collective singing is strong. The homilies are substantial. The music is inspirational and festive. The images of the camera express the vision of the church as the people of God.

4. Six Papal Masses: From Segmentation to Leadership. Discussion of the liturgies performed in St. Peter's Basilica in the Vatican. The mass in Latin, the singing of the choir in Latin and often in polyphony, and the non-participation of the assembly reflect a pre-Vatican II vision of the church, which is reinforced by images mostly of cardinals and seldom of the faithful. The homilies of Pope Francis reflect a different vision of the church, one based on dialogue and participation.

5 & 6. Two Ordinary Parishes: Strategies for Growth and *A Lay-Run Parish: the Need of Ecclesial Communion.* Presentation of the research undertaken by the Willow Creek Church about strategies for growth, followed by the description of three parishes: an average church satisfied with low achievements, a ritual-centered church struggling with change and emphasizing inner spirituality rather than external acts of charity, and a dynamic parish where most parishioners are involved in social action but with no common spirituality. For each, a strategy for growth is suggested.

7. Growth and Development at an Evangelical/Pentecostal Church. This chapter discusses spiritual growth, first as intensity of beliefs and practices, and second in terms of development according to Fowler. At the Bayville church there are exceptional levels of religious intensity, yet in terms of stage development, the main characteristic is conformity to church teachings and social expectations.

8. The Liturgical Imagination at St. Sabina. This chapter discusses how the pastor of an African American parish in Chicago experimented with liturgical innovation in the 1970s and 1980s, thus testing the limits of liturgical creativity.

9. The Zairean Rite and Usage: Creativity versus Authority. The dioceses of the former Zaire have been granted permission to use a Zairean adaptation of the official order of the mass. My field trip observations revealed exception levels of participation.

10. Method and Vision in Worship Analysis. This chapter shows how method and vision in worship analysis moves from social drama to mystagogy in the liturgy, the preaching, and spirituality.

2

American TV Masses

Sacramentalism and Ritualism

HAVING REVIEWED THE GREAT insights of Schillebeeckx, Chauvet, and Brown, we turn to a pre-Vatican type of mass that have little room for encounters with God because they are mainly videos to be watched. TV masses are probably the simplest form of Catholic worship. They only involve one main actor, the priest; there is no assembly. Like the pre-Vatican II silent masses in Latin, they follow diligently the liturgical prescriptions. They must be performed in less than thirty minutes.

TV masses are different from other televised masses, for instance the papal masses in Rome or at World Youth Days, where the participation of the faithful is often shown. In TV masses, the main actor is the priest and the second most important actor is the cameraman who decides what will be shown and what will be skipped. In contrast to televised masses where the purpose is participation in the sacrifice of the altar, in TV masses the purpose is to produce a video that can be watched later, alone, and without participation.

In the United States there are three major Catholic television networks that broadcast TV masses daily. CatholicTV is run by the archdiocese of Boston. It is the biggest television network under ecclesiastic control; its programs are aired in 16 states. The next in size is Telecare Television from the diocese of Rockville Centre, which broadcasts in the three states of New York, New Jersey, and Connecticut. The biggest Catholic network in the world is EWTN, which was founded by Mother Angelica, but the American hierarchy has no direct control over it.

There are slight variations within and between networks. CatholicTV broadcasts three daily TV masses from its studios on weekdays, Mondays to Fridays, and four such masses on Sundays. These studio masses have no choir and no assembly. On Saturdays there are two TV masses with a choir broadcast from two chapels, not studios, but their main purpose is broadcasting, not participation. On Telecare there are three daily TV masses, two from Rockville Centre and one from St. Patrick's cathedral in New York City. At EWTN the three daily masses last one hour, with little or no participation from the assembly as in TV masses.

At CatholicTV there are 17 TV masses during the week, 4 TV masses on Sundays, and also two participatory (or non-TV) masses on Sundays, In short, 21 out of 23 are TV masses. At Telecare there are 18 TV masses and also two participatory (or non-TV) masses on Sundays. In short, 18 out of 20 are TV masses. Hence TV masses are the favorites by a ratio of about by ten to one.

In my analysis I will concentrate on the Boston CatholicTV studio masses celebrated without attendance and without a choir. These masses only involve a priest, an altar server and a lector. Only the area around the altar is shown since the rest of the chapel or studio is occupied by the television crew. Because there is no assembly, there is no entrance and no exit song, no offering of gifts, and no communion of the faithful. It is like a pre-Vatican II private mass but it is broadcast. In order to understand this type of mass, let us begin with a short review of the reform movement leading to Vatican II.

The Tridentine Mass and the Liturgical Movement

In the Tridentine liturgy from 1570 until its replacement in 1969, a major distinction was between low (or private) masses and high (or solemn) masses.[1] A low mass involved only a priest and an altar server. A parish with several priests would have several low masses each day of the week at the main altar, and sometimes also at the side altars. There was to be only one solemn mass without communion on Sunday, with one or several low masses with communion earlier in the morning. What characterized the high mass was the participation of a deacon and a subdeacon (or two priests serving as deacon and subdeacon), the use of incense, and the participation of a choir. The Introit, the Kyrie, the Gloria, the Gradual, the Alleluia, the Credo, the Offertory and Communion antiphons, the Sanctus, and the Agnus Dei were sang by the choir, of course in Latin.[2] The assembly usually remained silent, except to sing a few hymns in the vernacular, often not related to the mass.

During low masses, the celebrant and the faithful prayed in different languages, the priest in Latin from the missal, and the faithful in the vernacular, often reciting the rosary. At solemn masses before the liturgical

---

1. See "Tridentine Mass" at: https://en.wikipedia.org/wiki/Tridentine_Mass.

2. *The Catholic Encyclopedia* (1917): http://www.newadvent.org/cathen/09790b. htm.

movement (and in fact often until Vatican II) the priest, the choir, and the assembly prayed as if belonging to three different worlds. It is still so at the papal masses, as we will see in chapter 4. The priest followed exact liturgical instructions called rubrics, and he prayed in Latin in a low voice. The choir sang the Latin prayers, often in polyphonic arrangements made popular by the Italian Renaissance, but incomprehensible to the faithful. As to the assembly, people were invited to sing hymns in the vernacular at the beginning, middle, and end of the mass but these hymns were often unrelated to the liturgy.

The Catholic liturgical reform movement began to gain influence around 1900. Prosper Guéranger, a Benedictine in the Abbey of Solesmes in nineteenth-century France, had pioneered the restoration of the Gregorian chant because church music had become overgrown with Renaissance polyphony. Giovanni Palestrina, who lived in the sixteenth century, was the Catholic equivalent of John Sebastian Bach: he had composed 105 masses, 68 offertories, 72 hymns, 35 Magnificats, and more. By the eighteenth century, works by Palestrina and other Renaissance composers had largely replaced Gregorian chant at high masses. Guéranger and other leaders in the liturgical reform movement sought to make Catholic worship less like a theatrical performance and more like the communal prayer found in monasteries.

> In the Tridentine mass, the priest, the choir, and the assembly belonged to three different cultural worlds, two using Latin and one the vernacular; one was centered on the liturgy and the other on piety.

Their efforts bore fruit when, in 1903, Pius X created a commission on church music that began to have some effect on Catholic worship about a generation later. By the middle of the nineteenth century, small missals for the laity had become popular, but none included translations of the Latin prayers and readings of the mass since this was prohibited by canon law.[3] The first bilingual missals for laypeople, with Latin on one side and a modern language on the other, were published in Germany at the end of the nineteenth century. This was originally done in defiance of church law, but bilingual missals eventually received ecclesiastical approval when they were shown to have a positive effect on Catholic piety. Once such translations were available, the faithful could "pray the mass" by following the priest's prayers. The next step was the so-called dialogue mass in which people were encouraged to chant the Gloria, the Credo, and the Sanctus in Latin, together with the choir during a high mass, at first without Roman

---

3. See "The History of the French Missals" at: http://www.bdnancy.fr/missels-histoire.php/.

authorization. Sometime later, people were also encouraged to join the prayers of the altar servers. Again, Rome acknowledged and approved the changes some time later.[4]

The liturgical reform movement sought greater participation of the faithful in the mass, and the efforts of the reformers eventually led to the famous Vatican II statement, "Mother Church earnestly desires that all the faithful should be led to that fully conscious and active participation in liturgical celebrations."[5] Although such participation is desirable, it was never required. Actually by law, "participation in the mass is satisfied by assistance at a mass" (canon 1248). TV masses follow this minimalistic requirement by eliminating the assembly and keeping only the priest and a single server. Hence TV masses are a return to the pre-Vatican II type of liturgies. Let us now turn to interaction analysis.

I. The Interaction Processes at TV Masses

In 2016, I recorded 16 TV masses from the Internet, where they are easily available. Most of the images of these masses are nearly identical because there are very few shots a camera can take, such as showing the altar, the priest, the lectors, the altar servers, the host, the chalice, and the surroundings such as stained glass windows. These TV masses are recorded over 300 times a year in the same church or studio; as a consequence, four to six recordings should have been sufficient to make an analysis. However, because homilies during TV masses were very short, a larger sample was needed in order to include an analysis of the homilies.

I recorded 10 TV masses produced in the CatholicTV studios and six produced in actual churches. I will first present the 10 studio masses and next the variations found in the other six TV masses. I will follow Collins's model presented in the previous chapter. Here again is a chart of the model shown as an interaction chain over time.

---

4. See the history and development of the dialogue mass at: https://en.wikipedia.org/wiki/Dialogue_Mass.

5. *Sacrosanctum Concilium*, 14, in Abbott, *Documents of Vatican II*.

	Processes	Outcomes
	1 Basic Information and description	5 What we learned: leadership and growth
Expectations	2 Description of the ritual process	6 Patterns of relationship
	3 Emotions and attitudes	7 Moral consensus
	4 Closeness to others and to God	8 Spiritual and emotional energy

When one visits a new church, one is affected by one's expectations, the ritual performance on that visit, the attitudes and emotions around oneself in the pews, and one's sense of closeness to others and God. These variables will affect the interaction outcome (spiritual energy) of that day, which in turn will affect one's expectations about returning to this church.

1. Expectations

The CatholicTV network explains what we should expect. In the words found on one of its web pages, we read, "The Sacrifice of the Mass is . . . the center of CatholicTV's mission." Elsewhere we read, "The Mass is the greatest act of Evangelization that the Church can offer the world." The celebration of many masses appears to be at the center of the network's mission. Moreover, these masses are a major form of evangelization because all masses give graces. Participation is not necessary. As stated by the Council of Trent, private masses "are celebrated by a public minister of the Church, not for himself alone, but for all the faithful who belong to the body of Christ" (1747). From this we can infer that a private mass with no one in attendance is, no less than a public mass, a great act of evangelization for spreading the message of Christ.

It must be remembered that TV masses are produced for the benefit of individual spectators; they are not televised celebrations in actual parish communities. Usually a different priest performs the TV mass every day. These masses cater to isolated TV spectators who can watch a mass on television or at any time on the Internet. These are individual practices, a major characteristic of traditional Catholic piety.

Priests are the main actors. They are expected to perform the mass in less than 30 minutes, which therefore requires the homily to be short. They must follow the rubrics without any personal touch or innovation because there is no time for it.

The camera director is the second most important actor in the production of a TV mass. The TV director might include video clips or announcements during the mass, show stained glass windows or flowers instead of the priest, or offer close-ups of the host and chalice. In short, the camera director decides what the public will see, and often explains visually what it means.

At all TV masses there was a lector for the readings of the day. In the 16 recorded masses, there were two female and 14 male altar servers, and four female and 12 male lectors. With the priest as the main actor and mostly male servers, the traditional male structure is strongly in evidence.

2. Ritual Performances

We must first describe the behavioral performance of the various actors. Their significance will be discussed later, in the sections on emotions, closeness, relational patterns and moral consensus. In TV masses, the actors are the priests, the television crew, the lectors and altar servers, the off-screen singers, and in church masses (as opposed to studio masses), the assembly. I will describe their behavior in a typical TV mass.

a. The Priests

In the studio masses the celebrating priest has only to take a few steps to be at the altar. There is no entrance and no exit song. He immediately begins, "In the name of the Father, the Son, and the Holy Spirit." The penitential rite at the beginning of the mass is usually the triple "Lord/Christ have mercy" (or Kyrie). As there is no Gloria during the week, the Kyrie is followed immediately by the opening prayer read from the missal. In the Roman rite on a given day the opening prayer is the same all over the world.

b. The Homilies

The major contribution of the celebrant to the liturgy of the Word is the homily. In the 16 TV masses, the average length of time of the homilies was three and a half minutes, ranging from two and a half to five minutes. They could be shorter: one was 50 seconds long and another 90 seconds in two TV masses that were not in my sample. How useful are such homilies? Let us first consider eight homilies somewhat related to the readings of the day; the others will be reviewed later.

In reference to the Good Samaritan, the main comment of one homilist was: "It is shocking that our neighbors may be people from a different race, religion, or morality. But we have to help them simply because it is Jesus's teaching." Another recommended the example of Mother Teresa. "One day as she was walking down the street with a reporter, she went to hug two homeless people and take care of them." The conclusion was, "Go and do the same."

In reference to Jesus saying, "Let the dead bury the dead" (Matt 8:18–22), a priest commented that "Burial has a specific place in the life of a believer, but the gospel must come first. Christ wants us to follow him because he created us and because we should be with him at all times."

With regard to denying oneself (Matt 16:24–28), one homilist said, "To deny oneself means giving up being the center and making Jesus the center. This is something we have to do again and again. It is like giving a thousand dollars to the Lord, one quarter at a time."

A priest applied the parable of the mustard seed (Mark 4:26–34) to daily life by saying, "This is about preventing relapse into drug addiction. We should be attentive to signs of growing seeds in our relationships with others and Christ. We often miss these signs and fall into negativity and sadness."

A homily on the Lord's Prayer (Luke 11:1–13) proposed, "The first word is 'Our.' Jesus could have said 'My Father' or 'Your Father.' Jesus said '*Our* Father.' We are in this together. We cannot do it alone. Thanks to God we have the church to support us, the Holy Spirit, priests, bishops, family and friends." This was the theme of the entire homily.

c. From Presentation of Gifts to Communion

There is no presentation of gifts at TV masses because there is no assembly. At this point altar servers normally present wine and water to the priest, but their contribution was eliminated in several of the recorded TV masses. At one mass, the priest fetched the wine and water by himself. With no presentation of gifts and only a lector and/or an altar server in attendance, TV masses tend to be minimalistic performances.

In masses broadcast from a church as on Telecare (as opposed to studio masses), one can count the number of communicants when they come forward. At one mass I counted eight, at another nine. At another mass a TV image made it possible to count 20 people dispersed in 22 pews. At these masses, the church appeared to be almost empty.

When it is time for communion during studio masses, the "Act of Spiritual Communion" is shown on the screen. It reads, "My Jesus, I believe that you are present in the Sacrament of the Holy Eucharist. I love you above all things, and I desire to receive you. Since I cannot at this moment receive you sacramentally, come at least spiritually in my heart. Never let me be parted from you. Amen." At the masses broadcast from the crypt of the National Shrine of the Immaculate Conception in Washington, the following text was shown on the screen: "If you cannot attend mass but would like to receive the Eucharist at home, please contact your parish directly."

d. The Camera

Everything that the public sees on screen is filtered by the director. By showing only the priest and the area around the altar, the camera propagates the view throughout the mass that the main actor of Catholic worship is the priest.

A camera can show images whose meaning is given by association or contrast, which is a common strategy in advertising. In one studio mass, the camera showed a woman sitting alone in the front pew, and shortly afterwards a female voice was heard singing. This sequence suggested that the voice off-screen was that of the woman just seen. But at the mass on the Fourth of July, when the homilist exclaimed, "How grateful we should be for the men and women who serve us in the military!" we were shown the woman who was previously associated with singing. Since she did not seem to be related to the military, the meaning of the visual association was not clear; yet it raised questions since at no other mass could a woman be seen.

In other cases, the meaning is only too obvious. For instance, images of bread, grapes, the chalice, and the host are shown repeatedly during the mass. The Boston studio masses usually begin with a video clip showing first a jug of wine, a jug of water, a chalice, and a bunch of white, red, and pink grapes. We next hear some pre-recorded singing while seeing a sheaf of wheat and more grapes superimposed over the image of the altar of the studio chapel. Next, there are two hands holding a host and lifting it up superimposed over the image of the crucifix above the altar. The video clip ends with a close-up of grapes, a host, and the base of a chalice. Thus the camera functioned as a reinforcement of the traditional eucharistic theology.

e. General Intercessions and the Prayers of the Faithful

Who writes the prayer intentions? In the 16 TV masses, six were read and had probably been written by the priest or deacon, and ten appeared to have been written by the lectors. Out of the 76 intentions of prayer, we may distinguish those that appear to be stereotypical: prayers for the pope, the church, the civil authorities, the armed forces, the persecuted, the parish, the poor, the sick, the departed, and clerical vocations. This type of request is more prominent among those read by priests or deacons. In the whole sample, about half of the prayer requests are of this type. Among the remaining, there are calls for a divine blessing for day laborers and migrant workers, people without healthcare, families in conflict, the sick and abandoned, those needing healing from terrorist attacks, and so on.

From the above, it is clear that these prayer intentions are "general intercessions" and not individual prayers of the faithful. The down-to-earth needs of ordinary people find no place in these general intercessions, contrary to what we will find at the Church of the Resurrection presented in chapter 6. People may, however, submit mass intentions. In two TV masses the priest mentioned such intentions. According to canon law, the faithful can make an offering for a mass intention (canon 945), and the stipends are quite low (about $15 to $20). In many people's perception, however, to have to pay for a personal intention is unattractive.

3. Emotions and Attitudes

Any interaction carries an emotional value, whether people go bowling or go on a date. In Collins's model of interaction, emotions are an important factor in the decision to continue or drop a relationship.

TV masses promote the relatively cold attitudes of dedication, loyalty, and devotion to the church and its sacramental theology. All of the priests and liturgical ministers exhibit these values, but we know nothing about the TV spectators.

There was one example of strong emotion, namely the enthusiasm expressed by Bishop Robert Reed in his homily on the Fourth of July. He said, "I still get chills when in a crowd I sing the Star Spangled Banner. I sometimes get tears in my eyes when I say the Pledge of Allegiance. I love this country and I am proud to say that I am an American citizen." Bishop Reed spent his whole homily (over 4 minutes) eulogizing the American way of life. One may conclude that he is a great patriot. But he did not say, "I love Jesus Christ and I am proud to be a member of the Catholic Church." He did not mention having chills and tears in his eyes when he celebrates mass. Why not?

The sacramental theology of the Council of Trent centers on deeds, not feelings such as devotion or love of God. The sacraments are the surest way to salvation; they are ritual deeds not involving emotions or even participation. The sacraments "contain the grace which they signify," i.e., they produce what they are supposed to. They are "conferred by the performance of the rite itself (*ex opere operato*)," even when performed by unworthy priests. There is little room for either thinking or feeling.

4. Closeness to Others and to God

One possible sign of emotional closeness is the exchange of the sign of peace, but at TV masses the exchange of peace is mainly perfunctory. Some priests only greet the lector and not the altar server, or only the deacon and no other liturgical ministers. In one extreme case the priest shook hands with an arm protruding into the screen because the camera was expected not to show the people in the assembly (if there were any). In no mass is the presence of the camera crew even acknowledged. Clearly in TV masses there is little opportunity for emotional closeness.

One may wonder whether 30-minute rituals can create closeness. At the beginning of mass, the recitation of the Kyrie only takes 15 to 20 seconds. Homilies last only three and a half minutes on average. The mass ritual includes moments of silence after the homily and communion but they usually only last a few seconds. Before Vatican II, priests were required to recite prayers before and after mass, but these requirements were abolished by the liturgical reforms, so there is no more praying before and at the end of the masses.

Closeness to God is difficult to assess, but the faces of people easily betray prayerful concentration or absentmindedness. In the TV masses most priests show signs of devotion, like holding joined hands and saying the missal prayers reverently, but these external behaviors can also be role-playing.

We have covered the four aspects of ritual interaction. Let us now turn to the four variables that analyze the results achieved during the interaction.

II. Interaction Outcomes

At the end of any encounter, one may reflect on what has been accomplished. What did I learn? What kind of relationship did we establish? What is our moral consensus? What does the future hold for us? Shall we meet again?

5. What We Learned

In order to understand the interaction processes we must review the information gathered from the sermons and interviews with the pastor and staff members. In TV masses, there can be no interview of the celebrant and there is no staff or assembly. In order to understand the ritual processes of TV masses we must turn to other sources of information, namely the theology of the Catholic Church and canon law. Let us take a look at these outside sources before turning to the analysis of the sermons.

The Sacraments in the Catechism of the Catholic Church (CCC)

Older Catholics remember the Baltimore Catechism definition of a sacrament as "an outward sign instituted by Christ to give grace." The definition found in the 1994 Catechism of the Catholic Church is quite similar:

"The sacraments are efficacious signs of grace, instituted by Christ and entrusted to the Church, by which divine life is dispensed to us."[6]

The Church makes at least four major claims about its sacraments. First, they are necessary in light of the traditional doctrine of original sin. "Adam and Eve committed a *personal sin* but this sin affected *the human nature* that they would then transmit *in a fallen state*,"[7] that is, eternal damnation. To be saved from such a fate, one must receive baptism, to be followed by the other sacraments in order to remain in a state of grace. "By baptism *all sins* are forgiven, original sin and all personal sins, as well as all punishments for sin."[8]

Second, they are *fruitful* because they give many kinds of graces. Sanctifying grace is a "stable and supernatural disposition"; it is a type of habitual grace or "permanent disposition." Actual graces are produced by "God's intervention" during the pursuit of holiness. There are, in addition, special graces "also called charisms," sacramental graces, that is, "gifts proper to the different sacraments," and graces of state, that is, divine assistance in the performance of one's responsibilities as a husband or wife, parent or pastor, ruler or subject, and so on.[9] According to the *Catechism*, Catholic life consists of acquiring graces, the more the better.

Third, they are *valid means of salvation* when performed according to the requirements of church prescriptions. They do not require personal prayer on the part of the recipient, only rote or missal prayer on the part of the priest. They do not necessarily involve a community as a private mass is as fruitful as participation in a mass celebrated before thousands. They require behavioral conformity to rules and regulations, not personal transformation. They are ritual products rather than spiritual processes. Hence they are within the easy reach of all.

Fourth, "They are *efficacious* because in them Christ himself is at work."[10] Since the time of the Middle Ages, sacraments have been understood to produce their effects *ex opere operato*, that is, as a result of the ritual action being performed. In simple (even simplistic) terms, sacraments have an automatic effect.

I would define sacramentalism as the belief that sacraments are necessary *and sufficient* for salvation. The four characteristics of sacraments given

---

6. Anonymous, *Catechism of the Catholic Church*, 1131.

7. Anonymous, *Catechism of the Catholic Church*, 404.

8. Anonymous, *Catechism of the Catholic Church*, 1263.

9. Anonymous, *Catechism of the Catholic Church*, 2000–2004.

10. Anonymous, *Catechism of the Catholic Church*, 1127.

above tend to foster sacramentalism: they are necessary, give graces, and have an automatic effect if performed according to the requirements of the law.

Ritual and Ritualism in Canon Law

Sacramentalism emphasizes the need of Catholic sacraments, but these can also be received with great devotion and inner fervor. By contrast, canon law will tell us that inner devotion and participation are not necessary; they only need to be performed according to the minimum requirements of the law to be valid. Hence canon law seems to foster ritualism.

The purpose of canon law is to define the necessary and sufficient conditions for valid processes according to the law. The US tax laws similarly define which incomes are taxable and which ones are not; moreover there are many deductions like professional expenses and humanitarian donations which are justified by the tax laws. As the US tax code does not intentionally encourage professional and humanitarian deductions, similarly canon law cannot be said to encourage ritualism. Yet, in fact, most people maximize their deductions, the way students aim for the highest grades for the least amount of studies, and we all hope for the highest pay for the least amount of work. The temptation of ritualism is inherent in ritual performances even if not fostered by canon law.

The 1983 code of canon law defines the conditions for the sacraments to be valid. They indicate which rituals and words must be followed for each sacrament. There are some administrative canons that specify how the various sacraments are to be administered. Thus for baptism and confirmation, there ought to be sponsors (canons 872 and 892) but their absence does not invalidate these sacraments. Infant baptism is to take place within a few weeks after birth (c. 867), but there is no indication of age for confirmation (c. 891). There are also recommendations and moral rules. Before holy matrimony, confession and the reception of communion are recommended (c. 1065). Some moral rules make very low demands. Catholics are to receive communion at least once a year, around Easter (c. 920), but at the time this canon was published (in 1983) it was already the custom to receive communion at every mass. On the other hand, Catholics are supposed to confess grave sins once a year (c. 988), but many disagree about the gravity of sins, and so they seldom go to confession. Catholics must also observe the eucharistic fast by abstaining from food "one hour before Holy communion" (c. 919), but if it takes one hour from the time one leaves home to the time that communion is distributed at mass, it is quite easy to observe the eucharistic fast. Canon law is mainly concerned with basic requirements, which is actually its purpose. The same can be said about the rubrics or liturgical rules printed in the priests' missal. As will be detailed further below, at TV masses the priests follow all the rules but nothing more. Hence TV masses tend to foster both sacramentalism and ritualism.

The Homilies

What is the main message conveyed by the homilies? In reference to the love of one's neighbor, we were told we should do so "simply because it is Jesus's teaching." With regard to discipleship, we learned that "Christ wants us to follow him because he created us and because we should be with him at all times." To deny oneself "means giving up being the center and making Jesus the center." From the parable of the mustard seed, we can get hints to "prevent relapse into drug addiction." In the Our Father, from the single word "Our," we were told that "We cannot do it alone."

These reflections show no theological knowledge. They are not much different from what an educated catechist might say. Their major characteristic is religious moralism, which requires no knowledge of Scripture and no clear reference to the readings of the day. The homilist may simply add "this is Jesus's teaching" to a few moralizing sentences, or "because he created us" to the invitation to follow Jesus. Actually any reference to the Bible is unnecessary. "We cannot do it alone" may be said at any time and out of time, and no scriptural justification is needed. Why is religious moralism so prevalent?

Role-playing is a common practice. Doctors, teachers, and parents play roles each time they behave the way society expects them to. Role-playing is also present at TV masses because they are repeated every day of the year. The term "TV mass" is commonly used on the CatholicTV network. It could have been coined by someone thinking of TV dinners that require minimum preparation and no effort. At several studio masses, Bishop Reed, the director of the network, appeared at the beginning to introduce the celebrating priest the way we introduce speakers and actors at the beginning of a performance. At the end of these masses he appeared again, thanking the priest for his performance, wishing people to enjoy the day, and "Thank you for watching"—thus implying that the mass was essentially a show to be watched. Role-playing is inimical to engagement in the sacred, and it may be the absence of such engagement that reduces homilies to mere moral exhortations.

6. Ecclesiology and Patterns of Relationship

What is the ecclesiology of the TV masses? In *Models of the Church*, Avery Dulles has outlined six church models but the TV masses seem to fit none of them. They are clearly clergy-centered because the laity plays no role in them except as lectors or altar servers. They are scheduled productions taking 25 to 30 minutes, not interactive processes. The high point is the moment of consecration when the bread and wine become the body and blood of Christ, and only the priest and his servers take communion. The focus on the *Eucharist as object* is endlessly emphasized by the camera repeatedly showing images of wheat, grapes, the chalice, and the host, but veneration of the Eucharist seems to be no part of it as the priests depart immediately at the end of the service. Because the mass is "the highest form of prayer we can have on earth," not much else seems necessary, and watching it on television seems as good as attending a Sunday service.

The model of church that comes out of this description is that of the church as sacramental instrument of salvation. This view is rooted in the Tridentine doctrines of no-salvation-outside-the-church and no-salvation-without-sacraments. This view is different from the Vatican II model of the church as "sacrament of intimate union with God and of the unity of all mankind."[11]

The kind of relationship that this model fosters is one of obedience to the laws of the church and the rubrics of the liturgy. There is much role-playing, of the priests when performing mass, and of the faithful when attending or watching. At the masses celebrated in a church rather than a studio, the majority of the people attending appear to be seniors. The pre-Vatican II cohort born before 1943 accounted for only of 6 percent of Catholics in 2016.[12] If seniors are the main audience of TV masses, one may wonder why the production of such masses should be "the center of CatholicTV's mission" as stated by this network.

7. Moral Consensus

In the Durkheimian tradition, a group is seen as a "moral community" when its members share strong common emotions, values and rituals. Such a group is called "moral" because of its common mores, not necessarily because people's behavior is seen as ethical. The strength of a moral community depends on the degree of its social integration.

TV masses suggest great moral consensus—or maybe social conformity—on the part of the producers. All studio masses begin with the same video showing eucharistic symbols, and they proceed by faithfully following the rubrics without creativity. All priests perform within the expectations of the television networks described above; there is no hint of disagreement or

11. *Lumen Gentium*, 1, in Abbott, *Documents of Vatican II.*

12. 2016 survey of CARA reported in its blog at: http://nineteensixty-four.blogspot.com/2016.

dissent. In their exhortations and main themes, the homilies exhibit a great moral similarity, that of religious moralism. The pervasiveness of this type of preaching suggests a strong consensus about it, although it may be due mainly to uniform training and a group ethic of obedience.

The TV masses have the implicit approval of the American hierarchy. Cardinal Dolan of New York appears frequently on Telecare to advertise for it, as does Cardinal O'Malley of Boston for CatholicTV. Both networks compete to enlist members of the hierarchy to promote their respective television programs. These masses also seem to have the approval of the Vatican since Robert Reed, who has been the director of CatholicTV since 2005 and appears in many of its shows, was elevated to the rank of bishop in 2016. No other Catholic television network in the world has a bishop at its head.

8. Spiritual and Emotional Energy

The spirituality that inspires TV masses is that of the traditional sacramental theology. Earlier we distinguished four characteristics of this theology, which are also found in TV masses. They are understood to be efficacious in and by themselves because it is Christ who works in them; hence they are "the greatest act of evangelization that the Church can offer the world." Second, sacraments and TV masses take little time and can be performed rather quickly if needed. They are individualistic practices in which the faith community is not involved. TV masses are designed to be watched alone by people sitting alone in front of a television screen. Most individualistic is the practice of spiritual communion, which consists of the very short prayer, "Since I cannot at this moment receive you sacramentally, come at least spiritually in my heart. Amen." This prayer can be said at any time during the day, at one's convenience. Finally, bearing fruit requires proper dispositions. The purpose of the homilies is to dispose the faithful to the proper moral attitudes, but they only give basic moral exhortations.

To what extent are the TV masses of CatholicTV representative of the archdiocese of Boston, its sponsor, and of other dioceses throughout the United States? We have seen above that this program has the support of various cardinals and even of the Holy See, which promoted Fr. Reed to the rank of bishop. In most parishes the family Sunday mass involves a choir and a longer homily. During the week, however, when in parishes mass attendance is very low, it is very likely that these early masses are similar to the low masses of the pre-Vatican II era. TV masses are apparently a viable model of worship for the hierarchy, but probably not for the faithful. They will last only as long as the American hierarchy draws on pre-Vatican II sacramental theology.

Conclusion: The Social Drama of
Sacramentalism and Ritualism

Collins's model of analysis allowed us to cover objectively the various aspects of ritual processes and then to engage in sociological and theological reflection. The possibility that masses can lead to ritualism and sacramentalism threatens any worship, and the American TV masses illustrate well this social drama of low input and low outcome.

Sacramentalism is the view that salvation requires the reception of the sacraments and, more specifically, attendance at the Sunday mass. This theological view is the ultimate justification for three masses every day, weekdays and Sundays. It is not universally accepted; for instance, the Guatemalan Catholic network, JesusTV, and the French Catholic television network, KTO, do not broadcast a mass on weekdays. Sacramentalism also implies that attendance at the Sunday mass is required for salvation. This view seems to be counter-productive: for US Protestants, Sunday worship is not mandatory, yet attendance is higher today than among Catholics. This obviously raises the question of what makes some Protestant worship more attractive. The answer seems quality, but quality also comes with its own cost and its own dramas. It is quality worship that we will pursue in the coming chapters.

Ritualism is a threat to all forms of worship. I have attended many very creative worship services yet after a while I got tired and wanted a change. Endless creativity is a necessity not only in public worship but also in private devotions. How creative can Catholic worship be, considering the constraints of the many liturgical rules of Catholic celebrations? This question will ultimately lead us in chapter 9 to investigate the place of creativity within the limits of Catholic obedience.

Let us now turn to a totally different type of mass, one of pomp and music.

3

Pontifical Masses at Notre Dame of Paris

Faith and Culture

ANY LITURGICAL SERVICE IS a synthesis of people's faith and their culture. Every mass is a synthesis between universal Catholic rituals and the culture of a given country, city, town, parish, and neighborhood. The 8 am Sunday mass is likely to be different from both the 10 am family mass and the 11 am Spanish mass.

The data for this chapter are taken from televised masses from the Cathedral of Notre Dame in Paris. The Cardinal Archbishop of Paris, André Vingt-Trois, raised the issue of faith and culture in my first recorded pontifical mass. This is an inescapable issue in worship analysis. It is the dialectic of Christ and culture discussed by Richard Niebuhr in *Christ and Culture*.

In order to understand this televised liturgy, we need to consider some characteristics of French Catholic television. There is only one national Catholic television network in France, KTO, while there are three in the US (CatholicTV, Telecare, and EWTN). The differences between the two are theological and cultural. Let us begin with the latter.

Most KTO programs are documentaries either for information or for discussion and enlightenment. There are five weekly one-hour documentaries or reports about events, places, or individuals (e.g., a pilgrimage, a local church, a writer) in the light of Christian values and traditions. There are also three weekly reports about the world, dioceses, and the papacy. Of a more reflective nature are two weekly programs: one is a theological debate, and the other addresses questions about faith. There is practically no top-down preaching of doctrine.

KTO offers three types of religious services: lauds in early morning and the midday office by the Monastic Fraternity of Jerusalem, daily vespers in the Cathedral of Notre Dame at the end of the day, and the pontifical mass on

Sunday evening, but no daily mass. The implicit spirituality that emerges from these services tends to have a double focus. There is the corporate dimension of the church in its collective prayer, as seen in the recitation of the hours, the vespers, and the Sunday liturgy. But there are also documentaries and discussions fostering personal reflection and individual growth. Neither of these was of noticeable importance in American Catholic television.

I recorded six Notre Dame pontifical masses, the first and the last celebrated by Cardinal Vingt-Trois, and the other four by two auxiliary bishops and an African bishop. This combination was a product of coincidence and will give variety to my analysis. I will again follow Collins's model of ritual interaction.

I. Interaction Processes at Notre Dame

Although I could raise many issues about the pontifical masses broadcast by KTO, we will concentrate on faith, art, and culture, the issue that confronted the audience in my first recorded mass.

1. Expectations about Art, Professionalism, and Prayer

June 12, 2016 was the twenty-fifth anniversary of the foundation of the cathedral's Association for Sacred Music. On this occasion, Cardinal Vingt-Trois expressed his gratitude for the contribution of the ministry of culture, the city of Paris, and the choir. He then added, "The beauty of the building which carries us in prayer is not sufficient by itself. To architectural beauty must be added instrumental, vocal, and liturgical beauty through which we try to express our faith and prayers." In other words, at Notre Dame, prayer should be enhanced by art, singing, and music. The school of Sacred Music at Notre Dame provides the professional training for this synthesis.

There is in France a strict but flexible separation between church and state. Most cathedrals are the property of the state as historical monuments, so the state provides for their upkeep. Public schools are strictly neutral, but Catholic private schools are supported financially because of their contribution to public education. The state also supports the Notre Dame Music School. High quality music is part of the national heritage. Hence twenty-five years ago the ministry of culture found it appropriate to subsidize this school of sacred music.

The Notre Dame School of Sacred Music (*la Maîtrise*) consists of two choirs. There is the children's choir that trains 35

> The Notre Dame School of Sacred Music is financially supported by the State, as are the upkeep of the cathedral and the running of most French Catholic schools.

to 40 children in 10 to 16 hours of classes and vocal practice every week. The adult choir involves about 20 students training for either a certificate in singing from the Notre Dame School, a certificate in music from the city of Paris, or an MA in singing from the University of Paris. The school employs three choirmasters and five organists.[1] Both choirs and their teachers serve in the liturgy.

The professional preparation of acolytes is given to volunteers of ages 16 to 25 who commit to serve the church under the responsibility of the rector of the cathedral. They are the "Acolytes of Notre Dame" (*les clercs de Notre Dame*). They engage in prayer and professional training as lectors, thurifers, cross- or candle-bearers, or masters of ceremony.[2]

Over the centuries the cathedral itself has constantly been improved. It was King Louis IX (St. Louis) and Bishop Maurice de Sully who founded it in 1163—a joint venture of church and state. After twenty years of marriage, King Louis XIII still had no heir. By a decree in February 1638, in order to have a child, the king consecrated his kingdom to Notre Dame. Nine months later Louis XIV (the Sun King) was born.[3] Louis XIII also pledged to renovate the choir of Notre Dame. The new main altar was decorated with a *pieta* and statues of Louis XIII and Louis XIV by the greatest artists of the time. The choir has been renovated once more in recent times. Besides the Louis XIII altar, it now also has, facing the assembly, a bronze altar with four male sculptures (the evangelists) in cubist style appropriate for the artistic tradition of Paris. Finally it has been fitted with the latest technology of hidden cameras, loudspeakers, and lighting for broadcasting.

Based on this history, we should expect to find a broad integration between faith and culture during the pontifical liturgies in the cathedral. In particular, performances should balance prayer and professionalism. The musicians should produce sacred music rather than religious concerts or oratorios. The liturgical action should be mystagogical (explained below) rather than ritualistic. The camera should convey prayer through images rather than simply record the rituals.

Moreover, the integration of art, professionalism, and prayer ought to be based on some reflection about art. Catholic teachings about art include the Vatican II Constitution on the Sacred Liturgy, Pope John Paul II's "Letter to Artists" of 1999, and "Built of Living Stones: Art, Architecture and Worship,"

1. See "Sacred Music at Notre Dame" at: https://www.musique-sacree-notreda-medeparis.fr.

2. About the acolytes of the Notre Dame cathedral, see: http://www.notredamede-paris.fr/Les-clercs.

3. About the vow of Louis XIII, see: https://fr.wikipedia.org/wiki/V%C5%93u_de_Louis_XIII.

the guidelines issued by the United States Conference of Bishops in 2000. Simply put, these directives insist that religious art must "lead beyond itself to the invisible God."[4] This is the purpose of any kind of religious art.

2. Description of the Ritual Performances

This section will present the various parts of pontifical masses the way TV masses were analyzed in the previous chapter.

The Entrance Procession

The first few minutes of the pontifical masses are crucial, just as the first few minutes of any social encounter or ritual performance are crucial to the experience and evaluation of the interactions.

The entrance ritual in four of the recorded masses was very spare, having only a minimum of participants: the thurifer, the cross-bearer, the gospel-bearer, one or two priests, and the celebrating bishop. At these masses, two acolytes of the procession also served as readers, candle-bearers, altar servers, and masters of ceremonies. The choir consisted of four members, two men and two women. When plainchant was used, one of the four choir members served as director and the others sang the verses. In polyphony, they sang in four voices, while one of the four also served as director. This simplicity was not linked to the rank of the celebrant, whether cardinal or bishop.

> Kataphatic rituals emphasize divine immanence through a profusion of images which apophatic religions emphasize transcendence. Both are found at Notre Dame.

Two more elaborate entrances involved a profusion of actors: the rector and master of ceremonies walking first, then the thurifer, the cross bearer, six candle-bearers, a few more acolytes, the gospel bearer, about twenty priests in albs, stoles, and chasubles, and finally the celebrating bishop. The exit procession was augmented by ten to twenty knights of the Holy Sepulcher and by the whole choir of about fifty. The first mass that I recorded with the cardinal archbishop as celebrant was simple, and the last one was elaborate. The mass for the feast of the Assumption was also elaborate, but the celebrant was a visiting bishop from Africa.

The entrance procession was accompanied by the antiphonal singing of a Psalm, so from the very beginning the liturgy was Bible-centered and antiphonal. There was some great originality in this practice. In one mass, the entering procession was greeted with the responsorial "God welcomes us to his house. God invites us to his banquet. Alleluia." Psalm 122 was also very appropriate: "I rejoiced when they said to 'Let us go to the house of

---

4. US Conference of Catholic Bishops, "Built of Living Stones," no. 148.

the LORD.'" At another time the entrance process was elaborate, using the refrain, "God made us free in Jesus Christ. All is for him. Let him be our deliverance!" This refrain was repeated by the whole choir of 50, singing in unison and in harmony, making a powerful impression.

At all times during the entrance procession, the camera showed the people and the actors from various angles. The cathedral was full from the very beginning and there were no latecomers. The attendees had the texts of the songs in their hands, and all sang, or so it seemed, because it was not possible to distinguish the voices of the choir from those of the assembly. The impression was a symphony of Christian unity. From a theological perspective, this was not a priest-centered service but a liturgy of the people of God worshiping together.

I will now present in succession the Kyrie and the readings, the homilies, the common prayers, the inspirational singing of the choir, the behavior of priests, and the announcements.

From Kyrie to Gospel Reading

There was great variety in the singing. In some masses, the choir consisted of four members (either two men and two women, or no men and only women, or a combination of the two), or nine members (four men, four women, and the director), or the whole choir of 50 members. During the liturgy, either the soloist was female and the song leader male, or vice versa, or both were female. One acolyte was the first reader one Sunday and the second reader another Sunday; on a third Sunday, neither of the acolytes did the readings. Two candle-bearers accompanied the reading of the gospel on some Sundays but not at others. The gospel was read by the archbishop or the celebrating bishop on two Sundays, and by a priest on the other Sundays. The Knights of the Holy Sepulcher in full regalia attended two pontifical masses out of the six, and one of their members read a Scripture passage at one of these masses. This variety in carefully planned choreography demonstrated serious attention to details and indicated that creativity was important to those who designed the liturgical performances.

> Singing by the choir can be both a prayer and a concert performance. Even concerts can be inspirational. At Notre Dame they are not art for art's sake.

Was the singing a prayer or a concert? Let us focus on the Kyrie in order to avoid having to analyze each of the pieces sung by the choir. Three aspects of the performance led me to interpret it as a prayer rather than as a concert, namely, the attitude of the clergy, the quality of the singing, and the implicit message of the cameras. First, during the singing of the Kyrie, all the priests and acolytes turned toward the main altar. They did not sit down as if listening to a concert but they stood in reverence. Second, the quality of the singing was exceptionally high. Beauty is neither religious nor secular. Beauty is found in art, and beauty is also considered an attribute of God. A traditional poetic image of paradise is one of polyphony in harmonious unity. The impression one could get from listening to the singing at Notre Dame is one of reverence for a transcendent reality. Third, the message of the cameras was inescapable. At the mass with full choir, the first image during the Kyrie was a wide-angle shot from above showing the 60 to 80 priests and acolytes turned together toward the bronze altar, with the cardinal standing alone behind it, the whole assembly with the Knights of the Holy Sepulcher on the right side, and the comparatively small choir seen in the vastness of this sacred space. This was not the picture of a concert. The message of the camera was clear: the choir sang towards the altar as a prayer and not towards the assembly as a concert.

The Homilies

This section will discuss the performance of the homilists; the content of the homilies will be examined later.

The cardinal archbishop presented his thoughts in a very lecture-like manner. He was fond of presenting intellectual challenges, such as reconciling the importance of living moral lives with the idea that we are saved by faith and not by good deeds.

Bishop Eric de Moulins-Beaufort spoke extemporaneously while following a prepared outline. He sometimes struggled with words, as if inviting the audience to struggle with him in his reflection. He compared Jesus confronting the evils of the world to our confrontation with "the deadly powers that surround us."

Bishop Denis Jachiet preached twice. Most memorable was his homily of July 17, three days after a terrorist attack that killed 86 people and injured 484. He began with the words, "Pain. Confusion. These are our feelings after the bloody massacre at the *Promenade des Anglais* in Nice." He concluded with comforting words about national fraternity.

Bishop Eugene Houdekon of Aberney in Benin (a small country between Nigeria and Togo) spoke for 21 minutes on the Feast of the Assumption. Central to his homily was the story of a personal miracle. Describing his lonely agony with malaria in Rome in the middle of summer, he invited the audience to share both his pain and the joy of the miraculous outcome, which he attributed to Marian intercession.

The Participation of the Assembly

In many parishes, participation by the assembly in singing is rather tepid. Not so at Notre Dame. There seem to be three reasons for this. First, the song leader invited participation through body language and by singing in a way that was not overwhelming, both of which reflected professional training at the Notre Dame School. Second, the melodies and texts were simple and singable, a quality found in the entrance songs, "Lord, deliver us for the glory of your name," and "God invites us into his house." Third, the singing of the Gloria and Credo in Latin were strong because people were given the Latin texts to read and the plainsong chants were traditional. One could say that singing at Notre Dame answers the Vatican II call for full and active participation in the liturgy.

Here, as in many churches, the assembly participated most fully in the liturgical prayers when invited to do so by the celebrating priest. The voice of the | Participation in prayer and singing by the assembly is often conditioned by the inviting or non-inviting voice of the celebrant.

cardinal in the "I confess" was strong but not dominating, that of Bishop Moulins-Beaufort was subdued and prayerful, and that of Bishop Jachiet was robust but melodious. The African bishop began with a loud personal prayer but his recitation of the liturgical prayer was in a low voice. The assembly was highly engaged in the calls and the responses leading to the Preface, and even more so during the recitation of the Our Father, during which many lifted their hands in unison with the priest. In these masses, it was the high point of lay participation.

The Choir and the Organ

The choir and the organ fulfill a triple function: they are supportive of the singing of the assembly, devotional to uplift the auditors, and festive to celebrate the liturgy with greater pomp. At Notre Dame, the organ provided a powerful accompaniment to the entrance and exit processions, it supported the singing of the assembly during the liturgy, and during the distribution of communion it filled the silence with soft inspirational music. The choir supported the assembly during the entrance rite, the Gloria, the Credo, and the responsorial Psalm. It provided devotional music by singing special pieces during the preparation of gifts and during communion. In addition, the choir enhanced the feeling of celebration during the singing of the memorial acclamation and the Great Amen.

There are churches in which the choir produces polyphonic pieces during the service. Are these concerts or | When polyphonic choir singing is followed by applause it was probably a concert; usually one does applaud after a minister's personal prayer.

sacred music? In a concert, the performers use their skills to produce an exceptional piece of art and draw attention to the music and ultimately to themselves. In sacred music, the performers must become invisible and their intension must be to elevate, not to impress. Here is a good example. At one time, during the preparation of gifts, a group of eight women sang a wordless melody, endlessly vocalizing the sound, "Eh," in one stanza, the sound, "Oh," in a second stanza, and the sound, "Ah," during a third, more joyful, melodic development. The camera left no doubt about its sacred quality. During nearly all the time of the singing we saw the cardinal incensing the altar as if the music were incense rising to the heavens. Next the cardinal washed his hands and stood in front of the altar. Then the camera returned to the singing group but slowly zoomed out of it, and progressively included not only the celebrant, the altar, and the church choir, but also the nave and the whole assembly. At the end of the singing, viewers were given a view of the whole cathedral with the nine women lost in the immensity of this sacred space. The attention was at no time drawn to the performers but instead to the mystical vocalization of the melody behind a visual foreground of ritual and incense.

During the Eucharistic Prayer, from the Sanctus to the Agnus Dei, the singing may appropriately be celebratory. In one mass, the cardinal struck a celebratory note by singing rather than reciting the Preface dialogue and the Preface itself. He was then majestically surrounded by about twenty concelebrating priests. The singing of the Sanctus was particularly joyful as it was accompanied by the full choir of fifty, with the twenty concelebrating priests all singing in full voice together with the assembly. The music, the choreography, and the visual effects of the camera worked in perfect coordination. After the consecration there was a crescendo from the memorial acclamation sung in unison to the polyphonic doxology and the triple Amen. The crescendo started with "Through him, with him, and in him," to which the whole church responded, "Amen!" Next, "In the unity of the Holy Spirit," to which the choir strongly responded, Amen!" The crescendo culminated at, "All glory and honor is yours, forever and ever," to which the choir responded in powerful polyphony together with the assembly, all singing, "Aa-men! Aa-men! Aa-men! Amen!" During this whole time, the camera showed in a motionless picture the whole cathedral singing in unity, in harmony, and in full voice.

3. Attitudes and Emotions: Engagement

Emotions are important in any encounter, for they determine whether one will continue, increase, or decrease a relationship. Emotions are important in religion because few people will return for long to boring churches, while it is positive emotions that attract new members.

The entrance procession usually included a wide-angle shot of the whole cathedral, revealing that the church was full, and every seat taken. There were no latecomers. During the exit song, those least involved in the liturgy often rush to the door, but not here. There was at Notre Dame a steady emotional attitude of engagement.

During the homily, the camera at times showed the listening assembly. What was striking in these images was that practically nobody moved, as though people were frozen in attentive listening. There was no noise: no sneezing, coughing, or babies crying. There was evidence of respect and intellectual engagement.

The assembly was also strongly engaged in the singing. Because the choir and the assembly sang together, it was not always possible to separate the contribution of each. During the entrance procession, however, the participation of the faithful was particularly strong, even enthusiastic. Why is this so? Credit can be given to the soloists and song leaders who skillfully led the assembly. The combination of art, professionalism, and prayer worked together in harmony, and the fruit of this trilogy was strong assembly participation.

In summary, the major emotion of the faithful could be defined as engagement, that is, a calm and mature sense of worthwhile participation.

4. Closeness to God

Personal encounters can bring people closer emotionally and intellectually. This is also true in religion. The concepts of liminality, piety, and mystagogy can help evaluate closeness to God.

The notion of liminality was first introduced by Arnold van Gennep and later developed by Victor Turner in *The Ritual Process*. It refers to the transitional stage in initiation rituals, *limen* in Latin meaning threshold. I use liminality to refer to the

> Closeness to God can be inferred from the observation of liminality or separation from the world, personal piety, and the mystagogy of the ministers.

threshold separating the sacred from the profane. In many religions, rituals require different vestments, behaviors, and attitudes. Notre Dame was the highest building in Paris for centuries. In the past and today, cathedrals were taller than palaces, cathedrals rising upwards like prayers and palaces spreading horizontally as a symbol of power. Liminality also requires an attitude of respect and proper attire according to local customs. During the entrance processions described above there was a sense of liminality, of moving from a secular to a sacred space and time.

Piety was the traditional Roman virtue of dedication and devotion to one's parents, clan, and gods. Religious devotions are traditional forms of dedication to the saints, the Virgin Mary, the Sacred Heart, and so on. Inner devotion is expressed in external behaviors and facial expressions. Devotional participation in the liturgy is expressed in gestures, body language, and tone of voice. I noticed many signs of inner devotions in the celebrants and the ministers of the pontifical masses. All walked slowly and meditatively so as not to disturb inner and outer silence. The readings were read in a devotional tone. Often the celebrant raised his gaze to heaven at the end of the recited prayers when he said the words, "Through Jesus Christ Our Lord who lives and reigns . . ." The Eucharistic Prayer was recited with gravity. During the recitation of the Our Father, the faithful raised their hands and often their gaze, and raised them highest during the climactic, "For the kingdom, the power, and the glory are yours, now and forever." Everyone recited with devotion, "Lord I am not worthy to receive you" before communion. The pontifical mass always ended with the singing of the *Salve Regina* as a devotional practice and not a ritual prescription. In short, art, professionalism, and prayer characterize the liturgies at Notre Dame, but piety and devotion are highest when prayer trumps art and professionalism.

> Mystagogy is introduction to divine mystery, existentially rather than doctrinally.

Mystagogy in the early church referred to the instructions of catechumens in the mysteries of faith. Today it is part of the Rite of Christian Initiation of Adults. Using the term in the general sense of introduction to divine mysteries, we can see that liminal separation from the world during worship and devotions are often mystagogical. In the past, initiation was mainly doctrinal, focused on teaching and preaching. Today there is more emphasis on intuition than on reason, more on feelings than doctrines, and more on community participation than individual assent. For many people today, especially the younger generations, music is a major introduction to transcendence, and for them the music must be contemporary. At Notre Dame, much of the singing is contemporary and of European taste, from the entrance responsorial to the *Salve Regina* at the end. Most importantly, singing is communitarian because the assembly is strongly engaged in it, as noted above. While liminality enables ascetic separation from the world and inner dedication in religious practices, mystagogy requires art and music inspired by mystery. There were times at Notre Dame when closeness to God came through music more than through ritual.

II. Interaction Outcomes

After an encounter or in the course of a relationship one may pause to reflect about it. What did we learn from the interaction processes at the pontifical masses? What ecclesiology do they portray and what type of relationship do they promote? Finally, what kind of moral values and community do they foster? These questions are interrelated, and we could begin with any of the three.

5. What We Learned: Leadership and Growth

Let us look at what can be learned from the homilies and from the announcements at the end of the mass, after which we can talk about the spiritual energy being generated by the liturgy.

Each of the homilists addressed a different aspect of spiritual growth. Cardinal Vingt-Trois's homily was doctrinal: "The function of God's law is to help us discover sin in ourselves by defining what is right and what is wrong. Yet it is faith in Christ, not the law that justifies. God's mercy is not for the righteous, but for the sinners." Here sin was looked at in relation to mercy, not just the law, which avoided the pitfalls of moralism commonly found in many homilies.

Bishop de Moulins-Beaufort promoted a spiritual rejection of the world: Jesus went to Jerusalem "to confront the deadly power of evil that goes on in the world . . . and to reveal the deadly power of evil in us." God's mercy exposes the "deadly and death-dealing" effects of evil in history. Christ does not unveil evil to condemn it, but to give hope because he saves us from "the prison of death and the deadly powers that surround us."

Bishop Jachiet explained Luke's reading with testimonies. Mariam is "the wife whose husband has been decapitated. She is proud to be the wife of a martyr and she said that it reinforced her love of God." He also gave the experience of a lecturer in a business school: "Power has meaning only to help others. The purpose of economic growth is social justice." These are examples of Christian living within the secular world, not of rejection of the world.

> Homilies are supposed to lead to spiritual growth; pious generalities and religious moralism are not enough.

Finally in the long sermon on Assumption Day, Bishop Houdekon recounted his miraculous healing from malaria thanks to the intercession of the Virgin Mary, whom he had implored at his deathbed. This was an example of devotional piety.

In summary, the homilists addressed various aspects of spiritual growth: increased understanding of doctrine, liminal distance from the deadly world of evil, involvement in the world through testimonies, and personal piety.

All announcements at the end of the mass were related to liturgical and paraliturgical activities that were to take place in the cathedral in the week or months to come, like organ and choir recitals. Most obvious in these announcements was what was missing. There was no invitation to join activities in the people's own parishes, to participate in national events then taking place in the capital city like missions and congresses, and more generally, no invitation to join a ministry and live a Christian life in one's family and professional life. In short, the religious program of the pontifical masses is one of self-preservation in an inward-looking way, within the spirituality of Vatican II. This raises the question of church leadership. No doubt the homilies fostered spiritual growth but they showed no global vision about the future of the French church.

6. Ecclesiology and Patterns of Relationship

Social participation depends on the prevailing definition of social roles. In the case of Notre Dame, social involvement depends on the theology of the laity and the church at work there. Here is a tentative appraisal.

The ecclesiology of the masses at Notre Dame reflects the theology of Vatican II, which promoted both a reform of the liturgy and a non-reform of church structures. The council called for "full and active participation" at a time when the mass was in Latin and participation in the liturgy was very limited.[5] At the same time the council did not change the theology of "submission of mind and will"[6] that has been the norm since the Council of Trent, although the language about the hierarchical nature of the church was somewhat muted.

The majestic processional entrances and the full participation of the assembly in the pontifical masses, together with the somewhat divine quality of the symbolism, support this Vatican II ecclesiology of variety of charisms and equality of all. The prevailing synthesis of faith and culture fostered this perspective. Yet the relationship between clergy and laity remained hierarchical. Many of the faithful who attended the pontifical masses were tourists or members of other parishes who appreciated the quality of the masses and came back week after week. This stability also raises the question of

---

5. *Sacramentum Concilium*, 14, in Abbott, *Documents of Vatican II.*

6. *Lumen Gentium*, 25, in Abbott, *Documents of Vatican II.*

leadership and the significance of these pontifical masses for the rest of France, which will be considered below.

7. Moral Consensus

According to Durkheimian theory, a society is a moral community if it fosters common mores and common values. Moral communities are created more by organic than by mechanical solidarity, that is, through interactive communication rather than through disciplinary integration.

Notre Dame is not a parish. Hence people in attendance come because they are attracted by the quality of the masses. They are likely to be lovers of full and active participation in the liturgy and nothing more. Vatican II did not promote active participation in the institutional church, which remains the domain of the ordained clergy and was strongly promoted by John Paul II.

What characterizes those who attend the masses at Notre Dame is their knowledge of Gregorian chant, their understanding of common Latin phrases, their high level of literacy which prompts

> There is at Notre Dame a strong consensus about faith and art. But is it representative of the whole French society?

them to read the handouts whenever available, and their appreciation of high quality music. In short, they tend to belong to the cultural upper class.

If this description is correct, then the moral consensus at Notre Dame centers on the cardinal's call for a synthesis between art, technology and transcendence, and more broadly a synthesis between the church and civil society. This synthesis has always been the ideal in French society. It is illustrated by the foundation of Notre Dame by the king together with its bishop, and by Louis XIII's dedication of his kingdom to Our Lady in the cathedral named after her. The French state subsidizes the Notre Dame School of Sacred Music as well as all Catholic schools in the country. The state finances the upkeep of all cathedrals as historical monuments. This ideal of church-state collaboration was also an ideal promoted by Pope Leo XIII, who envisioned two perfect societies working together in harmony, and it is still the implicit ideal of the papacy today. The only problem of this model is that it is shared by only a fraction of the French people.

8. Spiritual and Emotional Energy

Any relationship must face the issue of its future. According to Randall Collins, the seven interaction variables create an emotional energy that is the total sum of all the variables in the process, from expectations to moral consensus. Considering all seven variables covered so far, the evaluations are all positive, meaning the pontifical masses are attractive and will remain so.

The spiritual energy that sustains the liturgical imagination at Notre Dame is clearly that of Vatican II, which fostered a spirituality of renewal in the church. Its document on the liturgy, the first one adopted by the council, did away with the uniformity that had been the norm for centuries. Yet after the initial post-conciliar fervor cooled down and the controversy over birth control engulfed the church, Catholicism became polarized in a culture war with the outside world and a polarization between left and right within the church itself. The papacy and the US bishops retreated from public discussions except about sexual matters; moreover in recent decades the church has been assailed by sexual scandals. Catholicism has been losing members in the West, but the hierarchy does not face this crisis. The "New Evangelization" was supposed to address this problem, but it became a rather internal matter, exhorting inactive Catholics to "come home."

The liturgy of the pontifical masses achieves a synthesis of faith and culture at the highest level, but it also reflects the inward-looking spirituality of the post-Vatican II era. Its religious imagination is mainly directed to its continuation and development, with little engagement with the outside world. Its strong leadership is directed to the present, not to the future. A change is needed. Will Pope Francis be able to lead the church out of the morass of this inward-looking posture that is aggravated by inner polarization and segmentation? This will be an issue for the next chapter.

> The spiritual energy produced by the Notre Dame liturgies is essentially inward-looking, reflecting a general trend in Catholicism in recent times.

Conclusion: The Social Drama of French Elite Culture

Cardinal Vingt-Trois used the word "culture" in the elitist sense of high culture, that of Mozart and Italian Renaissance art, not, for example, jazz, rock music, and pop art. This interpretation is different from that of the social sciences, where culture has been seen as belonging to all people, not just the upper classes, since the publication of Ruth Benedict's *Patterns of Culture* in 1934. But there is an even deeper cultural difference among French social classes. The Catholic Church lost the majority of the working class in the middle of the nineteenth century when the clergy allied itself with the upper class. After that, French society became increasingly anticlerical, leading to the separation of church and state in 1905 and the creation of state secularism. Cardinal Emmanuel Suhard, archbishop of Paris from 1940 to 1949, became concerned with de-Christianization in France; as a response he founded the so-called Mission of France in 1941. Some priests took jobs in factories to re-establish contact with the working class, but worker-priests were condemned by Pope Pius XII in 1954. Since then no significant effort has been made to regain the unengaged and alienated. Sunday mass attendance is in single digits but the hierarchy does not perceive this as problematic. The Catholic Church has been losing members since the middle of the nineteenth century and it has apparently gotten used to it.

Several conclusions can be drawn at this point. The integration of faith and art in the liturgy is remarkable at Notre Dame, as is the perfect coordination of all the actors (clergy, choir, assembly). There is, however, no trickle-down effect because the liturgy is essentially a self-centered performance, with no ministry to the outside world. It is a good place for visitors, a place of enchantment for foreign and national tourists who can come and go as they please. Being the only Sunday mass broadcast throughout France, it offers an elitist model of worship with no alternatives for parishes that are less able to create such a synthesis of faith and art. And there is certainly no synthesis between the faith expressed in these masses and the culture of the mass of the French people.

Quite different are the papal masses, to which we now turn.

4

Six Papal Masses

From Segmentation
to Leadership

IN TODAY'S CULTURE, SEGMENTATION is often endemic because social differentiation divides populations into subgroups that have little in common. People think and act in isolation from one another, believing that they are a unified society until the differences become obvious.

Segmentation can also happen in worship. When the celebrant prays in a distant and monotonous voice, the choir sings by itself, and the assembly remains passive at all times, segmentation is alive and well. This segmentation is invisible, however, when the integration is achieved through obedience, uniformity, and discipline. What is needed to overcome such segmentation is a type of integration in worship that is based on inclusion, participation, and leadership.

This chapter will deal with segmentation at papal masses, that is, the liturgies presided by the pope. They fall roughly into three categories: those celebrated in the St. Peter's Basilica, those that take place in St. Peter's Square, and those that take place abroad. We will look at two of each type.

We will look first at two World Youth Day celebrations. The mass in 1986 in Melbourne, Australia, was presided over by Pope John Paul II, and the mass in 2016 in Krakow, Poland, was presided over by Pope Francis. Comparing these two papal masses will enable us to point to differences in the liturgy itself, in papal teachings, and in audience reactions. Next we will look at two masses celebrated in St Peter's Basilica, the mass on Pentecost in 2016 and the celebration of the feast of St. Peter and Paul in 2016. In these two masses we will look primarily at the liturgical processes. Finally, we will analyze two canonizations celebrated in front of hundreds of thousands of pilgrims, that of John Paul II and John XXIII in 2014, and that of Mother

Teresa of Calcutta in 2016. In the canonization masses, we will focus mainly on the participation of the assembly.

I. Two World Youth Days, 1986 and 2016

Let us first look at the arrival of the popes up to the time when they reach the altar at the World Youth Day masses in 1986 and 2016. This sequence took 30 minutes in Melbourne but only two minutes in Krakow. The difference is due to the different interpretation of the event by the commentators and the cameras.

The First Moments

Australia is a very secular country where Catholics are not seen as part of its social elite, so the secular television commentator for the papal mass used two tools of distancing: endless comments and images of the pope from a distance. From the very first images, we saw the papal motorcade in the distance, but what pleased the Australian audience the most was the view of the Flemington Racecourse where the papal mass took place, with the majestic view of the Melbourne skyscrapers in the background—seen from a helicopter, we were told. We were shown the racecourse probably as much as the pope himself. This racecourse is to Melbournians and Australians what Royal Windsor means to the British or Yankee Stadium to New Yorkers. Actually in the first pictures, the papal motorcade seemed quite Australian. Four galloping horses mounted by police officers in uniform and helmet opened the way, then two official cars, the popemobile, two more official cars, and four more galloping horses to close the parade.

When the pope reached the platform of the altar under a large canopy, his personality clearly emerged. Leaving the concelebrating priests and acolytes behind, he walked alone to the end of the platform, waving and blessing the crowd, and then while people were cheering, he walked to the other end of the platform and repeated his blessing while people cheerfully waved at him. A short moment later, the wind blew the papal cross to the ground, which made the commentator quip, "No doubt the wind will be a slight problem, but His Holiness will continue as if there were no problem at all." Indeed, and from now on, the helicopter images of the racecourse became irrelevant.

Most striking for us today, many years later, is the attitude of mutual respect and even distance between the pope and the crowd. During the long motorcade toward the altar in Flemington Racecourse, the popemobile was always about ten feet away from the people behind the barricades, and the pontiff never leaned out to move closer or to stop the motorcade. At the end of the mass, as at the beginning, he moved alone to the end of the platform to bless the crowd, and moving to the other end, he did the same. He did bless some of the handicapped in wheelchairs on the way out after mass; he did so by touching their heads or making the sign of the cross over them. No handshakes and no ring kisses. The crowd, too, was very different from what we see often today: no banners and no flags, except the small yellow flags of the Vatican.

> At the 1986 World Youth Day the pope did not stop to plunge into the crowd to shake hands and kiss babies. There was still distant respect for the pope.

Quite different was the arrival of Pope Francis in Krakow. From the very first images on KTO (the French television network that broadcast the event in France), we saw the papal procession, and within a minute, the pope himself. While the Australian television used panoramic and general shots taken from towers or a helicopter, KTO favored close shots showing only a few people, often leading to a close-up of the main character, namely the pope himself. In less than two minutes, Pope Francis was at the altar to incense it. No motorcade. No waving crowds.

The theme of the 1986 World Youth Day was: "Always be prepared to make a defense to anyone who calls you to account for the hope that is in you." That of 2016 was: "Blessed are the merciful, for they shall obtain mercy." The first theme directed the faithful to the outside world in an invitation to defend their faith and account for their hope; the second invited

> The theme of 1986 was, make a defense of your faith. That of 2016, be merciful. We have moved from social to individual engagement.

them to look inward. In 1986 the camera showed the open spaces of cheering crowds; in 2016 the focus was on the altar and the celebrant. The choirs also gave different messages: the Melbourne choir loudly sang English hymns that were picked up and sung by the attenders; the Krakow ensemble softly sang Latin hymns nobody understood. As to the crowd of several hundred thousand attending in Krakow, we saw them only at the end of the mass.

Differences in Liturgical Performances before the Homilies

Here we will examine the performance of Pope John Paul II in greater detail because the next section will cover the Pope Francis's masses from beginning to end.

From the very start, John Paul took command in a proclamation tone, "In the name of the Father, the Son, and the Holy Spirit." He continued in short phrases pronounced in proclamation fashion: "It is—with heartfelt joy—that we have come together—on this day of the Lord.—We are many—men, women, and children . . . We are one—one people—bound together—in Jesus Christ." Clearly he wanted each word to be listened to.

The choir played an important role in this 1986 papal mass. The Kyrie was introduced by a male cantor in a strong and clear voice and was repeated by participants at the invitation of the song leader standing next to him. The camera showed the cantor in a close-up and the response of the crowd in a wide-angle view. The Gloria was similarly a dialogue between the choir and the crowd. We could see successively the choir in a general view, the pontiff in prayer in a close-up, and, at the sound of trumpets, the response of the crowd. The participation of the faithful was shown in a panning shot: turning from right to left, the camera showed in rapid succession the faithful in the front row, showing briefly their behavior without giving them the time to react. We could see them singing and holding the text in their hands. This technique was repeated many times during the mass, always scanning the faithful briefly in general shots, never in close-ups.

"Let us pray." The pope observed a minute of silence. He covered his face with joined hands. He then read the opening prayer in a proclamation tone and a strong and slow voice, "God our Father—your Son—promised—to be with all who gather—in his name . . . May he fill us—with his grace."

After the first reading, the responsorial Psalm displayed a perfect musical integration between the cantor, the assembly, and the choir, with none of the three dominating. After each verse sung by the cantor the assembly repeated, "We are his people, the sheep of his flock," together with the choir singing in harmony. The images of the crowd were innovative again: the camera would show the singing people from the side and from a distance so as not to intrude and reveal their inner spirit by showing their faces.

At the World Youth Day celebration thirty years later, the mass was in Latin, perhaps because Pope Francis did not speak Polish, or perhaps because Latin was chosen by the master of pontifical liturgical ceremonies, about whom I will say a few words later.

> Nineteen-eighty-six: integration and coordination between the liturgy, the choir, and the participating crowd. Two-thousand-sixteen: fragmentation between the liturgy in Latin, the choir singing in Latin, and the non-participating crowd.

With the camera fixed on him, the pope began in a low voice, "*In nomine Patris, et Filii, et Spiritus Sancti.*" Continuing in an intimate voice, "*Pax vobis,*" to which a few around him responded "*Et cum spiritu tuo.*" After these ten seconds of prayer, the pope sat down to listen to an eight-minute welcome speech in Polish by the archbishop of Krakow. (In contrast, the welcome of John Paul II in 1986 lasted only a minute and a half.)

The invitation to repent was followed by a brief moment of silence. Then Francis began the recitation of the *Confiteor*. Only a few voices around him could continue in Latin, "*Deo omnipotenti . . . quia peccavi in cogitatione, verbo et opere.*" More than five decades earlier, this Latin prayer was recited by altar boys. Today only a few seniors may remember that at the words, "*mea culpa, mea culpa, mea maxima culpa,*" one was to strike one's breast three times.

The polyphonic singing of the Kyrie in Latin was introduced by close-up images of the numerous violinists in the orchestra. At the Krakow event, the choir consisted of 150 to 200 voices, accompanied by an orchestra of about 50 various instruments. From the beginning of the singing, the pontiff bowed his head in meditation. The images of the camera alternated between a general view of the whole choir and a close-up of the pope in meditation. The assembly was not shown since it had no role in the singing.

The Gloria was introduced with a close-up view of violinists. The camera tried to reflect the spiritual mood of the singing through general views of the choir from right to left, with the movement of the camera following the rhythms of the singing. At the words, "*Qui sedes ad dexteram Patris,*" the music and the images became more inspirational, ending with a triumphal Amen! But nobody sang besides the choir.

In short, Pope Francis appeared to be most comfortable with the Latin mass said in a low voice, as was the norm in the pre-Vatican II days. He often withdrew into personal prayer during the mass and paid little attention to the singing. The two popes, John Paul and Francis, clearly had different styles of presiding at the liturgy, but their differences are better understood in light of their homilies.

The Homilies

Pope John Paul II sized every opportunity to reaffirm the eternal teachings of the church. In his homily in Melbourne he made no mention of the liturgical readings. His main theme was about the role of the laity in the world. Here are some approximate quotations.

"The laity is called to bring the message of the gospel to the everyday world of family, leisure, and work . . . The priestly people of God finds much to do in the field of social justice, the poor and the disadvantaged in our consumer society." Then came a series of basic moral challenges. "Will the Christian community stand firm in defense of marriage and the family? Will the Christian community defend the gift of life from conception to the moment of death?" (Applause.) "Take a firm stand on the side of life and love, truth and justice, and the dignity of every human being. I am asking

you to take a stand for God!" (Applause.) To the young: "A society is deca-
dent when it does not want children . . . Australia needs young people who
will live chaste lives and bear witness to God's love in marriage." As a reminder that attendance at Sunday mass is still the norm, the pope said, "To
those who have drifted away from the practice of the faith, I say this. 'Listen
to Christ, and you will discover once more the meaning of his love. You will
hear him calling you to his Father's house which is the church.'" More generally, "No human life is safe in a world without moral principles, in a world
where everything is relative." (Applause.) "If science is separated from its
moral and ethical demands, it will never be able to lead humanity to a better
life." (Applause.) He ended with great conviction, "God made us. We belong
to him. Our task is to serve him with gladness." (Long applause.) He had
spoken, standing, for 32 minutes. Clearly he had won over his audience.

Totally different was the Italian homily of Pope Francis in Krakow. It spoke in
a soft voice, like the mentor in a graduate
seminar speaking to a circle of students.

> John Paul II: public proclamation of
> church doctrine. Francis: individual
> meditation on the gospel.

He did not try to convince, like John Paul; he tried to speak to the hearts.
Here are his first words. "Dear young people, you have come to Krakow to
meet Jesus. Today's Gospel speaks to us of just such a meeting between Jesus
and a man named Zacchaeus, in Jericho . . . Jesus wants to draw near to us
personally, to accompany our journey to its end, so that his life and our life
can truly meet."[1]

The tax collector of Jericho had to overcome three typical temptations:
low self-esteem due his small stature, fear of ridicule by climbing a tree, and
the pernicious effect of gossip about being called a public sinner.

Low self-esteem and fear of ridicule are not just adolescent issues; they
are issues of spiritual identity. "Faith tells us that we are children of God . . .
That is what we are. We have been created in God's own image . . . So, not
to accept ourselves, to live glumly, to be negative, means not to recognize
our deepest identity." In more colloquial terms, "[God] is our biggest fan . . .
even when we turn in on ourselves and brood over our troubles and past
injuries. But such brooding is unworthy of our spiritual stature!"

The fear of ridicule can be paralyzing. "Zacchaeus was a public figure, a man of power. He knew that, in trying to climb that tree, he would
become a laughingstock to all." Yet he overcame the fear of shame. He took
a risk, he put his life on the line. The crowd looked down at Zacchaeus as
a public sinner but "Jesus did otherwise: he gazed up at him (v. 5). Jesus

---

1. Text available at: https://www.vaticannews.va/en/pope/news/2018-10/synod-youth
-2018-final-mass-pope-francis-homily.html.

looks beyond the faults and sees the person." This is one of Francis's favorite themes: see the people behind the system, recognize the inner good behind the social mask. "Don't stop at the surface of things. Distrust the worldly cult of appearances and the cosmetic attempts to improve your looks . . . The joy that you have freely received from God, freely give away: so many people are waiting for it!"

Liturgical Performances after the Homilies

The liturgies of both 1986 and 2016 illustrate two different theological visions. John Paul's message was clear: "[God is] calling you to his Father's house which is the church." The Father's house *is* the church and Peter's successor is the pope. At all times during the liturgy, John Paul tried to rally his flock around Peter's voice. Quite different was Pope Francis's message: "Dear young people, you have come to Krakow to meet Jesus." The 2016 liturgy was totally geared to meet Jesus personally and individually. The Eucharistic Prayer and the singing were in Latin, which allowed the gaze to turn inwards.

Immediately after his 33-minute homily, John Paul began in a loud voice the recitation of the Nicene Creed: "We believe—in one God—the Father almighty—the maker of heaven and earth." The crowd responded with equal fervor. The dialogue between the pontiff and the people came to a peak during the Preface. The pope sang: "The Lord be with you!" The response was roaring," And also with you!" Then the pontiff read the Preface with emotions in a proclamation tone: "Father—all powerful and living God—we give you thanks—through Jesus Christ our Lord!—Through his cross and resurrection—he freed us from sin and death!—and called us . . . —to be a holy nation—a people set apart."

The Words of Institution or consecration, the culmination point of the Eucharistic Prayer, were pronounced with reverence and fervor. Then came the invitation to proclaim the "mystery of faith" and the people's response, "Christ has died, Christ is risen, Christ will come again." This Memorial Acclamation was sung together by the choir and the crowd, ending in polyphony. The Great Amen similarly responded—in unison and polyphony—to, "Through him, with him, and in him... all glory and honor is yours."

In summary, the 1968 liturgy showed integration between the roles of the celebrant, the choir, the crowd, and the images recorded by the camera. John Paul's voice was powerful but not overwhelming. The choir fulfilled its triple function of support, inspiration, and celebration. The images reflected the emotions of the participants. The crowd was cheerful but not casual.

In Krakow, shortly after the homily, a cantor sang the first words of the Gregorian Credo in the "missa de Angelis" version, the one sung every Sunday in pre-Vatican II days. Very few people remembered it. The choir members could only sing it by reading from their musical sheets. The camera showed in a slow motion the long line of about twenty officials attending the WYD but none could be seen moving their lips. At the end of the row, representatives of the Polish government stood motionless. Pope Francis did not sing. The Preface dialogue was in Latin and in a low voice: "*Dominus vobiscum*," with "*Et cum spiritu tuo*" by the clergy around the altar. Francis read the Preface in a low and monotone voice, as in a private low mass. The "*Sanctus, sanctus, sanctus, dominus Deus Sabaoth*" was polyphonic and inspirational. Francis recited the Latin Words of Institution in a low voice. The "mystery of faith" and the Memorial Acclamation were sung in Latin by the choir. The rest of the mass was similarly in Latin recited in a low voice. During the communion distribution Pope Francis sat in front of the altar, meditating.

At the end of the mass, three women and one man from the choir came forward to the end of the platform, far away from the choir and close to the crowd, and be-

> The European crowd of Krakow comes to life singing in English, not in Polish or Latin.

gan in English, "Jesus Christ, you are my life, alleluia. Jesus Christ, you are my Lord, alleluia!" It was an instant explosion of sounds and motions. The whole crowd repeated the chorus, moving hands and bodies, supported by the whole choir. The camera showed young people waving. The male singer sang the verses—all in English. Now the priests in the first rows were waving their hands and bodies rhythmically. The camera showed one singing woman in a close-up like a rock-star. The whole choir also tuned in, everyone swinging at the sound of the music. Before a general applause at the end, we could see waving hands in a close-up and the vast crowd in a panoramic view. Finally the crowd had been invited in. Of course one can meditate without understanding Latin but it is easier in English, which is the most common foreign language in Western Europe.

The general impression conveyed by the 2016 liturgy was one of segmentation: the pontiff read the Latin prayers like at a private mass, the choir sang Gregorian chants long forgotten, the crowd had no part in it, and the camera looked at the scene like an unimaginative spectator. This segmentation needs to be explored further, first at the masses inside St. Peter's Basilica and next in the two canonization masses.

II. Processes in St. Peter's Basilica

In looking at the papal masses in St. Peter's Basilica, we will again follow the eight variables of Collins's interaction model, the first of which is the formulation of expectations.

1. Expectations in 2013 and 2016

Expectations about an encounter condition one's satisfaction or dissatisfaction with it. When doing scientific research, expectations define what one will find or not find; without expectations (or hypotheses) a scientist searches in the dark. In order to understand what could be expected from Pope Francis, we have to review the situation of the Catholic Church before his election.

The pontificate of Benedict XVI ended in a triple crisis of unprecedented proportions: there were leaks from inside the Vatican, there was an international investigation of the Vatican Bank, and there were ongoing sex scandals involving priests.

In May 2012, Gianluigi Nuzzi published *His Holiness: the Secret Papers of Benedict XVI*, containing confidential letters and memos exposing power struggles and corruption within the inner circle of the papacy. These documents had been leaked by Paolo Gabriele, the pope's personal butler, but confidential information had been leaked during the previous months as well. At his trial, Gabriele argued that he wanted to fight "evil and corruption" within the papacy and put the Vatican "back on track." In October 2012, he was sentenced to 18 months in prison but was pardoned two months later. The long-term issues of secrecy and accountability were never investigated.

> The resignation of Pope Benedict for health reasons left uncovered the triple crisis of Vatican leaks, irregularities at the Vatican Bank, and the clergy sex scandals.

The Vatican Bank had been under international investigation for money laundering for quite a while. Many international banks were about to stop making financial transactions with the Vatican because about 25 percent of its financial transfers were in cash with no information given about the senders and the receivers as required by law. Benedict resigned at the end of February, 2013. His resignation was greeted with admiration and support, but the given reason, health, kept all the secrets pertaining to the crisis hidden behind the walls of the Vatican.[2]

---

2 About the Vatican finances, see: https://www.timesunion.com/opinion/article/Vatican-can-t-escape-financial-crisis-4295430.php.

The sex abuse scandals emerged in the late 1980s and continue to this day in courts. Most cases of sex abuse by priests were kept from the public until *The Boston Globe* broke the silence in 2002 and triggered investigations around the world. At the March 2013 conclave; these three crises in the church were discussed among the cardinals who elected Jorge Mario Bergoglio as pope.

What were their expectations? The vast majority of the cardinals at the 2013 conclave had been nominated by John Paul II or Benedict XVI. Faced with the multiple crises in the church, they wanted to uphold the John Paul II legacy and were opposed to any structural or doctrinal change (the so-called liberal agenda). They wanted, however, a reform of the curia through moral reform—the agenda promoted by Cardinal Bergoglio in Buenos Aires, which consisted of prophetic denunciations of abuses, pastoral support for innovations, and moral exhortations to all. To this day the whole church supports this moral agenda, and the cardinals did not wish for more than that.

What about liturgical innovations? Popes reign but the curia governs. Ruling over the Catholic Church is like a US president trying to govern with the cabinet inherited from his predecessor. Such a president would not be able to dismiss the cabinet; he could only replace members one by one over the years. The pope's actions are even more limited; he can only replace bishops and cardinals when they retire or die. The curia consists of secretariats, dicasteries, congregations, tribunals, councils, offices and commissions, all relatively independent one from another. When elected, Pope Francis inherited the curia from his predecessor, more specifically Monsignor Guido Marini as his master of pontifical liturgical celebrations. Marini was appointed to this office in 2007 and he is known for his support of the (conservative) "reform of the reform" in the liturgy. The director of the Sistine Chapel choir was (and still is) Fr. Massimo Palombella, appointed in 2010. His authority is independent from that of the master of the liturgy. The director of the Vatican press office was (and still was until recently) Fr. Federico Lombardi, appointed in 2006. He was previously the director of the Vatican Television Center. Hence the papal liturgies and their diffusion throughout the world are operated by three or four independent actors: the master of the liturgy, the choir director, the Vatican television director, and to a lesser extent, the Vatican press secretary. Specialization and segmentation are part of the Vatican organizational structure. When Bergoglio was elected pope, therefore, it was clear that the curia would resist reform.

Given this context, we can expect to find segmentation in the papal liturgies, both those inside St. Peter's Basilica and those in St. Peter's Square.

2. Description of Ritual Performances

Our initial focus will be on the entrance processions, the liturgy of the Word, and the Eucharistic Prayer. Afterwards, we will look at the cardinals, the choir, the camera, and the crowd.

Entrance Processions

The first minutes indicate the tone of a celebration and suggest some of the issues that need to be addressed. In one procession it took less than three minutes for the pontiff to reach the altar, in another it took more than 30. Let us look at one in the basilica and one outside, as recorded and broadcast to the world.

The largest basilica in the world provides the ideal stage for papal splendor, beginning with a majestic entrance procession consisting of scores of acolytes, priests, bishops, and cardinals. On the day of the recording the procession moved in one column that divided into two lines around the chancel where the prelates found their seats, while the papal escort climbed the steps to the altar under the magnificent baldachino cast in bronze by sculptor Bernini. The camera then showed the whole basilica, the nave full of attendees, scores of prelates already seated in the first pews, and the procession moving to the altar—all within the splendid marble walls. Such images evoke a baroque aesthetic of sumptuous splendor.

Since its completion in 1626, St. Peter's Basilica has been the setting of papal pomp and liturgical splendor, and one of the architectural marvels of the world.

During this entrance procession the choir sang "*Veni Sancte Spiritus.*" The assembly, however, never sang, neither during the entrance and exit nor during the mass. The assembly did not sing, the cardinals did not sing, and the pope did not sing. For instance at the beginning of canonizations, the choir began the Litany of the Saints and the assembly was to answer "*Ora pro nobis*" (Pray for us) after each saint's name. The prelates in the procession, the bishops, and the attendees in the first rows were obviously not singing. Since "*Ora pro nobis*" was repeated more than fifty times, it could not be said that they did not know the words.

The Liturgy of the Word

The integration of faith and language is central to the liturgy of the Word since the Scripture readings are meant to be understood by all in attendance.

At the four papal masses that are the subject of this section, one could hear Latin, Italian, Spanish, French, Chinese, Vietnamese, Greek, Polish, and more. The people who did not understand must have felt somewhat excluded. Most of the singing and the entire Eucharistic Prayer were in Latin. This means that from the Preface to the final blessing by the pope, those who do not understand Latin had to pray on their own, as in pre-Vatican II days.

The issue of faith and language needs to be raised, not only in terms of linguistic translations but also in relation to cultural traditions. Today the Catholic liturgy is celebrated in the vernacular, i.e., the local languages of around the world, but many people still feel that the liturgy is foreign to them.

Liturgical practices are governed by rules often known only to specialists. Canonizations are rare and their rules are unknown. The canonization of John Paul II and John XXIII took three and a half hours in the video of the Vatican television, and the canonization of Mother Teresa of Calcutta took two and a half hours. Nonetheless, one could argue that canonizations are unnecessarily long and excessively choreographed. A close analysis reveals that it only takes about two and a half minutes to canonize a saint. The process begins with the official request: "Holy Father, we beg Your Holiness that the above mentioned be included in the list of saints." This was a ten-second formula to which the Holy Father replied in a longer formula ending with, "After mature reflection and having implored divine inspiration and at the advice of our brother cardinals, we declare and define John XXIII and John Paul II as saints to be listed in the catalog of saints." Since this was spoken in Latin, few if any understood what was being said. On top of this, a papal mass is not needed for the canonization to take place. The whole process could be done in writing. Thus for the beatification of Oscar Romero, Pope Francis authorized the prefect of the Congregation for the Causes of Saints to publish a decree of martyrdom which made the cause of Romero open for beatification, which took place three months later in San Salvador on May 23, 2015.[3] Therefore, even the presence of the pope is not needed for a canonization.

> By itself the canonization ritual only takes a few minutes: a one-sentence request for canonization and the pope's one-sentence reply—all in Latin.

It would appear, then, that far from being totally rigid, many liturgical rules can be adapted to circumstances by those who know them.

The Liturgy of the Eucharist

In all of the papal masses in Rome, the camera focused on the pope and the altar, or the area around, but occasionally the camera also looked at

3. About the beatification of Oscar Romero, see: https://en.wikipedia.org/wiki/%C3%93scar_Romero#Basis_for_canonization.

the cardinals and at people in the pews. Everything was in Latin: the liturgical prayers spoken by the pope and the priests, and the Gregorian chant. Thus images and sounds conveyed the message that the mass is something done by the clergy with the support of the choir.

> The camera can present theological views, e.g., by showing the pope elevating the host seen from behind, like in the pre-Vatican II days with priests' backs turned to the assembly.

One memorable elevation of the consecrated host suggested—visually—a pre-Vatican II theology. The camera showed the pope not facing the assembly as is the case in the post-Vatican II mass, but from behind. Thus the public saw Pope Francis from behind as he raised the Blessed Sacrament, with two priests standing on his right and two priests on his left, the master of the liturgy kneeling on his right and the master of ceremonies on his left, one deacon kneeling on his right and one deacon on his left, and one priest kneeling on the right and another on the left. All had their backs turned to the camera. For viewers old enough to remember, this image of priests with their backs to the people was a clear reminder of the past. Unintentionally, the camera portrayed a theological vision from the past.

In three instances, the camera showed hands holding a rosary in extreme close-up, as if the picture were taken from only a few feet away. The implicit message was that during mass and especially during the liturgy of the Eucharist, the faithful should pray the rosary since they have nothing else to do. In one case, the camera zoomed in on a one-inch cross on a rosary, suggesting that this little cross was more important than the cross on the altar. In this case the camera upheld the individualism of private devotions.

Francis supports popular devotions, but he also urges the church to be a public hospital for the poor and the wounded. The ritualism of the papal masses is contrary to such an ideal. For an integration of papal teaching and papal liturgy, serious reform would be needed.

The Cardinals, the Choir, and the Camera

Since the cardinals and bishops were seated in the first rows near the altar, they were open to the scrutiny of the camera. Some appeared to be inwardly engaged in prayer but more expressions of piety and prayer were found on the faces of laypeople than on those of prelates. Cardinals and bishops residing in Rome have seen many papal masses. At the recorded pontifical masses described here, their attitude was one of solemn respect and formal obedience, but apparently not much more.

The Sistine Chapel Choir was established in its present form by a *motu proprio* of Pope Pius X in 1903. It consists of 20 male professionals and 30 young boys—rather than women—to sing soprano and alto parts in polyphonic pieces. The repertoire of the choir under its first director, Don Lorenzo Perosi, included many of his own compositions, and his immediate successor did the same.[4] Queen Elizabeth of England has similarly a choir of 12 male professionals and 23 boy choristers at Windsor Castle.[5] Both the British and the papal choirs give concerts throughout Europe, and both choir directors choose the music to be sung. More importantly, in neither case is the director expected to support the singing of the faithful, and this was clearly the case in the papal masses being discussed here.

Since the choir sang the entrance song, the Kyrie, the Gloria, the Credo, the Sanctus, the Pater Noster, and the Agnus Dei, all in Latin, there was nothing left for the attendees to do. Gregorian chant was supplemented by polyphonic hymns or motets. Some of this singing was quite inspirational and of great vocal quality but it was treated by the camera as a concert. We could follow in close-ups the facial expressions of the artists straining to produce high quality sounds in response to the animated motions of the choir director. In short, since the time of Palestrina, the Renaissance composer appointed as director of the papal choir in 1551, the papacy has promoted high quality polyphonic performances but not involvement by the faithful in singing during the liturgy.

The camera has at least five options and all were used during the papal masses. First, it can concentrate on the celebrant, the choir, and the other actors of the liturgy. This was the case most of the time, but with variations. This vision implies that the clergy is the church and the church is the clergy. Second, the camera can illustrate prayers with images associated with the prayers, for instance, a dove representing the Holy Spirit during the singing of the "*Veni Creator Spiritus*." Such images are hardly found in masses that are broadcast live, and when such images are found, they add nothing substantial. Third, the camera can seek images with a human touch. This is the general trend in secular television and also on Vatican television. The following images were all close-ups covering the whole screen: an adorable sleeping baby with a lollipop in mouth, a mother kissing her baby, a wife resting her head on her husband's shoulder, and a father gently swinging a babe in his arms back and forth. Also shown were the cherubic faces of boys comparable to those in secular and religious paintings from Raphael to Renoir. The camera stared several times at blond

As in secular television reporting, the camera can show images with a human touch unrelated to the liturgy, as was the case in papal masses.

---

4. See: https://en.wikipedia.org/wiki/Sistine_Chapel_Choir.

5. About the Choir of St. George, see: https://en.wikipedia.org/wiki/Choir_of_St_George%27s_Chapel,_Windsor_Castle.

British choristers singing like angels, and it also focused on faces of attractive women. A potentially emotional image was that of emeritus Benedict XVI struggling to put on his glasses. Note that none of these images had anything to do with the mass. Fourth, the camera could zoom in on the picturesque and the unusual. One shot showed African women in colorful clothes and elaborate headgear. Others showed architectural features of St. Peter's Basilica. One time the camera zoomed in on a cardinal's ring in extreme close-up, and another time it found a reflection of the basilica in a man's sunglasses. These pictures filled the entire screen even though they had no religious value. Fifth, the camera can visually suggest theological concepts. One of the more striking pictures was a view from a walkway above the massive baldachino, showing the altar below, the pope and the clergy around him, the half circle of cardinals in red, a few rows of prelates seated in the nave, and a few rows of laypeople. Clergy and hierarchy therefore predominated in the views shown by the camera, again suggesting that the church is a clerical hierarchy.

The Crowds in St. Peter's Square

The canonization mass of John Paul II and John XXIII was a media event attended by delegates from many countries. Vatican television dedicated 30 minutes to the arrival of the delegates and 33 minutes after the mass to Pope Francis welcoming the delegates and the crowd.[6] The event was attended by six royal families and 18 presidents, plus many prime ministers and other officials. As the delegates came out of the basilica one by one, they were greeted by a Vatican official and taken to their seats on the platform. The camera singled out the king and queen of Spain. Finally, after about 25 minutes needed to seat all the delegates, the papal procession emerged from the basilica.

After the canonization mass of John Paul II and John XXIII, Pope Francis went to greet the dignitaries. They waited in a long line of maybe 200 delegates. Francis shook hands with each of them, exchanging a few words, having pictures taken with them, showing warmth and patience during the 33 minutes it took to speak to them individually. Then he toured the crowd in his popemobile.

The crowd that could be seen in Rome in 2016 was very different from that of Melbourne in 1989. People were invited over the loudspeakers to "refrain from raising banners or waving flags"—in Italian, English, Spanish, and Polish but to no effect—in contrast to Melbourne where people

---

6. About these canonizations see: https://en.wikipedia.org/wiki/Canonization _of_Pope_John_XXIII_and_Pope_John_Paul_II.

only waved small papal flags at the passing popemobile. At all times people waved banners and flags indicating where they came from. Various means were used to attract attention. One banner was attached to balloons floating perhaps 30 feet in the air. Another six- to eight-foot long banner was waved in front of the camera obstructing its view of anything else. More importantly, the flags and banners were mostly about themselves, their nationalities and towns. I counted flags of no less than ten different towns of Poland. There were also flags from many other countries. In fact, so many flags were being waved that one could hardly see the people behind them. At one time we could see a ten-foot long banner attached to the fence and reading "Bergamo is here" as people waved to the camera. Another banner obstructed the view of the camera saying "Tijuana Mexico sends greetings and blessings from Rome."

Most significantly, people wanted to be seen by the camera. At the beginning of the mass, the camera pointed to a few people in the front row. Within seconds a man responded by waving back, taking off his hat to straighten his hair in order to look better. During the communion distribution, which lasted half an hour, it was appropriate to show images of people in prayer—and there were many—but wherever the camera turned, people waved back. When the camera showed a small group of people receiving communion, people around them waved at the camera. At the end of the mass, wherever the camera turned, people waved back or waved banners with their local identity. Clearly, people wanted to be seen.

During the motorcade after the mass, most people cheered enthusiastically, extending their arms to take pictures with their smartphones. A few tried to attract attention in unusual ways. A pole with three Ukrainian flags was lowered on top of the passing popemobile to force the pontiff to see it. At the same time, someone threw a red balloon into the popemobile. A few more balloons or objects were thrown at the pope. Some of the delegates were no less eager to get the pope's attention. Several delegates drew a smartphone from their pockets and insisted on having a selfie taken with the pope. One woman wanted to be prayed over, then wanted a picture taken with the pope. Among the prelates, many wanted to shake his hands and convey a personal message to him. It seemed that the outdoor mass had become a meeting of celebrities, with Pope Francis being the prime celebrity of the day.

In these and other media events, Pope Francis appears quite comfortable. Half a million pilgrims had filled St. Peter's Square for the canonization, many having arrived before dawn. They had been standing for six or eight hours in the blazing sun. They could hardly see the altar. Obviously they could not be engaged in the liturgy and show any sense of sacredness.

They were different from the other crowds discussed earlier. They resembled the Zacchaeus whom Francis had described in his homily in Krakow, having low self-esteem because of size or looks, and fear of humiliation among peers. Francis clearly wanted to see the people behind the system. To the young in Krakow, in Rome, and elsewhere he repeated, "Don't stop at the surface of things. Distrust the worldly cult of appearances and the cosmetic attempts to improve your looks."

3 & 4. Emotions and Attitudes & Closeness to Others and to God

Two different publics can be seen at the papal masses in Rome. There are the prelates who appear to fill most of the basilica because the camera is not much interested in people in the pews, and the crowd in St. Peter's Square. Both publics exhibit different attitudes and emotions.

Cardinals, who are the pope's senate, are expected to attend all major papal ceremonies. Their prevailing attitude appeared to be that of a dignified fulfillment of their duty. The cardinals nominated by John Paul II and Benedict XVI very likely had attended many such masses, hence their faces betrayed little enthusiasm. There is a long tradition that cardinals attend but do not sing, the singing being the exclusive responsibility of the papal choir. Like the faithful in the pews, the cardinals as a group played no role in the celebration of the mass, even when it was concelebrated. Hence their attitude could be described as one of formal attendance, similar to that of the Knights of the Holy Sepulcher at Notre Dame in Paris.

> Dignified formalism was the major attitude of cardinals, excitement was that of the crowd in St. Peter's Square.

Formalism was a major characteristic of all papal masses. The rules of the rituals were followed and applied quasi-mechanically. Thus the rubrics call for a brief moment of silence at different times during mass. No exceptions were allowed, not even after a 30-minute homily or after a 33-minute communion distribution; the rule of silence was mechanically followed.

For the prelates, the formal fulfillment of their duties is based on obedience to the papacy. Before being promoted to the rank of archbishop and receiving directly from the pontiff the pallium as a sign of their authority, each new archbishop must take (as recorded on June 29, 2017, the Feast of Saints Peter and Paul) an oath of allegiance which states: "I will always be faithful and obedient to Peter, the apostle of the Holy Apostolic Church of Rome, and to you, his legitimate successor." It is noteworthy that in secular societies, the traditional oaths of fidelity to the sovereign have been replaced by oaths of fidelity to the constitution or some foundational document. In the Catholic Church, fidelity to the teachings of Christ is still identified with fidelity to the papacy, in a Latin formula that has hardly changed over the centuries.

If fidelity to the pope is fidelity to the gospel, then religious formalism (the formal attendance at rituals) can be identified with closeness to God—at least in appearance. Throughout the papal masses, the camera showed images of the faithful in prayer, with their eyes closed. Significantly no such images were shown of cardinals. Yet no traditional Catholic would doubt that the clergy, being closest to the altar, should also be seen as closest to God.

Quite different were the attitudes and emotions of the crowds in St. Peter's Square. There was excitement, expressed in the endless waving of banners and flags. There was little outward sign of piety, except the fact that most had come from afar, had waited for hours before the beginning of the ceremony, and had stayed long after the mass was over. This crowd seemed to have little taste for religious obedience in a hierarchical church. They tended to favor improvisation rather than formal ritualism, and outbursts of emotions rather than formal attendance. They represent a new generation of believers.

II. Interaction Outcomes

It is time to look back at the ritual interactions described above and draw conclusions about what we learned concerning the patterns of relationship, the moral consensus, and the spiritual emotional energy found in all the variables.

5. What We Learned

In order to get some insights into the pervasive segmentation found in the papal masses, let us compare them with the pontifical masses in Paris.

Pontifical versus Papal Masses

The rector of the Notre Dame in Paris seemed to have total control over the Sunday liturgy, which was his primary responsibility. The acolytes of Notre Dame were under his direct control; they functioned as lectors, thurifers, cross- or candle-bearers, and masters of ceremony. All of the participants understood that the liturgy must be pastoral and that the choir must involve the faithful. They worked hard at their roles because the liturgy was different every Sunday. For the entrance procession there had to be an antiphonal responsorial that could be repeated easily by the assembly. The rector had to decide whether the liturgy would be simple or elaborate. This choice determined whether the choir would consist of four voices, nine voices, or the whole choir of fifty, and how many acolytes and priests would participate. The rector was likely to get in touch with the school of sacred music so that the best soloists would be chosen for the pieces to be sung each Sunday. He would also be in contact with one of three organists. As master of ceremonies, the rector needed to communicate with the celebrating bishop, who was different every week. Recall that the rector of the cathedral, Msgr. Patrick Jacquin, had supervised a complete rewiring of the cathedral to improve the broadcasting of the liturgies on television, so he might also consult with the television crew in order to improve the recording. In sum, the rector was the central figure at Notre Dame ensuring a highly integrated liturgy at the cathedral.

By contrast the papal liturgies are highly segmented. What is the likelihood that this could change? In order to assess the difficulty of reform, let us look at a few paraliturgical details of the papal liturgy.

> The difference between the Parisian pontifical masses and the Roman papal masses is one of organization: centralized and unified in Paris and decentralized and fragmented in Rome.

The zucchetto is a skullcap that was originally just a protection against the cold. It had no religious meaning, but it has become a sign of ecclesiastical rank. The one worn by the pope is white, the one worn by cardinals is a scarlet red, and the one worn by bishops is amaranth.[7] Priests have long ago given up wearing their black zucchetto (and also the biretta) but cardinals always wear their red skullcap in church and also at times in outdoor appearances. There are many rituals of power to show the superiority of the pope over the bishops. Popes never put on or off their zucchetto or miter; this is the function of a priest. The pope has a special staff surmounted by a cross called ferula but the staff or crosier of bishops is not allowed to have a cross.[8] All bishops can consider themselves as vicars of Christ, but since the Middle Ages the popes wanted this title to be used exclusively for themselves.[9] To make some changes in these rituals of power would require rewriting liturgical manuals and change customs developed over the centuries.

If symbols of power are hard to change, reform of the papal liturgy seems even more difficult. Even minor changes, like replacing the boy

---

7. On the zucchetto, see: https://en.wikipedia.org/wiki/Zucchetto.

8. Description of the ferula at: https://en.wikipedia.org/wiki/Papal_ferula.

9. On the use of "Vicar of Christ," see: https://en.wikipedia.org/wiki/Vicar_of _Christ.

choristers by women or allowing the pope to put on and take off his miter by himself would shake the whole ritual establishment. As was said before, popes reign but the curia governs. In practice, popes are often prisoners of the Vatican bureaucracy. Yet the reform of the curia is the task that was given to Francis by the conclave that elected him. Given the segmentation of the church's government, what is the likelihood that he will succeed?

Papal Leadership

Even if Francis cannot easily change Vatican rituals, he is free to teach and preach *urbi et orbi,* in Rome and in the rest of the world. In this way he has shown great leadership.

Like in the painting of Washington crossing the Delaware, a leader must be on the front line. The day Pope Francis was elected, he refused to live in the Apostolic Palace where popes have lived for over a hundred years. Instead, he took up residence in an apartment in the Casa Santa Marta, a Vatican guesthouse for visiting clergy. Shortly afterwards, he visited migrants and prisoners. The image of his washing the feet of a Muslim woman is symbolic of his leadership in action. But he also leads by speaking.

The pope's numerous speeches and three encyclicals cannot be easily summarized, but we can catch a glimpse of what is on his mind by looking at the speeches he made during his visit to Washington, DC, on December 23 and 24, 2015.[10] In his speeches we can discern four basic themes that characterize his papacy.

1. First, there is an appeal to conscience rather than authority. "I have not come to judge you or to lecture you. I have no wish to tell you what to do. I trust completely in the voice of the One who teaches all things" (in his speech to the bishops). Francis did not come to lecture but to invite people to listen to the inner voice that teaches all things. Authority in the church should similarly appeal to conscience rather than authority.

2. Second, there is a primacy of people over systems. Francis reminded administrators at the United Nations that "above and beyond our plans and programs, we are dealing with real men and women who live, struggle and suffer" (Speech to the UN). More generally, "In opposing every attempt to create a rigid uniformity, we can and must build unity on the basis of our diversity of languages, cultures and religions . . . Together we are called to say 'no' to every attempt to impose

10 All the speeches of the 2015 visit are available at: http://www.usccb.org/about/leadership/holy-see/francis/papal-visit-2015/2015-papal-visit-speeches-homilies.cfm (Accessed December 3, 2018).

uniformity" (Speech at Ground Zero). Of course this rejection of rigid uniformity also applies to the church.

3. Third, there should be a new ecclesiology of dialogue. To the American bishops Francis said, "We are promoters of the culture of encounter. Dialogue is our method. Dialogue among yourselves, dialogue in your presbyterates, dialogue with laypersons, dialogue with families, dialogue with society. I cannot ever tire of encouraging you to dialogue fearlessly" (Speech to the US bishops). This is a remarkable invitation considering that dialogue is very limited in the church.

4. Fourth, there is a call for leadership rather than centralized authority. To the American Congress Francis stated, "A good political leader is one who, with the interests of all in mind, seizes the moment in a spirit of openness and pragmatism. A good political leader always opts to initiate processes" (Speech to US Congress). This principle applies to the church, not just to the civil society.

There is another theme of the pope that overrides all others: get out of your comfort zone! Francis said, "I prefer a Church which is bruised, hurting and dirty because it has been out in the streets, rather than a Church which is unhealthy from being confined and from clinging to its own security."[11] This is a program of radical change.

Segmentation can be overcome by uniformity, discipline, and centralization—which is the traditional Catholic way. But it can also be overcome by leadership. Francis has provided a new description of leadership for the church: appealing to conscience, the primacy of people over systems, dialogue, a decentralized ecclesiology, and getting out in the streets. But can a program like this succeed?

6. & 7. Patterns of Relationship & Moral Consensus

We must again consider separately the two publics already identified: the public consisting of prelates in St. Peter's Basilica and that of the crowd in St. Peter's Square. The prevailing ecclesiology of the papal masses is expressed visually by the predominance of prelates in the sanctuary where they occupy most of the visible space. In a striking video taken from high above Bernini's baldachino, the camera looked down at the altar, the celebrant, and the priests around him, the circle of prelates in the chancel, more

The ecclesiology betrayed by the Roman liturgy is best illustrated by the oath of obedience of the new archbishops to the pope rather than to the gospel, to the papal institution rather than to evangelical values.

11. Francis, *Joy of the Gospel*, 49.

prelates in the first pews of the nave, and a few rows of laypeople. Images of clergymen occupied most of the picture framed by the camera. This image, repeated many times, suggested that the hierarchy is the church. Laypeople had no part in the liturgy except when presenting the gifts at the offertory.

The type of relationship portrayed by the papal liturgy was one of obedience, respect for the authority, and formalism. The assembly in the basilica and the worldwide television audience watching the ceremony seemed invited to say with the new archbishops, "I will always be faithful and obedient to Peter . . . and to you, his legitimate successor." Respect for hierarchy is basic in all unequal societies. Not only do cardinals, bishops, and priest wear vestments and skull-caps of different colors, they are also seated according to rank, the highest rank being given first places. The seats may also be of different quality: red upholstered seats with armrest for the highest rank, upholstered seats without armrest for the next rank, and plastic seats for those at the bottom. The consensus about this pattern of relationships portrayed by all the participants was that the Catholic Church is governed by an ethic of obedience, as were the European societies in the past.

While some of the pilgrims who attended the canonizations came in groups, most of them came individually, and all belonged to the smartphone generation. It is difficult to define the ecclesiology that inspired them and the patterns of relationship they entertained with the Catholic Church. They tend to be critical of all institutions. Americans' confidence in all three branches of the US government has fallen, with only seven percent having a great deal of confidence in Congress.[12] Confidence in religion has also declined, the churches now ranking lower than the military, small business, and the police. "The Catholics' confidence dipped to a record low in 2002 and again in 2007."[13] Our contemporaries have little taste for obedience in organized religion.

At the same time, the pilgrims flocking to Rome for the canonizations also showed great attachment to the church and to gospel values. Although our contemporaries tend to be more spiritual than religious in the narrow sense, they are also very open to evangelical ideals, as indicated by the number of conversions to evangelical forms of Christianity. Pope Francis reached them at the right level when he compared his young audience of Krakow to Zaccheus, the marginal Jew who colluded with the Roman Empire in order to make a fortune. Like Zaccheus, many people suffer from low self-esteem, fear of ridicule, and loss of face through gossip. Zaccheus struggled

12. Gallup statistics from: http://www.gallup.com/poll/171992/americans-losing-confidence-branches-gov.aspx.

13. See: https://www.livescience.com/21581-american-confidence-religion-low.html.

with identity as a renegade Jew. The social media generation likewise needs to find its identity as made in the image of God. It was fitting to tell them, "Don't stop at the surface of things. Distrust the worldly cult of appearances and the cosmetic attempts to improve your looks." Such evangelical messages are very relevant today.

8. Spiritual and Emotional Energy

There are two forms of spirituality at work here, that of the prelates and that of Pope Francis. The traditional Latin mass has been celebrated in St. Peter's Basilica ever since its completion in 1626. Vatican II did not change much: at the papal masses the Eucharistic Prayer is still recited in Latin, the choir still sings Gregorian chant and Latin hymns, and the laity still attend in silence. The only difference today is that the Scriptures are now read in modern languages. The cardinals are the princes of the church and the pope's closest advisers. They have been wearing red vestments since the Middle Ages. The unchanging ritual of the traditional Latin mass, the choreography of the cardinals around the altar, and the centrality of the pontiff celebrating mass under Bernini's baldachino suggest a spirituality of permanence that defies the centuries. This is a spirituality of clerical grandeur and superiority that is impervious to the changes in the outside world. It is a spirituality of collective security, based on the belief that "the gates of hell will not prevail against it." The basic attitude inspired by the palatial setting of papal liturgies is one of dignified fulfillment of duty and the exact enactment of the liturgical rubrics. The main emotion is one of loyalty and formalism. This spirituality has ensured the permanence of the curia over the centuries.

The spirituality of Pope Francis can be seen as a call for a new world order. "I prefer a Church which is bruised, hurting and dirty because it has been in the streets, rather than a Church which is unhealthy from being confined and from clinging to its own security."[14] Francis is looking beyond the confines of the sanctuary to face the insecurities of the outside world. The four points of his agenda described above call for a new form of being for the church. They are: a call to conscience rather than to authority, a spirit of encounter and dialogue, the primacy of people rather than rules, and leadership rather than centralization. These principles are similar to those of co-responsibility of the 1970s. They recapture the spirit of the Vatican II while also appealing to the smartphone generation. The main emotion is excitement, or to use one of Francis's favorite terms: "joy."

14. Francis, *Joy of the Gospel*, 49.

Conclusion: The Papacy and the Drama of Segmentation

The tension between specialization and social integration is a major issue in sociological analysis. As specialization increases with social development, so does segmentation, and greater segmentation results in less integration.

Until the middle of the twentieth century, it was common to believe that a strong society should be integrated through the uniformity of one race, one culture, and one religion. Minorities were often persecuted and their cultures repressed. Nazi Germany promoted this ideology of racial purity to the extreme, resulting in genocide. Today this model is still favored by many young nations that practice ethnic cleansing and the expulsion of minorities. In this view, pluralism is weakness and democracy inefficient. Historically, integration in the Catholic Church was achieved through obedience, uniformity, centralization, and control from above. The differences between clergy and laity were seen theologically as God-given. In parish life the great functional differences between the celebrating priest, the choir, and the faithful were seen as normal because this was the way it had always been.

Pope Francis calls for a new form of integration based on inclusion, dialogue and the primacy of conscience. This is the model of organic solidity found in differentiated societies, as opposed to mechanical solidarity in less developed nations. Organic solidarity is best seen in business when all aspects of production are integrated through constant communication. Segmentation appears when there is little consistent interaction among the various agencies. Similarly, church segmentation becomes obvious when the singing, the praying, and the rituals are not integrated. They appear as independent units pursuing their own goal at the expense of spiritual integration.

Segmentation seems to be inherent in the hierarchical structure of the church. The papacy nominates bishops, but the latter are independent from one another. Bishops nominate parish priests, but the latter are independent from one another. The pastor organizes his education department, his outreach program, his choir, and his school, but each of these units may work independently from the others.

There is a high price to be paid for the social drama of segmentation. As indicated by the title of this chapter, what is needed for overcoming segmentation is leadership, which is what we found in the new management style of Pope Francis. Such new leadership is also needed in parishes, to which we now turn.

5

Two Ordinary Parishes

Strategies for Church Growth

I. The Measurement of Church Growth

IN THIS CHAPTER AND the next ones, there will be less emphasis on Collins's model and more on theoretical issues. As indicated in the first chapter, an important goal of this research is to suggest strategies for renewal, which is a theoretical issue. The first part of this chapter will be dedicated to a discussion of growth and the measurement of religiosity, two basic theoretical questions.

There are programs for parish renewal based on small groups, for instance RENEW,[1] or on staff training, for instance the Catholic Leadership Institute,[2] but the evaluation of these plans is primarily qualitative, often based on subjective satisfaction. No objective measurements are used, as evaluations are based on observations with suggestions for improvement. At the same time, there are agencies that provide survey tools, such as the US Congregational Life Survey and the Gallup Member Engagement Survey. These agencies provide detailed statistics but they give no guidance about using them. The research generated by the Willow Creek Community Church, located in a distant suburb of Chicago, provides both survey data and strategies for growth, e.g. the research by Hawkins and Parkinson to be presented shortly.

The Willow Creek research is not academic; the questionnaires and the data are private property and have not been made public for peer review, yet the main findings seem sound because they tend to confirm what could be regarded as common sense. The results of this research can be

---

1. RENEW International was founded in the Archdiocese of Newark in 1976 to promote parish small groups. See: http://www.renewintl.org/.

2. The Catholic Leadership Institute was founded in 1991 to promote leadership in parishes through conferences and seminars. See: https://www.catholicleaders.org/.

summarized in five points. First, religious activities by themselves do not lead to much long-term spiritual growth. Second, spiritual development can be defined in terms of closeness to God. Third, three basic areas of growth are beliefs, practices, and other-centered activities. Fourth, guidance by church leaders is the most common catalyst of spiritual growth. And fifth, various levels of beliefs, practices, and activities suggest a variety of strategies for parishes and individuals rather than a uniform one. Let us look at these findings more closely.

A Revolutionary Finding

The Willow Creek Community Church had been surveying its members since 1992, but in 2007 it made an astonishing discovery, namely, that "Involvement in church activities does not predict or drive long-term spiritual growth."[3] This finding was based on 5,000 replies from its members as well as from six satellite churches located in and around Chicago. This finding contradicted the major practices of Willow Creek Community church. In the sixteen years prior to this survey, there had been a 50 percent increase in church attendance. Moreover, "Participation in small groups has increased by 500 percent, and we have witnessed a dramatic increase in the number of people who serve the poor."[4] Like many churches, Willow Creek sought to increase attendance, have people join small groups, and encourage altruistic activities. Now data showed that the Willow Creek flagship church scored only average on spiritual growth. Clearly church attendance and small groups were not sufficient to foster spiritual growth.

There is no denying that church activities do produce spiritual growth in the short-term, measured by increased church attendance and participation in small groups. After the initial growth, however, people reach a plateau, and in the long term, there is little additional growth. Thus joining a new church may be spiritually uplifting, but during the following five or ten years people may experience little new growth.

In this chapter, growth is measured by examining three variables—religious beliefs, practices, and altruistic activities—as will be explained more fully below. The absence of long-term individual growth could mean, for example, that after five or ten years, someone who attends church regularly might have the same level of beliefs (for instance, stereotypical beliefs about Christianity and other religions), the same level of practice (for example, just coming to church on Sundays), and the same level of charity (for example, giving 1 percent of income for Catholics and 2 percent for mainline

3. Hawkins and Parkinson, *Reveal,* 33.

4. Hawkins and Parkinson, *Reveal,* 14.

Protestants). Similarly, a no-growth parish would be one where within five or ten years the pastor offers no deeper theological insights into the life of faith, does not encourage additional devotional practices, and hires new staff without much input from church members.

> We may find it counter-intuitive that involvement in church activities does not by itself lead to long-term growth, because it does actually lead to short-term improvement.

This analysis suggests two things. On the one hand, people have to grow in their faith and they must be challenged to do so if they are not going to stagnate at the same level. On the other hand, churches themselves must constantly suggest new growth activities for their members lest the church itself stagnate in place. Roman Catholicism is prone to such stagnation because, as an institution, it promotes mainly sacramental behaviors, even though some parishes and religious communities may move beyond these limitations.

Measurements

Since the late 1960s, sociologists consider religiosity a multi-dimensional variable. Rodney Stark and Charles Glock in their pioneering work, *American Piety*, distinguished four basic dimensions: belief, practice, experiences, and knowledge. Factor analysis made possible the creation of empirically derived measurements, but these are usually considered too involved and too complex by researchers, who often prefer to rely on a simple question about the frequency of church attendance. The Willow Creek researchers, on the other hand, created their own measurement for closeness to God, measured both subjectively and objectively.

Subjectively, the respondents are asked to locate themselves on a continuum consisting of four levels of closeness to God. At the lowest level, usually that of regular attenders, people tend to agree with the statement, "My faith is not a significant part of my life," or, "I attend church regularly but have no personal relationship with Christ."[5] The highest level is "Christ-centered." People at this stage would say, "My relationship with Jesus is the most important relationship in my life. It guides everything I do." These people "represent the most active hands and feet of Jesus on the planet."[6] They are the backbone of the church; they are the leaders of its activities. There are two intermediary levels between these two.

Besides this subjective self-assessment, closeness to God can also be measured objectively in the three areas of beliefs, spiritual practices, and altruistic activities. These three variables are a good compromise between

5. Hawkins and Parkinson, *Move*, 77.

6. Hawkins and Parkinson, *Move*, 87.

the single variable of attendance and a complex scale of five or more dimensions. Within these three measurements, we can further distinguish between low intensity faith, practices and deeds, and high levels on these three variables. But in order to study them, these three areas of growth need to be operationalized.

The first area is cognitive; it refers to beliefs. The question is not just what people believe but also how strongly they hold to these beliefs and what impact these beliefs have on their lives. In the area of

> For research based on interviews and observation, the three variables of beliefs, practices, and good deeds are most practical and most effective.

morality, a basic understanding could be the recitation of the Ten Commandments, but a deeper understanding leads to a more sophisticated application of biblical norms. Preaching and teaching must deliberately lead to cognitive transformation; it cannot just be a catechetical repetition of some basic formulas.

The second area of development relates to religious practices like prayer, meditation, Scripture reading, small group discussions, and traditional religious devotions. Involvement in these practices is likely to intensify beliefs but may also lead to questioning them and growing beyond basic understandings. They can increase the experience of closeness to God and the desire to transform oneself and society. Moreover, research revealed that "Reflection on Scripture is the most powerful spiritual practice for every segment" of the churches growing in faith.[7] Such practices need to be fostered though preaching and teaching, and by exhorting people to engage in them.

The third area of growth is that of deeds of faith and charity—or in more neutral terms, altruistic activities. Here love of God and love of neighbor become one. While beliefs and practices are mainly private, deeds of faith may require that one's faith becomes public. Overcoming the fear of going public "marks this 'final frontier' of spiritual growth."[8] The most common forms of altruistic activity are giving financial support to the church and engaging in charitable activities such as staffing a food pantry or helping people to pay utility bills. More challenging activities would include challenging racial injustice, improving schools and social services, and working to change governmental policies unfair to the poor. Church leaders need to encourage involvement in such activities, and they need to lead by example.

At Willow Creek, the subjective and the objective measurements of closeness to God are clearly related. The church's research shows that each of the four levels of closeness to God correlates with a corresponding

7. Hawkins and Parkinson, *Move,* 117.
8. Hawkins and Parkinson, *Move,* 122.

level of faith, spiritual practices, and altruistic activities. Moreover, it is the church leaders who are the most significant catalysts of growth, at least at the lower levels of development. The pastor and other leaders must challenge beliefs, encourage spiritual practices, and promote social action in the neighborhood because the pastor plays a key role in the members' spiritual development.

Strategies of Growth

The above findings of the 2007 survey have been replicated from 2008 to 2010 in over a thousand churches involving 250,000 congregants.[9] Another study in England using different tools came to similar conclusions.[10] Every congregation that participated in the Willow Creek research received the results for its church, but pastors were often more puzzled than helped by the avalanche of statistical data. What were they to do next?

A new statistical analysis presented in *Rise: Bold Strategies to Transform Your Church* found eight basic church patterns, depending on their levels of beliefs, spiritual practices, and works of faith. The eight patterns of church were labeled troubled, complacent, extroverted, average, introverted, self-motivated, energized, and vibrant.

- In the troubled churches (14 percent) the levels of faith, personal practices, and faith in action were lower than average, and these congregations were in conflict with their pastors.

- In complacent churches (9 percent), the scores on faith, practices, and action were even lower than in the troubled churches, but people were satisfied with their pastor and the status quo.

- In extroverted churches (9 percent), faith development was low but deeds of faith were strong.

- In average churches (13 percent), people's scores were average and showed no direction for growth.

- In introverted churches (17 percent), faith and personal practices were strong, but public manifestations of faith were lacking.

- In self-motivated churches (10 percent), the three measurements of spiritual life were higher than average but the congregants tended to be dissatisfied with their leaders. Most initiatives came from individuals rather than from pastors.

9. Hawkins and Parkinson, *Move*, 263.

10. Francis et al., "What Helps Christians grow?" Table 12.

- In energized churches (12 percent), faith and religious practices were growing and people loved their church.

- In vibrant churches (8 percent), "Faith was strong and mature but still growing, and people loved their church."[11]

This classification of churches ranks them from low (the troubled and the complacent), and medium (the extroverted, average, and introverted) to high (the self-motivated, energized, and vibrant), but each type has its advantages and disadvantages. Complacent churches may appeal to many people but not to those who want more from their church. Average churches accommodate most people but do not produce much growth. Extroverted churches may thrive on high demands but they may also become spiritual deserts. In troubled churches and self-motivated churches there can be some conflict between a pastor's demands and the wishes of the people, leading to a no-win situation but also possibly to a new beginning.

Two findings of the Willow Creek research can be easily applied to many Catholic parishes. First, "church activities do not predict or drive long-term spiritual growth." For Catholics this means that sacraments, by themselves and in the way they are practiced, often have no discernable effects in the long-term, even if they do have short-lived effects. Thus, after years of mass attendance, parishioners are often at the same spiritual level as when they were adolescents. Likewise, the thousands of masses said by priests over ten or twenty years do not necessarily lead them to progress spiritually beyond where they were when they were ordained. More dramatically, confirmation often has the opposite effect, for instead of confirming young people in their faith, it often leads to their reduced participation in Sunday worship. In short, sacramental practices in and of themselves have few or no long-term spiritual effects.

This flies in the face of the traditional understanding of sacraments. According to Catholic theology, sacraments confer spiritual benefit called grace. As noted earlier, "by baptism *all sins* are forgiven, original sin and all personal sins."[12] Furthermore, sacraments are said to have automatic effects "*ex opere operato . . .* by virtue of the saving work of Christ."[13] Sacramental effects are generally other-worldly, but the sacra-

> There is no empirical evidence that the sacraments by themselves and in the way they are generally practiced have a discernable long-term effect, even if they have a short-term impact. This is a challenge to Catholic teaching.

11. Parkinson and Lewis, *Rise*, 3.

12. Anonymous, *Catechism of the Catholic Church*, 1263.

13. Anonymous, *Catechism of the Catholic Church*, 1128.

ment of reconciliation is supposed to bring about moral improvement and even reparation for sins, even though this is not often the case. Personal prayer and doing good deeds for others—two things that promote spiritual growth—are not required in the reception of most sacraments, and sacraments usually do not lead to increased prayer and works of charity.

From the perspective of ritual structure, most of the sacraments are rites of passage that ought to result in a person acquiring rights and responsibilities that he or she did not have before. For example, a person who is sworn into public office can make decisions that ordinary citizens cannot, such as making laws and approving public budgets. This is still true of ordination, but how is a baptized infant different from a non-baptized one, how is a confirmed child different from a non-confirmed one, and how are married Catholics different from those who live together without the benefit of marriage? It seems that people are not changed by the sacraments even if they change their status in the church. Hence regular sacramental practices do not usually lead to long-term growth.

The second finding of the Willow Creek research that is applicable to Catholic parishes is that the initiative for spiritual development changes over time. At the lowest spiritual level, progress is mainly the result of church initiatives. Pastors encourage prayer and promote the formation of prayer groups, and people invite acquaintances to come to their church. Sermons and homilies are very important at this stage, whereas self-direction and personal quest play a larger role at later stages.

If personal growth depends on pastoral guidance, then parish priests should help and promote people's favorite devotions—which is not what they do in the two parishes to be presented below.

From a Catholic perspective, the lowest level of sacramental practice is one of ritual performance without encouragement to spiritual growth. This is certainly the case of the TV masses where the priest performs the rituals without an assembly.

The remainder of this chapter and the next one will present parishes with an eye toward spirituality as manifested in the three dimensions of beliefs, spiritual practices, and faith in action. In this chapter, the two parishes of the Holy Family and St. Benedict tend toward the lower level of expectations. In the next chapter we will look at a Catholic church with high standards but with its own special problems.

In the Willow Creek surveys of various churches, the assessment of spiritual growth was based on questionnaires filled out by parishioners. There is no such data for the Catholic parishes that will be discussed, but information about spirituality can be inferred from sources such as homilies, the announcements at the end of mass, and interviews with the pastor and staff. Since the pastor is usually the main catalyst of growth in a parish, we can learn from his homilies and interviews to what extent he challenges the beliefs and attitudes and encourages spiritual practices. From the parish web page, mass announcements, and the parish bulletin we can learn about the practices available in a given parish, and also something about the actual practices of parishioners.

II. The Holy Family Parish

This suburban parish is similar to many others in the same part of the country. It is warm, welcoming, and not very demanding as it provides little guidance for faith, devotional practices, and good deeds. It has a school with declining enrollment, a convent but no sisters in residence, a balanced budget with no debt and no financial worries, and only a few devotional groups and activities for the devout. The pastor in his seventies, Fr. Michael, is relaxed and friendly. The parish governance is hierarchical but without friction. As is common in the Catholic Church, the parish structure is segmented since each function or unit is quasi-independent from the others. It is one step above the minimum participation level of TV masses since it has a choir, ten-minute homilies, and a Sunday church attendance of about 20 to 25 percent—as in the rest of the nation.

There are in fact two parishes within the Holy Family: an Anglo community and a Latino one. But they do not communicate with one another. Fr. Diego, who is in charge of the Latinos, speaks no English, and Fr. Michael speaks no Spanish. Fr. Diego never comes to the monthly pastoral meetings because he would not understand what is being discussed. He follows pastoral strategies of his own like an independent pastor. Most adult Latinos speak little English but their children learn it at school while speaking Spanish at home. The Anglo community offers no help, which it could through language classes in its Catholic school. Having no contact, the communities are conflict-free. It is a perfectly working segmentation—but at a very high social cost.

Liturgical Processes in the Latino Community

There are liturgical practices that are special to Latinos such as, according to Fr. Diego and my own observations, the participation in mass of *servidores* or commentators, the use of typically Latino songs and music, uneven participation in the singing and praying, holding hands during the Our Father, and much silent prayer. "There is much spirituality in Latin America," according to Fr. Diego, "especially the popular devotions to the rosary, the Virgin Mary, and the saints. People still recite the rosary at home, more or less often. People have pictures of Mary and the saints at home." These practices have maintained the faith of the people over generations. In colonial times the church was part of the political power structure, and after the wars of independence the clergy often sided with the social elites, keeping people in a subordinate position. This history may explain the uneven participation of the Latinos in the church liturgy.

The Latino masses at Holy Family follow a common format. After the introductory song by the choir, the liturgy begins with a general introduction to the readings of the day by the commentator. At the beginning of the mass on October 2, 2016, the commentator said, "Welcome to the first Eucharist of this month of October. We are the 27th Sunday of Ordinary Time. We are moving towards Advent when we will begin a new liturgical year, but there is still time until then." Many priests also begin their homilies with similar generalities. The commentator continued, "The apostles in today's reading ask Jesus to increase their faith. Their request is logical and very human because it is easy and often we have doubts, but the answer of the Master implies more than what he says." Then followed another set of generalities. "If our faith is authentic, even if very small, we certainly will begin at once to improve the world which is faithless and without love. Today we have the opportunity to question at the deepest level what we believe in and how we believe." Latino rhetoric tends to follow an esthetic of profusion rather than of parsimony: speakers say in many words what could be said in few. This is often the case in Latino homilies as well.

The first reading was presented by the commentator as "a beautiful passage from the book of prophet Habakkuk. This sentence from Habakkuk 'the just will live by faith' is totally certain." The singing of the Psalm of the day was introduced as "a prayer that is full of awe for our Lord the Creator of all things and all people." The second reading was introduced as "the very interesting letter of the apostle Paul to his friend Timothy. It deals with a catechetical teaching that may well be useful to us. Let us pay attention." The introduction to the gospel of the day was also lengthy: "The request of the apostles to Jesus that God increases their faith is a permanent and universal request of all men and women of all times. Without his help, faith is not possible." Such generalities are common in this Latino community, so there is no need for additional examples.

The entrance, presentation of gifts, communion, and exit songs were all introduced by the commentator, who indicated the page of the song in the hymnal. Very few people opened their hymnal, and maybe only half of the people had one. There was never any invitation to sing and there was no song leader. The singing was mostly done by one or two singers of a music ensemble that consisted of a synthesizer, a drum set, two guitars, and occasionally a flute or a violin. The ensemble performed in the back of the church, behind a powerfully blasting loudspeaker.

The Kyrie repeated many times "*Ten piedad de nosotros. De nosotros ten piedad*," on a very upbeat melody played by the synthesizer. This song is well-known to outsiders and is available on YouTube, but few people sang. The Gloria was a very joyful tune introduced by the synthesizer. It is also well-known. The same Kyrie and Gloria were sung at all the five masses I attended, yet few people sang along, with the exception of Fr. Diego, who sang a few times while at the altar.

A major characteristic of the readings was their poor quality. Most readers, including the priest, stumbled over words. Often the readings were choppy, covering just a few words at a time, as if the text was being read for the first time with no preparation. Another characteristic was a great tolerance towards children. Many prayers and readings were interrupted by crying babies. A few children played with toys, distracting people in the pews around them.

A special characteristic of the presentation of gifts was the symbolic introduction of activities done in the whole church, more specifically the work of missionaries, since the month of October was designated as the month of missions. The following objects were processionally carried to the altar from the back of the church: a lit candle as the light of God to the world; a cross, the symbol of salvation; a gospel book, the message of the missionaries; an image of Europe, for which the church was praying that week; the image of Pope John Paul II, the pope of missions (applause); and lastly the bread and wine. Such a symbolic procession took place every Sunday. It can be found in other Latino churches.

Unexpectedly, the whole assembly, previously silent, sang the Our Father with the accompaniment of the synthesizer. People raised their hands and formed a chain across the two halves of the church. They raised hands highest when they sang, "For the kingdom, the power, and the glory are yours, now and forever." The whole church came to life at this symbolic expression of Latino identity through the recitation of Our Father. An ethnic sense of community and family closeness are major traits of the Latino community, inside and outside the church. The common recitation of the Our Father was an expression of these common values.

Fr. Diego was trained in the Carmelite spirituality of St. John of the Cross and Teresa of Avila, which focuses on the contemplation and experience of the divine mysteries. In his homilies, he often emphasized prayer and missions. "Without missions the church has no

> The Latino religiosity is traditional; it is personal without much involvement in the liturgy, and as such it is a conservative force in the church.

future," he said in an interview. He has carried this emphasis into his ministry here. He introduced the offertory procession described above. He also created teams of missionaries who visit homes, and these are blessed at the end of the mass. On one Sunday there were two missionaries to be blessed, on another eight, and on another ten. The priest extended his hands over them; the whole assembly similarly extended their hands over them from a distance.

Latino religiosity is very pious. Instead of participating in the singing, people may engage in silent prayer. Fr. Diego is also very pious, as suggested by a tone of sincerity when he recites liturgical prayers, and by the conviction with which he preaches his homilies. His apparent purpose was to uplift hearts rather than instruct minds, and he spoke from the heart rather than from the intellect.

In summary, Holy Family is fragmented into an Anglo and a Latino church. The Latino liturgies are further fragmented by the different levels of participation: of the priest, the commentator, the loud singing band, and the silent assembly. Fragmentation comes with a high social cost, namely apathy and low participation; it seems a recipe for decline.

Liturgical Processes in the Anglo Community

The leadership of the Anglo pastor is non-directive: lay initiatives in the parish are welcome but are not sought after. Participation in the mass at Holy Family is also non-directive: one can sing or remain silent as there is little encouragement to participate. This can be called religious *laissez-faire*, and it leads to segmentation. Generally speaking, the louder the choir and the song leader, the more passive the assembly.

The song leader at all Anglo masses was a woman in her fifties or sixties. When she sang at the lectern in the front of the church, it was usually a hymn from the hymnal available in the pews. Her voice was loud and it was accompanied by loud organ music except that a few times she was joined by female voices from the choir on the balcony in the back of the church. Very few people opened the hymnal and sang. The scenario of non-participation at the entrance was usually repeated at the offering of gifts, the communion, and the exit song. At times, the organ was very loud and it was not possible to tell whether anyone in the assembly was singing.

The song leader also introduced the responsorial Psalm. Her strong voice gave a vibrato ending to every line that she sang, and this created a problem of comprehension. Excessive vibration (or vocal wobbling) comes with age, and singing vibrato often leads to the words becoming incomprehensible because the vowels are clear but the consonants get lost. Thus "alleluia" easily becomes "a-e-u-i-Aa-Aa-Aa-Aa." The verses of the Psalm were likewise incomprehensible. The song leader invited the assembly to repeat the responsorial line of the Psalm after she sang it, but to no avail. Nor could the priest very often be seen as singing.

When a choir (either of children or of adults) was part of the liturgy, the songs were not taken from the hymnal and the assembly was not invited to join in the singing. Thus on the feast of the Epiphany, as the entrance song the children's choir sang "The Little Drummer Boy," at the offertory, "We Three Kings of Orient Are," and for the exit song they sang, "Long Time Ago in Bethlehem." These songs were accompanied by guitar rather than by the organ. At times the singing was inspirational, at times it was awkward, but at all times it was a concert-like performance.

The adult choir of five women and two or three men often sang in polyphony, which excluded the assembly from participating. During the offertory procession at one mass, they sang *Adoro te devote, lateens deitas* (I adore you, hidden deity), which is a hymn written by St. Thomas Aquinas. The music is well-known, but the Latin lyrics are incomprehensible to non-Latinists. The exit was similarly a concert piece. Much of the singing of the adult choir was of high quality and it could have been intended for individual meditation.

There was one mass without a choir, without an entrance and exit song, with only organ music during the presentation of gifts and during communion. The rationale for the various types of music is difficult to explain. The adult choir sang in polyphony at a Sunday of no special importance, while the following Sunday there was no choir and little singing. This absence of rationale suggests organizational segmentation.

The assembly usually participated in the singing of the Gloria, the Alleluia, the Sanctus, and the Agnus Dei, but most people did not sing during the entrance song, the presentation of gifts, and the exit song. In general, the people participated most fervently when the melodies were well-known, and they remained quiet when the song leader or the choir introduced new tunes. Since the Gloria ("Glory to God in the Highest") was the same week after week, the people sang joyfully. There was also a common version of the Alleluia which people liked to repeat. The same was true for the Sanctus ("Holy, Holy, Holy") and the Agnus Dei ("Lamb of God"). Participation was strongest when the choir joined the assembly without overpowering organ music, and weakest when the organ played loudly. When the song leader introduced a new melody, singing "Alleluia" five times, few people repeated it. When a steady voice from the children's choir introduced a new tune for the Alleluia, only the choir repeated it.

And when the choir sang in modern dissonant polyphony, people were necessarily excluded from participating in the singing.

A pattern emerges from the above observations. People did not sing old hymns from the hymnal, but they liked to sing some more recent post-Vatican II songs. At the mass without a choir, the participation of the assembly in the songs was weakest, while it was strongest when the choir played a supportive role. As elsewhere, a choir wanted to shine during its polyphonic performances, but such concerts increased passivity. In short, participation was weakest at both the masses without a choir and masses dominated by the choir. Good planning is needed to foster liturgies in which the choir, the organ, and the assembly can perform together.

The assembly also participated in the recitation of the Kyrie, the Creed, the Our Father, and Lord I Am Not Worthy. The recitation of the Kyrie ("Lord Have Mercy") was strong but it only consisted of three words. The recitation of the Creed was weakest because many people did not remember the words, and even the priests usually read from the written text. The recitation of the Our Father was probably the strongest recited prayer, but with less enthusiasm by those in the back of the church. In these prayers and the singing, it seemed that some people took advantage of the strong participation of others to get a free ride, as it were. Free riding during worship is facilitated by a *laissez-faire* strategy in the liturgy.

Interaction Outcomes

Turning now to the interviews, here is what I learned from Fr. Michael. Currently, there are only a few devotional groups, and they are "getting extinct," he said. There is a steady group of 25 to 30 people who come for the weekly adoration of the Blessed Sacrament. The religious education program is active with about 80 volunteers. There is a yearly retreat during Lent that attracts 80 to 100 people. The youth program meets only twice a month for social activities. "The Knights of Columbus are not very active here. They are generally older men." There is a parish council, but "I am not too good at using it." There is a liturgy committee but its job is "to do things like decorating the altar, or having prayer books in the pews." It is the music director who selects the songs and plans the singing, which means that the Sunday liturgy is designed by this one person rather than by a committee contributing various ideas.

The pastor and his staff have minimal expectations. Asked whether parishioners would welcome a longer liturgy, "No," he said, "People are content with the 45 to 50 minute mass, with a 10 minute sermon. People are creatures of habit; it's a cultural thing." Asked whether they would welcome more face-to-face interactions, he said, "No, knowing others by sight, that's enough." In light of his stated principle that "a lot of people do not function at a high level for a long time," his strategy is to offer a few programs lasting only a few weeks. "The wisdom is that six weeks is as much as people can take, twice a year, either in October or November, or during Lent." His strategy is to offer multiple short options. "That's the marketing strategy of today."

The social relations at Holy Family are warm, welcoming, and not very demanding. The parish has about 6,500 registered members but the church can only hold 400, so it is very satisfying to see the church 80 or 90 percent full. At the beginning of a mass the church may be mostly empty, but it fills up quickly. There is an empty convent that has been converted into a spirituality center where all groups are welcome, the most regular and popular offering being a yoga class. Within today's pluralistic society, this parish is a conflict-free harbor where Latinos and Anglos can worship separately.

The spirituality that animates this parish seems to be one of custom and tradition, where masses last only 45 to 50 minutes, the homily no more than ten, and people do not like to sing hymns, al-

> The spirituality of the Anglo community is one of comfort and low demands. It is threatened by decline in times of crisis like ours.

though they do join in some prayers during the liturgy. The median family income in this area code is $122,646 but probably most high-income earners are not members of Holy Family.

How should this parish be evaluated? Generally speaking, the pastor does not offer theological insights into the life of faith, he welcomes but does not encourage devotions, and he delegates outreach to a staff member who does not get much input from the rest of the parish. Given these variables, we can say that this parish ranks as low or average. Evaluated according to the eight types of churches described by the Willow Creek research, Holy Family is not troubled by conflict but it is complacent in its expectations. The social cost of complacency is very high, but one can find comfort in the fact that other parishes are probably no better.

III. The Church of St. Benedict

This parish is located at the fringes of a metropolitan area that was semi-rural when it was founded fifty years ago. It was then populated mainly by Italian Americans, and although the population is more diverse today, Italian Americans are still the old-timers in the parish. Among the unique features of this parish are the pastor's weekly reflections posted on the web and a yearly "state of the parish" report that summarizes the church's achievements and the challenges ahead. A detailed financial statement is also posted on the web every year, which also lists numerous devotional groups and outreach activities. From this information one may guess that this parish tries to move beyond the level of the Holy Family parish.

As stated in chapter 1, the Gallup research found that in all US denominations, about 30 percent of members are "engaged," 50 percent are "not-engaged," and 20 percent are "actively disengaged."[14] Among Catholics, fewer than 20 percent are "engaged," and more than 30 percent are "actively disengaged," according to Gallup. In his desire for parish growth, the pastor of St. Benedict, Fr. Patrick, took the Gallup survey in 2010. He was probably painfully surprised to learn that in his parish 42 percent were "actively disengaged," 35 percent were "not-engaged," and only 25 percent, the backbone of his parish, were "engaged." These data suggest that this parish is divided, with more apathetic and negative members than active participants. Fr. Patrick was appointed pastor in 2004. At the time of my research in 2016, things had not substantially changed.

Interaction Processes

This description of the ritual processes will point to the importance of silence, the singing of the choir and the assembly, and the participation of the people.

Sunday mass begins with five minutes of silence before the processional entrance. All lights are turned off. Most people tend to observe this religious silence while a few continue chatting. Lights are turned on again at the entrance of the priest. There are many moments of silence during the mass. A few are prescribed by the ritual, for instance after the homily and after communion. Many more are optional. Liturgical ministers move slowly in a very dignified way during which time there is silence. Thus it takes much time for the first and second reader to come to the podium and walk back, for the song leader to come to the podium and move back, for the reader of the general intentions to come to the podium and move back. There is a long silence during the presentation of the offerings, and another silence during the collection. During communion there is a long silence when the celebrant gives communion to each of the eucharistic ministers, that is, before he gives them the bread and wine for distribution to the faithful. Communion, pew after pew, takes some time; it is followed by the prescribed silence when the priest sits down. There are a few more silences before the exit hymn. As very

14. See: https://news.gallup.com/poll/14950/congregational-engagement-ascends. aspx.

few people sing besides the choir, silent participation tends to be either passive or meditative. At the Latino masses at Holy Family there was also much silence because people did not sing; their silence was cultural while at St. Benedict it is imposed, as will be explained.

The parish has three choirs, one of adults, one of teenagers, and one of children. During mass, the page location of the songs in the hymnal was usually announced. About one parishioner in ten opened the hymnal, mostly in the front pews. As a general observation, very few people sang, except in the front pews. Several priests explained to me that this is due to ignorance of the songs, but this can hardly be the case. During the Christmas season, the songs included all the most common traditional hymns: "O Come, All Ye Faithful," "Come, O Come Divine Messiah," and the universally known "Silent Night," yet very few chimed in. The Alleluia sung before the reading of the gospel is the same all year round; its melody is simple and well-known, yet it induced few people to sing along. People are not averse to singing as such, since at several masses the Our Father was sung rather than recited. In one mass the Our Father started as a recitation but quickly changed into singing. The absence of singing is a cultural habit that goes back to the pre-Vatican II days when attendance was mainly passive during the Latin masses. The refusal to sing can also be interpreted as a refusal to move out of passive attendance.

The singing of the adult choir represented what mass participation should be; it was heartfelt, committed, and never ostentatious as in a concert. The choir director was talented, playing alternatively the piano and the organ, depending on the song. One soloist functioned as song leader but without much success. Raising hands in order to invite people to sing, the practice found in most parishes, is just not sufficient to engage a crowd. Yet strong participation in the singing by the whole assembly is common in a parish to be described in the next chapters; it is inspired by a theology of active participation rather than one of silence.

Membership in the three choirs has increased substantially in recent years, at the encouragement of the pastor who values greatly the quality of the liturgy. The adult choir sang both in plainchant and in polyphony. The children's singing was more difficult to handle, as their voices and their sense of harmony were not yet formed. Their singing was often awkward and incomprehensible, especially when two or three performed as soloists, shrieking in full voice. Yet children's performances were greatly appreciated by parents who often expressed their appreciation with applause.

The faithful fulfilled an active role several times during the mass. At the Kyrie, they repeated three times, "Lord have mercy." During the readings, about two in ten opened the missalette in order to better understand the text. After each of the two readings, people responded, "Thanks be to God." After the reading of the gospel, most people participated in the profession of faith, although mostly in a low voice. Most people recited the Creed from memory while the priest and a few faithful followed in the missalette. After the long silence of the offertory, people responded to the priest's invitation, "Pray, brothers and sisters, that my sacrifice may be acceptable." The Preface dialogue was often enthusiastic. The recitation of the "Our Father" was the highlight of the faithful participation. Most people raised hands; some held hands across the aisles. The high point was reached at the singing of "For the kingdom, the power and the glory are yours, now and forever." As the Sanctus and the Agnus Dei were sung by the choir, this left to the assembly only the recitation of "Lord, I am not worthy to receive you . . . " The assembly probably spent less time participating vocally in the mass than the choir, and the participation of both the choir and the assembly probably took less time than the moments of silence during the mass.

One important aspect was the early exit of about 10 to 20 percent of the faithful who walked out at communion. Some walked to the door after receiving communion, others without receiving communion, and others walked out after a short prayer to a saint in the back of the church. This early exit is found in quite a few parishes I have visited. In some parishes 10 to 20 percent of parishioners arrive late, thus expressing little engagement in the liturgy. At St. Benedict few people arrived late; on the contrary, quite a few people arrived early for silent prayer; yet quite a few left after communion.

Silent piety is commendable, but it can easily turn into silence without piety. To prevent boredom in silence there needs to be enthusiastic teaching and preaching.

The main attitude that can be deduced from observation is one of silent piety. At the family mass at this parish, however, there was much distraction. Some children in the back talked and even fought with one another. Some parents seemed to attend mass mainly to take their children there. However, a certain reverential silence prevailed at all times. The 2010 Gallup parish survey indicated that individual piety at St. Benedict is higher than at a typical Catholic parish in the area.

Closeness to God requires liminality, that is, a separation from the profane. This is achieved at St. Benedict through the initial silence, which invited people to quiet down in order to open to a transcendent dimension. There must also be mystagogy, that is, the revelation of the divine through liturgical practices and ritual performances. At St. Benedict the adult choir provided an atmosphere of religious piety, although the assembly did not participate much in it. Mystagogy was mainly achieved through the celebration of the Eucharist. This celebration was ritualistic, in the Tridentine tradition, which was what the faithful were accustomed to. Hence they found closeness to God through reverential silence, their participation, strong or tepid, in the songs and the vocal prayers, and a sense of the sacred experienced during the mass ritual.

Interaction Outcomes

I learned a lot about parish life at St. Benedict from interviews with the pastor and his staff. In discussing these interviews, I will concentrate on the spirituality at work there rather than follow successively the four items of the interaction outcome.

The liturgy is the major concern of the pastor. "All my energy goes into the public prayer of the church, which consists of the Eucharist, the sacraments, and the liturgy of the hours." The purpose of the liturgy is discipleship, he said, which is more than devotional prayers; hence he has little interest in them. "Devotions are obviously private: they barely reach my radar. If people want to initiate them and lead them, that's fine but I have nothing to do with them." The private devotions at St. Benedict are mostly an Italian legacy, especially the devotion to the Sacred Face of Jesus and that of Padre Pio. Their meetings take place in the morning and attract mainly women and retired people, and they seem to have a limited future.

Fr. Patrick's position is in harmony with the liturgical reform movement described in chapter 2, which championed the idea that it is the liturgy, not private devotion, which is the "true prayer of the church." Vatican II adopted this view and stated in three passages that it is the liturgy (not devotions) that is the "source and summit" of Catholic spirituality.[15] The council also made it clear that popular devotions are an inferior form of piety because the liturgy "by far surpasses any of them."[16] The council abolished the celebration of many saints to highlight the priority of the liturgy.

"Much of my sense of the liturgy was formed by the Benedictines," said Fr. Patrick, who attended retreats in a Benedictine monastery. This explains his emphasis on silence. This type of liturgy has some similarities with the "Reform of the Reform" of Benedict XVI. "Everything in the liturgy must be conducive to adoration, including the music, the singing, the periods of silence," explained Msgr. Marini, the pope's chief liturgist.[17] Fr. Patrick has geared his parish in this direction.

15. The three references to "source and summit" are: *Sacrosanctum Concilium*, 10; *Lumen Gentium*, 11; and *Presbyterorum Ordinis*, 5, in Abbott, *Documents of Vatican II*.

16. *Socrosanctum Concilium*, 13, in Abbott, *Documents of Vatican II*.

17. On the Reform of the Reform, see: https://en.wikipedia.org/wiki/Guido_Marini.

Not all parishioners favored this orientation. "There were people coming to me on two sides," the pastor recalled. "For the seniors, that is the only time they get to see their friends, so for them the desire to socialize at church is quite natural. Other people, when they come to church, want some quiet time before mass. I got messages from both sides, so I opted for five minutes of silence before mass. We have been doing it for the last three years." Over the years, Vatican II has also been interpreted in two radically different ways. One emphasizes the liturgy, the subservient role of the laity, and a hierarchical nature of the church. The other puts the emphasis on the people of God, collegiality, and co-responsibility. This second interpretation was progressively rejected in favor of the first in the years following the council. This option was also the one adopted by the pastor of St. Benedict, which dissatisfied quite a few parishioners.

The spirituality prevailing at St. Benedict is that of John Paul II and Benedict XVI. John Paul II was a man of action who required obedience in his struggle against communism and what he called the culture of death. Benedict XVI added a touch of mysticism in his encyclicals on hope and God's love and in his sympathy for the traditional Latin mass. At the parish of St. Benedict, the emphases on the liturgy and outreach are both in the hands of the pastor, following the leadership model of these two popes.

The prevailing pattern of relationship is one of docility of the faithful to the pastor. As there is no social structure for lay participation, lay docility is the salve that makes everything run smoothly. But this apparent moral consensus hides a deep divide.

The purpose of the liturgy, I was told by the pastor, was to teach discipleship. It is hard to see how liturgy can teach discipleship, except perhaps through homilies. At one mass, the homily by a foreign-born priest was incomprehensible. Another homily was hard to follow because of the constant noise of children behind me. Another homily was directed to the children whom the celebrant had gathered around him. His message was: "Jesus means 'God saves' and Emmanuel means 'God is with us.' God is with us in our hearts, and at church in the Eucharist." This was a low-level message, appropriate for children. Another homily on a feast of the Virgin Mary can be summarized by its conclusion: "*Theotokos* means God's bearer. We must be God's bearers in our own lives. Where is God, in today's confusion? We are challenged to bring God to the darkness of the world." One more homily insisted on finding a direction in one's life. "Today many people have lost their sense of direction. Today, in order to stay on the right path, we must know where to go. Christ should be our light in the night. With discipline we will not be lost in the night but find our way in Christ." Discipleship was a major theme in the teachings of John Paul II and Benedict XVI at the theoretical but not the practical levels; according to my observations, homilies at this parish do not provide much direction for a life of discipleship in terms of personal prayer, devotional practices, and altruistic activities.

Sunday church attendance at St. Benedict is down to 9 percent, less than half the national average of about 22 percent. The Gallup survey also revealed that 42 percent of parishioners are actively disengaged, that is, dissatisfied with the parish. There exists a deep discontent in this parish, behind the general piety exhibited at the Sunday liturgies. The two deacons of this parish have become alienated to the point that they participate very little in its ministries; one deacon even goes to another church for Sunday mass. If attendance is only 9 percent, this means that half the parishioners have left in recent years. One may be tempted to blame Fr. Patrick, but he is only following with determination the official theology of the papacies of John Paul II and Benedict XVI about the church and the liturgy. It is also under John Paul II that the church experienced a great decline in mass attendance in North and South America and in Europe. Thus the Catholic exodus is not special to St. Benedict.

Let us evaluate the parish of St. Benedict in light of the criteria of growth outlined at the beginning of this chapter. There is little theological or spiritual teaching in the homilies to nourish the life of faith. Devotions do not appear on the pastor's radar, and hence they are likely to decline. Outreach is in the hands of the pastor's appointed minister. In reference to the eight categories of churches, St. Benedict seems average, even demanding, but also conflicted.

> Surveys by an outside agency like Gallup can reveal levels of discontent easily negated or repressed. Then an internal dialogue becomes a necessity—which is not taking place in this parish.

At this point, nothing would seem to be gained from comparing Holy Family and St. Benedict parishes. We will analyze one more parish in terms of beliefs, prayer, and good deeds, and then conclude about strategies for growth at the end of the next chapter.

Conclusion: The Social Drama of Low Expectations

There are two points we learned from the Willow Creek research that need to be discussed in relation to Catholic practices. First, church services do not by themselves produce long-term growth, and second, it is the clergy that must initiate the mechanisms of growth. Let us begin with the first finding.

All religious practices produce spiritual development initially, but after a while they reach a plateau of routine that is difficult to overcome because, as the saying goes, routine is the death of piety. This applies to the recitation of the rosary, mass attendance, and participation in a devotional group. After ten or twenty years of such practices, one is often not much transformed. There is, however, a difference between low and high intensity performances. A high intensity performance in one devotional practice can lead to others. By combining several high intensity practices, one is likely to reach long-term growth, but most people follow devotions with moderate or low intensity. The participation in the masses described above is mostly of low intensity. Popular devotions are also mostly of low intensity and they are often divorced from sacramental practices. In Latin America, millions of Catholics follow popular devotions but they seldom or never attend mass. Low intensity practices usually do not lead beyond themselves.

It is the responsibility of church leaders, according to the Willow Creek research, to lead to higher levels of religiosity, for instance, through sermons. The homilies given at the TV masses and those presented in this chapter are not likely to lead to high intensity religious practices. Moreover, Vatican II has prioritized the liturgy at the expense of devotions. Fr. Patrick has clearly stated "I have nothing to do with them," in line with Vatican II, and he does not expect much initiative coming from his parishioners.

Low intensity practices easily fade away. So it is with mass attendance. In pre-Vatican II days, participation of the faithful in the Latin mass was actually lower than today, yet few people dropped out because the church building was also the center of their private devotions. People were attached to the eucharistic devotions (First Fridays, Benediction, Adoration), and the many statues of Mary and the saints in the church and at home nourished their devotions. By making the liturgy the main or sole religious practice at the expense of private devotions, Vatican II has unwillingly undermined people's faith. It is like asking students to attend class without giving them homework. Class attendance and homework support one another; if one is dropped, the other is weakened. Instead of the Sunday liturgy being the "source and summit" of spirituality, the Sunday mass becomes an island in the ocean of secularity. Without personal devotions, mass attendance becomes devotion-less, that is, perfunctory, and the imposed moments of silence are filled with emptiness. This is the situation not only at St. Benedict but in many parishes.

We have reached the core of the social drama of many parishes today: low expectations on the part of the pastor, little support for private devotions, and strong official support for the liturgy but little local push for it. For many Catholics the social drama becomes the dilemma of leaving or staying. Let us now turn to a more dynamic church.

6

A Lay-Run Parish

Consensus without a Central Authority

THE CHURCH OF THE Resurrection is located in what used to be an Irish Catholic neighborhood close to a nearby railroad-switching yard. In the 1960s, railroad operations began to be computerized, reducing the need for manual labor, so families moved away and the area around the church gradually turned into an industrial park of factories and warehouses. When the parish was about to be closed, an energetic young priest gave it new life. Here is what an 82-year-old sister remembers about that time: "I was there two years after the parish was restarted. The pastor was mainly an instigator, not an organizer. He enabled people to do what they wanted to do. Governance was from the bottom up; it was based on social justice and the equality of men and women. The congregation selected its own readings, sometimes from the Bible, sometimes from contemporary literature, sometimes we wrote them ourselves. For the first time in my life I read the Bible."

A new pastor who was appointed in the 1970s was particularly concerned about what the US government was doing in Central America. He informed the congregation that America was supplying weapons and training to repressive regimes in El Salvador and other countries. Under his leadership, people in the parish were galvanized around issues of social justice, including the anti-war movement. After much debate, parishioners voted to become a sanctuary parish, meaning they agreed to house refugees fleeing from oppression in Latin America and helping them reach political asylum in Canada. The parish also became involved in local social justice issues such as rehabilitating local housing, providing financial services to poor people, and starting a gift shop that increased the income of Third World artisans by paying them fair prices for their hand-crafted goods. The church cooperated with other socially conscious parishes across the city and occasionally with nearby African American congregations.

The bishop at the time had attended the Second Vatican Council, and he gave permission to this church to implement the newly approved liturgical changes. Side altars and statues were removed, and a platform for a contemporary music ensemble replaced the imitation Gothic altar. The new altar was a large wooden table on casters so that it could be moved, but its usual place was in the center of the nave. Pews were replaced by comfortable folding chairs that face the center aisle, bringing everyone closer to the liturgical celebration. Contemporary songs replaced traditional hymns, real bread replaced communion wafers, lay preaching was allowed, and in general, full participation by the assembly was encouraged. The bishop fully embraced the spirit of Vatican II and gave tacit approval to how parish life was developing, even though it was not in full compliance with canon law. With the loss of nearby housing for railroad workers, the Church of the Resurrection became a non-geographical parish, drawing people from around the city and even across county lines. Eventually, due to the declining number of diocesan clergy, the church was given a lay administrator, and a priest from a nearby parish was appointed to preside at Sunday worship. The parish has now been staffed by laypeople for over a quarter of a century.

I. Interaction Processes

The church itself is a modest brick structure with a tall peak and low sides, typical of many Catholic churches built in working-class neighborhoods during the early twentieth century. The seating capacity is around 300. During Advent, in the small garden outside the main entrance, there may be 90 to 100 white crosses, one for each of the homicides in the city during the past year, many of which happen in the poor neighborhood on the other side of the railroad yard. Year-round, across the front of the church there is a large banner that reads, "Immigrants and Refugees Welcome."

Description of the Liturgy

As one walks into the church, a greeter hands out the participation sheet with all the songs and prayers of the day. The parish does not use a hymnal but has its own collection of songs, all of which are reproduced with permission. After entering, people stand around and chat with friends. There are no pews and no kneelers but chairs facing each other on both sides of the nave, with the altar in the middle.

At the appointed time for mass, the sound of a gong signals everyone to stop talking and take their seats. The greeter invites all to silence and suggests that the newcomers stand up and introduce themselves. When the liturgical team of the day (the priest, the greeters, the two readers, and the lay homilist, if any) come out of the vesting area in the rear, all rise for the opening song.

The orderly proceedings described so far are the result of careful planning by various committees. The worship committee oversees four liturgical planning teams. Each of these teams meets with the head of the music ministry and they decide which songs would be appropriate for the readings of the four or five weeks to come. They also decide which Kyrie, which Profession of Faith, and which Lord's Prayer is going to be used during the coming weeks. Besides the worship committee, there are also teams of greeters, lectors, eucharistic ministers, art and environment workers, volunteers for the stewardship collection, and Sunday bread bakers. All these teams are coordinated by the worship committee.

There is no choir but there is an ensemble of musicians under the direction of an accomplished pianist. The instruments include two guitars, a mandolin, drums, a flute, and a keyboard.

> There is no choir, no song leader, yet most people sing. There is a music ensemble but no director, and the music does not overshadow the singing.

The main function of the ensemble is to lead the assembly in song, so even though the instrumentalists also sing, their voices are often drowned out by those of the people. There is no leader as such; when the ensemble begins, all join in. Thus the ensemble basically fulfills a supportive function.

At one time, the celebrant began the mass with the words, "In the name of the Creator, the Redeemer, and the Holy Sanctifier." A recently-appointed bishop objected to this and other non-canonical practices such as allowing lay homilists and not kneeling during the Eucharistic Prayer. Faced with twelve diocesan mandates from the new bishop, the parish met monthly after worship to discuss and decide about them. After two years, with the mediation of laypeople in the chancery, the parish accepted four of the mandates as close to what they were already doing, they rejected four (including the attempted prohibition of lay preachers), and they made four adaptations. For example, instead of beginning with the Sign of the Cross using inclusive language, the liturgy now begins with the ritual gesture being performed in silence.

For years, the sacramental minister was a priest who also served in another parish, but since that priest has retired, the mass is celebrated by either one of two retired priests or a priest from a religious order. One of the priests always follows the Roman Missal, but the other two are more creative, either using prayers they have memorized or paraphrasing the prescribed texts.

The music of the Kyrie changes with the seasons, as do the regularly repeated parts of the liturgy such as the Gloria, the Creed, the Our Father, and the Sanctus. The two readings, the responsorial Psalm, and the reading of the gospel proceed normally. About half the time, however, the priest invites a layperson to give a "reflection" on the readings since the parish agreed not to have lay homilies—one of the compromises with the new bishop. There are about ten unofficial lay preachers in the parish, all of whom have theological training. They usually begin with a brief exegesis of the gospel, after which they offer general exhortations, just as many Catholic priests do.

For the profession of faith, the assembly may recite the Nicene Creed, or the Apostles Creed, or one of several that are available, such as one written in El Salvador. Out of about five that are available, the liturgy team selects the one most appropriate for the day, and it is printed on the participation sheet handed out at the church door.

The Prayers of the Faithful is read by the greeter who gave the introduction at the beginning of the mass. After four or five general intentions written by the greeter, there is a call for individual prayers. Individuals stand up and ask for prayers for special needs, for instance for an uncle in a car accident, a sick child, or a family problem. There may be as few as five or as many as twenty such petitions, depending on what is on individuals' hearts and minds. Thus the needs of those in the community are given voice and listened to.

> The food collected in the food baskets is enough to supply local food distributions at other parishes as well.

For the collection, four small baskets are passed through the four quadrants of the assembly. There is also a large basket by the altar for offerings of food that will go to the St. Vincent de Paul pantry to be distributed the following week. Often enough food is offered to supply other local food distribution centers as well.

Some priests read the Eucharistic Prayer from the missal, others to do not, as mentioned earlier. Some years ago, a visiting priest invited the congregation to extend their hands during the consecration, as priests do during a concelebrated mass. It has been the custom ever since.

Several versions of the Lord's Prayer are used, including one that uses a Native American chant. As mentioned before, it is the liturgy committee that selects the version to be used during a particular liturgical Sunday or season.

Rather impressive to visitors and newcomers is the sharing of the sign of peace. The greeting and hugging usually last from five to ten minutes. Some people start embracing others around their seats and then go around the church, greeting others. When the ensemble begins to play the music for the "Lamb of God," all go back to their seats.

For communion, the church uses bread that has been made by one member of the baking team. It is not always the same bread. Two eucharistic ministers distribute the consecrated bread near the altar, and four other ministers offer the cup at the front and back of the church. People proceed toward the altar in the middle before returning to their seats through the side aisles. All leftover communion bread and wine are consumed by the eucharistic ministers. Nothing is kept after the liturgy, although additional hosts are reserved in a small tabernacle in case they are needed for an overflowing crowd.

At the end of the mass there is often a blessing, for example, for young people going away for college, for couples celebrating an anniversary, or even an anointing of the sick for someone before undergoing surgery. During this blessing, one liturgical leader says a spontaneous prayer while laying on hands in blessing, and people in the pews likewise extend their hands in blessing.

The last item at the end of the mass is colloquially called "the liturgy of the announcements" which also lasts from five to ten minutes. Individuals come forward and announce coming events in the parish or the neighborhood for instance a march against poverty, a prayer group meeting, fundraising, financial requests, and so on. Taking advantage of this practice, I asked for volunteers to be interviewed for my research, and within minutes eleven people signed up.

Attitudes and Emotions

The major attitude is one of community engagement. Since Resurrection is not a geographical but an intentional parish, people come from many zip codes, happy to find a community that satisfies their needs. The interactions between people make this clear. Much time is spent chatting before the beginning of the mass, and many people voice personal needs at the Prayer of the Faithful, their own and those of others. Sharing the sign of peace is another opportunity for lengthy communitarian exchanges. At the end there are the individual blessings for special needs. And when one personally knows the individuals giving the homiletic reflections, it affects one's bond with them positively. My interviews also confirmed the importance of community engagement at the Church of the Resurrection.

Closeness to God and to Others

The mass begins with a short period of silence to create a liminal space between prayer time and secular preoccupations. Mystagogy, that is, an introduction to the divine, can be experienced during the singing, the liturgical ritual itself, and the homilies. Participation in the singing varied greatly at Holy Family and St. Benedict. At Resurrection, the community has taken ownership of its songs and prayers, to the point of having rewritten some of the common prayers and created some of their songs. There was also strong participation in the singing at Notre Dame of Paris thanks to the supportive role of the choirs and the dynamic action of the song leaders. At both Resurrection and Notre Dame, the musicians are subservient to the community; their role is to serve and lead, not to perform for their own sake, and such conditions favor active participation. If singing is praying twice, with one's voice and also with one's heart, then there is great possibility of mystagogy through singing at Resurrection.

In order to find out the kind of mystagogy that prevails in a given church, one should look at the high point of its liturgy. In the TV masses, it is obviously the consecration since there is no assembly, or at least none is shown by the camera. At the Holy Family and St. Benedict masses it is unexpectedly the recitation of the Our Father. Then the faithful are most active physically: many raise their hands while at the same time forming a chain, often between both aisles of the church and sometimes around the altar. Even when the faithful do not sing throughout the mass, they may sing the Our Father. For many Catholics, the recitation of the Our Father at mass is their main and often their only strong collective participation in the mass.

At Notre Dame the high points of the celebration are the Memorial Acclamation and the Great Amen. I have noted the crescendo in voice and music after the consecration when people sang, in unison with the polyphonic choir, the Memorial Acclamation and the triple Amen: a strong "Amen" of the whole church, next a *forte* and festive "Amen," and finally a powerful polyphonic "Aa-me-en!" Then the camera showed the whole cathedral singing in unity, harmony, and full voice.

Here the high point of assembly participation is the kiss of peace, not the recitation of Our Father nor the Memorial Acclamation.

The high point at Resurrection is the sign of peace when people walk around the church to greet friends and acquaintances. This exchange of greetings may be the continuation of a conversation started before the mass. The collective consciousness of the faithful is expressed again in the many intentions of prayer when they recall friends in need, in the special blessing for those who request it, and especially in the "liturgy of announcements" when everyone can come forward to ask for community action. Here the high point is community interaction. It was noted above that the main emotion and attitude was one of community engagement. This was also confirmed by the interviews. Note that the high points described above are those that are observed to be so, not the high points of the mass in a theological perspective.

A third source of mystagogy, the homilies, will be analyzed below.

II. Interaction Outcomes

In the two parishes mentioned in the previous chapter, I interviewed the pastor and his staff, but at Resurrection there is no pastor. The main sacramental minister who regularly comes to preside at the liturgy does not interfere with parish life in this community because he is primarily involved elsewhere. The lay parish administrator here has no power other than persuasion; she chairs the pastoral team, which also has no special power. The major initiatives originate in the pastoral planning council, which has no power. The ideas of the pastoral planning council are discussed at the parish assembly which meets four times a year, but it has no ultimate power. Here all decisions are made by consensus; the discussion continues until the vast majority of the participants are satisfied with the emerging consensus. Power is both a clerical and a secular concept, defined by canon law in the church and constitutions in secular societies. In a great reversal, Pope Francis emphasizes dialogue and consensus, away from decision-making through institutional power. This is what we find at Resurrection.

Here is the collaborative model of governance at work at Resurrection. Instead of a parish council offering proposals to the pastor, there is an interaction process between the pastoral planning council, the leadership circle, and the parish assembly to which all are invited and where all can vote. The pastoral planning council begins its work with a retreat to reflect on the needs of the parish. Its members are elected for two years, renewable once only, so that there is a constant turnover of members and greater participation. The pastoral planning council meets regularly with the leadership circle (which includes the heads of all of the committees) in order to seek feedback and inquire about possible implementations. When a consensus has emerged from these meetings, proposals are discussed at the parish assembly for adoption or further reflection. The process involves the maximum number of participants. This active participation in decision-making generates strong support from all, because about two-thirds of the parishioners are involved in some kind of committee or ministry, and

Sunday mass attendance is 60 to 70 percent, as opposed to 9 percent at St. Benedict, which does not promote participation.

The Lay Reflections

Here are a few concluding sentences taken from the lay reflections, which are printed and available for parishioners to take home for further reflection.

a. Put first things first. The realm of God is near, is here. God is with us. Seek relationship with God. Show up and do your part.

b. What we have to be is what we are . . . love-in-action! Risk something big! Let love-in-action proclaim your commitment to live in this wild and precious all-inclusive love.

c. When we are open, the Spirit can still breathe new life into a tired and tepid church. Let us pray on this Pentecost that it indeed does happen.

d. God wants to heal our world, comfort our sorrows, and lead us to herself. God is still at work. In the midst of our deserts, angels are here to wait on us.

e. The Gospel message is simple. Those who are not against us are for us.

f. Feeling threatened or jealous may be an honest reaction. Such fears are an invitation to dialogue and listening, and to find a middle ground.

g. It takes nurturing and attentiveness to be part of planting and tending God's reign of justice. So where is the seed in you today? And what will you do today to help God's reign grow?

h. Do we live for love? Or do we satisfy ourselves, numb ourselves with something that looks good but is a sad, sad substitute?

These concluding sentences are not very different from the two- or three-minute homilies of the TV masses described in chapter 2. These reflections were written by male and female laypeople, not clerics. There seems to be an implicit consensus that homilies should be moral exhortations, a kind of collective self-help for moral living. This conception is quite different from the pre-Vatican II sermons emphasizing doctrines of the faith, the Ten Commandments, mortal sins, and the Last Judgment. It is also very different from the exegetical explanation of the readings of the day, which is what homilies are expected to do, even if moral lessons are then drawn from the readings.

> The lay reflections may be no better than the priestly homilies, but people prefer them because they are more the voice of the people, not the voice of an outsider speaking from above.

Beliefs, Practices, and Altruistic Activities

How do these homilies relate to the three areas of growth: beliefs, spiritual practices, and altruistic actions? In reference to beliefs, one cannot underestimate the importance of theological visions. The Reformation and Vatican II were both based on new theological insights, yet such insights easily become catechism formulas and stereotypes over time, which is what is found in most parishes. In a previous research, I found few or no theological insights in the homilies in about a hundred parishes.[1]

In the Church of the Resurrection, spiritual practices are mentioned a few times. Here is an example: "This year I started doing Yoga. As I have become more committed to this activity, I have learned that it is referred to as a 'practice.' This has reminded me of the old-fashioned phrase 'practicing Catholic.' Why do we practice? Because being a practicing Catholic helps us take actions of justice and peace in courage and faith." Yoga and practices from other Eastern traditions are quite common at Resurrection. Another speaker explained that "daily commitment to prayer time . . . means choosing 'right action' in our work-place, our school, our home, and our relationships." In this speaker's mind, prayer is directly linked to (and even replaced by) action. Generally speaking, there was no real push for private prayer.

On the positive side, the lay reflections are at times quite passionate and eloquent about social justice and actions of faith. They often refer to popular iconic models: "Jesus washed feet. Gandhi went against caste laws and scrubbed toilets. Mother Teresa cleansed with love the terrible wounds of people dying on the streets." In another reflection: "Oscar Romeo began change . . . He paid with his life. Dorothy Day was so dedicated to those among us who live on the margins that she envisioned houses of hospitality where the poorest could come and be served. Martin Luther King, for his fearless challenging of systemic racism, laid down his life." These exemplary models have inspired many parish practices.

In this parish, there are no traditional devotional groups. No one mentioned the existence of a rosary society, an adoration society, a Padre Pio society, and no one who was interviewed

> There are no devotional groups here but involvement in many committees and social justice activities. Is this a model for other parishes?

mentioned reciting the rosary. These devotions seem to have completely disappeared in this parish. Committee services are seldom mentioned in interviews because so many people are involved in so many of them. Let us look at the list of committees. At the top is the pastoral planning council, whose eight elected members must propose visionary plans for the future

---

1. Hegy, *Wake Up Lazarus,* vol. II, ch. 4.

following the church's mission statement. Next comes the leadership circle, composed of the pastoral planning council plus the five standing committee chairpersons and a representative from each of the four outreach ministries. Their purpose is to implement the visionary plans of the parish. The five standing committees serve the community in music, administration, life-long learning, peace and justice, and service. The outreach committees are the CrossRoads Ministry offering retreats for young people, GuardiaCare offering financial guidance for people on disability and welfare, Just Creations selling fair trade goods in its own store, and New Directions Housing Corporation, which grew out of a concern for well-maintained but low-cost apartments in the city. Some of these committees have sub-committees; thus peace and justice has five. Finally, the worship committee consists of many sub-committees or teams: liturgy planners, greeters, lectors, eucharistic ministers, sacristans, collection counters, an art and environment crew, bread bakers, and liturgical dancers. It seems that there are enough committees to involve most people in the parish.

One outstanding parish ministry is the assistance given to a sister parish in Latin America. Resurrection pays for a community physician, it contributes to a clinic for expectant mothers, it subsidizes an organic farming project, and it teaches women how to grow nutritious vegetables for their families. The committee raises about $50,000 per year for these endeavors. To help get these projects going, the parish saved money by not installing central air conditioning in the church. In addition, every year four or five parishioners visit their sister parish at their own expense and report back, and every other year the parish pays the expenses for members of its sister parish to fly to the US and report on developments back home. One could say that a focal point of this church is action rather than prayer.

Sense of Community

As indicated above, the high points of the mass at Resurrection are the sign of peace and other opportunities of face-to-face interaction. Here the sense of community is very strong. "Resurrection is my community more than it is my faith community. It is the people. I live by myself, so that's where I get my weekly supply of hugs and connections." This statement suggests the ambiguity of the Resurrection community: it is a religious community where personal interaction may often be more important than the liturgy. The centrality of the human dimension is expressed thus by another parishioner: "What I could not stand any more about five years ago [in another parish] was the isolation and resistance to touch one another at the kiss of peace. Now I go to Resurrection every week for my fix. If there is something

I am addicted to it is the hundred people I get my arms around on Sunday morning during the kiss of peace." He concluded with these strong words: "It is as powerful as the Eucharist." Several people spoke of the therapeutic effect of attending church. "I like to sing, and I sing all the songs, because that is something so therapeutic. Singing is a real draw for me." And here is the attitude of someone raised in a very Catholic family: "We went to church every Sunday and we were also taught our prayers; we kneeled for prayer with mom and dad every night. We would also say the rosary." Now the emphasis is on the therapeutic. There is a strong sense of parish community, but little or no sense of ecclesial community. The parish seems to be an isolated island within the wider church.

When I asked people about their most important rituals, many mentioned family and friends. "Family and friends sustain my life; they are on my calendar before anything else." "What about church rituals?" I asked. "That's the ones I could drop." The melding of

> There is a greater need for community here than for mystagogy. In a sociological perspective, true mystagogy is communitarian and true community is mystagogical.

the sacred and the human is central in another testimony that was offered in reference to community: "On a scale from one to ten, it's a twelve. In terms of being nourished and instructed, I feel very blessed to be with the Resurrection community. If things were radically different, I would not go to another Catholic church." This statement exemplifies the preeminence of community over liturgy in many people's minds. Her conclusion about her church is very positive: "I don't have enough words to express how much nourished and supported I have felt, and how important the community is to me." Once again, community trumps liturgy; and the local liturgy trumps the sense of a universal ecclesial liturgy.

Moral Consensus and Patterns of Interaction

In the Church of the Resurrection there is no polarization between liberals and conservatives because decision-making by consensus leads extreme voices to become part of the mainstream or to quit. Indeed, some have left because the parish was too liberal and others because it was not liberal enough. Because all major decisions have to be discussed by the whole parish after having gone through various committees, the process brings the parish closer together. Years ago, after it had been decided to use only inclusive language, it was necessary to discuss every single objectionable word, find a substitute, and make a decision based on consensus. The process took about a year. Similarly when the bishop required conformity with his twelve rules about the liturgy, the parish discussed them all over a period of two years. The discussions dragged on because any compromise had to be accepted through a moral consensus in the parish. Building a consensus takes much time and those with the most patience ultimately win. At one point, the chancery insisted that the priest presiding at the liturgy implement a certain rule. After a few weeks, the priest forgot to do so, and the rule was never mentioned again.

Interactions at Resurrection are egalitarian because there is no power structure. Inequality in the institutional church comes from the distinction between the teaching church and listening church. Not here. Half the homilies given as "reflections" may be no better than those of the pastor but they have the enormous advantage, mentioned several times already, of providing variety and equality. Because there is no hierarchy but interaction between committees, all interactions are reflexive, leading to better mutual understanding. At the Church of the Resurrection, all are equal; hence the relationships are egalitarian. There is strong interaction among the members, and also between this church and the neighboring churches on issues of social justice. But there is little or no interaction with the larger institution known as the Roman Catholic Church.

Spirituality and Emotional Energy

Only a few people in this parish said they find their spiritual inspiration in the traditional practices of mass and Scripture reading, and these were mainly ex-priests and ex-seminarians. Most people tend to be more spiritual than religious, and quite a number of parishioners are alienated from the institutional church. "Prayer is an odd concept to me. Even when I was little and tried to pray, I felt I was talking to myself, and it did not make any sense. Prayer for me has the connotation of 'God, give me something.'" Such a negative attitude rooted in childhood becomes a blockage to adult spirituality. Some take a position of near rejection. "I do not expect any help from a supernatural power" was the response of someone from a devout family involved in the church for many years. And here is a statement from someone who spent nine years in a monastic environment: "Let's just be as good as we can, and let's not drag God into the equation, because he or she is not really in it anymore."

Secular activities are often taken to be spiritual, and to a certain sense they are. "While reading a mystery book, I am thinking about what happened during the day." Or, "Walking for me serves the purpose of what meditation does for other people." Or, "My thinking time is gardening. I have a hard time with whatever they call spirituality." Others may simply say that they used to pray as a child, but not anymore.

Yoga is usually a secular form of spirituality. According to a yoga practitioner, "I never understood the concept of a relationship with God or Jesus. It is the language I grew up with but it never made sense to me." Some forms of Eastern meditation are common at Resurrection. Buddhism and Christianity are not necessarily opposed. One interviewee's spirituality consists of "basic Catholic foundations with a generally Buddhist attitude towards life. The two are not in contradiction; the emphasis is on experience, not doctrine." Most practitioners of Eastern spirituality at Resurrection would probably agree. Here is a form of prayer which combines yoga and centering meditation: "I begin with a deep prayer, followed by measured breathing, breathing in, holding the breath and exhaling, controlling the muscles of the body to relax them, so that in my meditation I have peace in my whole body. It is like yoga plus centering prayer." Not much seems to remain from the nine years this person spent in a monastery chanting the holy office.

Several people practice passage meditation, a form of meditation that is very demanding. "Every morning at 5:30 I do passage meditation, seven days a week. You take Scriptures from all the world's religions, you memorize them, and you go over them in your mind slowly, sitting still for 30 minutes." Others do tai chi, which seems less demanding.

> If there is a greater need for community than for rituals, there is also a great need for personal meditation in one form or another.

Why is Buddhist meditation so popular? From a Buddhist practitioner I learned that there are Buddhist classes at the local cathedral. Its website lists six different courses of various levels and topics. Their purpose is "To purify the mind of mental defilement, [and] find inner peace." One may raise the question as to whether this kind of meditation fosters or replaces traditional prayer. Observation suggests the latter. Here is the main point: there is not much teaching of Christian spirituality at Resurrection and most parishes. Most homilies are moralistic, devoid of doctrine and spiritual insights, while Eastern meditation is easily available, even at the local cathedral.

There is, however, a spirituality of social justice at Resurrection. It is the main reason why many members have joined this church. The various ministries of peace and justice are engaging and successful. This spirituality is mainly ideological. "We are all products of the Big Bang," hence we are all brothers and sisters. Jesus is our model because he "stood up against all the injustices of his day, the injustices against women and the poor." These interviewees do not seem to need a more advanced level of Christian teaching.

Let us evaluate this church using the criteria of growth introduced in the previous chapter. On works of charity, this parish is outstanding. In reference to religious practices, there is a strong current in favor of Buddhist meditation, but not for traditional devotions. In terms of greater theological insights into the life of faith, I found nothing special here; so on matters of faith, Resurrection is just average. In reference to the eight strategies for parish growth mentioned in the previous chapter, Resurrection would be classified as an extroverted church, Holy Family as complacent, and St. Benedict as conflicted.

Interviews at the Church of the Resurrection revealed a problem that was not covered by our definition of spiritual growth borrowed from the Willow Creek research, namely, this parish is an island with little or no ecclesial connections, and the result is that it often stands in conflict with the institutional church. The problem is rather serious. The lay parish administrator has reached the age of mandatory retirement, and the bishop may not appoint another lay administrator. In light of past tensions with this parish, he may appoint a moderately conservative pastor who may enforce all the liturgical and administrative rules. Such a situation would be the worst possible, one of a troubled and dissenting church. Mass exodus from the Catholic Church might follow.

In hierarchical structures, creativity leads to conflict with authority but in democracies there can be even greater conflict is case of polarization and the absence of a superior authority.

Conflict with church authority seems embedded in the administrative structure of Resurrection because no one has ultimate decision-making power. Neither the sacramental minister, nor the lay parish administrator, nor the pastoral team, nor the parish assembly has ultimate power. All decisions are made by consensus, a very enviable process in the Catholic Church, but there is no central authority to guide the church. Consensus may actually turn into stonewalling in case of disagreement with a future pastor. In congregationalism, conflict may be solved by referring to common traditions and biblical principles (which is their central authority), but these are lacking in the church of the Resurrection. It is an isolated model of consensus with few ecclesial ties. Consensus is the wind that fills the sails to move forward, but when there is no wind, there is no central authority to guide out of the morass.

During mass, all recite the Nicene Creed or some other version of the creed, but in private there seem to be few common beliefs. Many parishioners are alienated from the Catholic Church. "I do not expect any help from a supernatural power," says one. "Prayer is an odd concept to me," says another. Buddhist meditation is more easily available than traditional meditation. According to Willow Creek research, it is the responsibility of the clergy to guide the flock to higher levels of spirituality, but here "reflections" have replaced traditional preaching, often with little gain. There is little connection with the ecclesial tradition of theology and Christian meditation.

The analysis of interaction at Resurrection has revealed the limitations of spiritual growth, because we encountered an unexpected variable, consensus without a central authority. No variable list can encompass all aspects of communal interaction. In the next chapter we will add one more variable, spiritual development, which is growth between stages. Ultimately we will have to confront the question of authority, which undergirds the synthesis between faith and culture, integration versus segmentation, and liturgical creativity versus obedience to church rules. Such a hard question has to be left for a later chapter.

Conclusion: The Social Drama of Polarized Democracies

Resurrection seems to have the best form of governance, democracy, which is the envy of many parishes, but democracy without a superior authority can lead to conflict and chaos in case of extreme polarization. Decisions can easily be made by consensus as long as there is no split into opposite camps, but in case of serious conflict there may be no ultimate recourse about which both parties agree. The highest authority in the United States is the Constitution interpreted by the Supreme Court, but what happens when neither is respected? The answer has been one of the bloodiest civil wars in history. Many conflictive democracies were overtaken democratically by dictators, as in Germany, Italy, and Spain, and in many countries of Africa and Latin America. In times of social concord it is assumed that the political leaders will follow their conscience for the common good, but what happens when the president seems to have no conscience, no notion of truth, and little respect for the institutions of government? This issue is real today.

Neither strong centralization nor broad decentralization seems desirable. The TV masses are an example of strong centralization. There the rituals are programmed in their slightest details, the performance is executed quasi-mechanically, and the result is little spiritual growth. At Holy Family there is flexibility in a *laissez-faire* type of parish management, but there seems to be not much spiritual growth. At Resurrection there is great decentralization, government by consensus, and a high level of parish involvement, but here growth is fragmented into a great variety of spiritual practices, many of which have little to do with traditional Christianity. The purpose of this book is to look at the social cost of the various forms of worship. Let us continue our exploration and turn to a church where there is strong pastoral leadership and real spiritual growth, but at what cost?

7

Growth and Development

An Evangelical/Pentecostal Church

WE NOW TURN TO individual growth, as opposed to church growth discussed in the previous chapter. Hence we have to introduce another set of variables to enable us to evaluate worship in reference to individual growth and development. James Fowler's theory of faith development will be presented in the first part of this chapter, and in the second part, it will be used to evaluate faith development at an evangelical/Pentecostal congregation.

I. Defining Individual Growth and Development

Although the words are sometimes used synonymously, growth and development are not the same: growth will be understood here as change within one's stage, while development is change from one stage to the next. In the case of a butterfly, the difference is obvious: it grows in each stage until it develops from egg to larva, from larva to chrysalis, and finally into a butterfly; first there is growth, then development. In humans, differences in development are not as clear. When an infant starts walking and talking, it is not a baby anymore, but it has developed into a child. When young people get married and have children, they are not teenagers anymore, but they have developed into young adults. Even retirement can trigger a new development after decades in the labor force.

Religions offer ways to grow spiritually, and also ways to develop. For example, one can develop from a naïve acceptance of religious beliefs to a critical examination of those beliefs, and further, to a sophisticated interpretation of those beliefs that is integrated with scientific and other knowledge.

We will look first at sociological research into spiritual growth, next at five levels of commitment in a prominent megachurch, and lastly at James Fowler's theory of faith development.

1. Growth as Increasing Intensity

A common way to look at people's spiritual lives is to appraise them in terms of fervor, zeal, and piety, or what can be called religious intensity. We have already seen that low-intensity faith, devotional practices, and altruistic activity easily lead to complacency. At Holy Family and St. Benedict, there seems to be little long-term growth. People keep believing what they believe, and they keep doing what they do, and they assume that this is all there is to being religious.

In the early days of *sociologie religieuse* (religious sociology) in France in the 1950s, religiosity was measured mainly by church attendance. In the 1960s in the United States, Charles Glock and Rodney Stark introduced multi-dimensional measurements of religious life in *Religion and Society in Tension* and *American Piety*. They measured beliefs, ritual practices, religious experiences, and religious knowledge. For each of these measurements, the respondents were asked to answer on a scale ranging from low to high. The next step was to combine several items into a single complex scale. The availability of computer programs like SPSS made possible the creation of empirically derived scales. The work of King and Hunt, among the first to use computer correlation techniques, appeared as the coming-of-age of sociology of religion as a scientific discipline. The authors found ten scales, six about basic religiosity and four additional ones derived from a total of 132 questions. The six basic scales were: creedal assent, devotionalism, church attendance, organizational activity, financial support, and religious knowledge. The weakness of empirically-derived scales is that factor analysis generates different scales from different sets of questions and different samples, and the names given to these scales often vary among different researchers. Today we have a few good scales of religiosity, each measuring a different aspect and adapted to a specific religious dimension. We do not have, however, a universally-accepted scale of religiosity, so today church attendance is still the most common measurement of religiosity in quantitative research.

I have adopted the three dimensions of religiosity used by the Willow Creek Church in its research, namely, beliefs, religious practices, and altruistic activities. These dimensions are very useful for fieldwork. Whereas for general surveys, questions about beliefs, practices, and activities must be worded unambiguously, in field research they can be adapted to different situations. These three dimensions have proven to be very helpful in the previous chapters because in any congregation one can find evidence of different individual and collective beliefs, religious practices, and altruistic activities. Interviews can also be used to obtain information about these three variables. In this chapter, information about these variables will enable us to investigate growth, that is, to learn how people move from low-intensity to high-intensity, and how they move from one level of development to the next.

2. Growth and Development at the Saddleback Church

Rick Warren's major contribution to spirituality in local churches was his recognition that there are several levels of commitment even though most churches recognize only two levels, namely Sunday attenders and church leaders. The traditional dichotomy of the teaching church versus the listening church has been prevalent in Catholic teaching since Trent, and the distinction between ordained ministers and the non-ordained is even regarded in canon law as of "divine institution." Warren's five levels of commitment are based on observation. They are: the community of the unchurched or occasional attenders, the crowd of regular Sunday attenders, the congregation of members who have signed a membership covenant, the committed who engage in discipleship, and the core of those who are committed to ministry.[1]

> It is common to recognize only two levels of development, that of priests and religious and that of the laity. The Saddleback church offers five levels of growth and development, and they are open to all to climb.

These five levels are not an abstract typology of believers but a dynamic path that leads one from one level to the next. It is the responsibility of pastors to move their members forward; it is also a major conclusion of the Willow Creek research. Both Saddleback and Willow Creek offer classes for spiritual progress all year-round.

The first level is that of seekers, that is, people who have not given up on religion but seek the divine by coming to church occasionally. It is very important not to turn them off by offering what they most complain about: boring sermons, asking for money, and making them feel unwelcome in a place that is unfamiliar to them.[2] The seekers want to listen but not to sing, to observe without being observed, and to be catered to without having to contribute financially. The immediate goal of the pastor is to make them want to come back.

The crowd is the group of regular attenders. Not much is asked of them except to come regularly and occasionally invite their friends.

The next level is that of members. The process of assimilation consists of turning regular Sunday attenders into active members. All Sunday

1. Warren, *Purpose-Driven Church*, 131.
2. Warren, *Purpose-Driven Church*, 191.

worshipers are invited to become members. Out of a crowd of 10,000 regular attenders, about half will take the necessary steps to become members. There are four requirements: to accept Jesus Christ as Lord and savior, to be baptized by immersion as a public profession of faith, to take the membership class, and to pledge to live according to the requirements of a signed membership covenant.

The next step is commitment to spiritual maturity. Here the requirements are much stiffer. The committed must acquire four basic habits (what in the previous chapters I have called religious practices): Bible study, personal prayer, involvement in a small group, and tithing. These habits are explained at length in the seminar called "Discovering Spiritual Maturity." The effect of this seminar is similar to that of the retreats at San Miguel and the charismatic movement, which will be discussed later. "People leave the class permanently changed. It is always a very moving moment when the people in each class commit their time, money and relationships to Christ."[3]

There is one more step that may take years to complete, namely, involvement in ministry, which is the mission of the core. Preparation for ministry begins by attending "Discovering my Ministry," a course spread over many months. There will be weeks of reflection about one's talents, a personal interview, supervised work in an area of interest, and finally an official commissioning to a given ministry.[4] The spirituality and theology of ministry are those of the universal ministry of all believers: "There are no laypeople in a biblical church: there are only ministers. The idea of two classes of Christians, clergy and laity" is absent here.[5]

This plan provides a stable pyramid of progress. At Saddleback, half the crowd will become full-fledged members, a third of the latter will move on to commit to maturity, and less than a third of the latter will become core ministers.

> The pyramid of two levels of ordained and non-ordained is static; one enters through a rite of passage. The pyramid at Saddleback is dynamic: one can move up and down at any time.

People at each level can look at those above as role models to follow.

This model is similar to what I have observed in several parishes and in the charismatic movement in Guatemala and elsewhere. At the lowest level is the weekly assembly or the Sunday mass open to all. A few will go on a retreat that will be life changing for most of them. They will meet weekly in small groups and get involved in ministries. They also follow courses for

---

3. Warren, *Purpose-Driven Church*, 349.

4. Warren, *Purpose-Driven Church*, 381–82.

5. Warren, *Purpose-Driven Church*, 391.

several years in Bible studies and ministries. There are about 73 million Catholic charismatics in Latin America who follow this model.[6]

The five levels of commitment at Saddleback can be seen as stages of development. Although there are no stark differences from one level to the next, there is a gulf between the lowest and the highest levels. There is also growth in intensity within each level; one can remain forever within one's stage and grow in zeal in it. Such is obviously the case at the highest level from which there is no higher stage to climb to. The Saddleback model of progressive commitment is important in this chapter because it is also the model followed by the Bayville church, which Rick Warren has visited.

3. Fowler's Stages of Faith Development

Traditional spirituality recognizes three steps in spiritual development: purification, illumination, and union (the threefold *via purgativa, via illuminativa, and via unitiva*), but these are theoretical stages that cannot be easily defined empirically. Starting with Piaget, however, psychologists began to discern specific stages of development, and Fowler found a way to apply this model to stages of faith development.

Jean Piaget was the first to show empirically that children's cognitive development goes through stages. At each stage, children can perform only the mental operations that characterize their level or below and not operations that are typical of higher levels. Lawrence Kohlberg did for moral reasoning among adults what Piaget did for the cognitive development of children. Moral reasoning goes through six stages grouped into three major levels. In what he called the pre-conventional level, people's moral decisions are based on obedience, fear of punishment, and self-interest. At the conventional level, moral thinking is dominated by conformity to social norms and the acceptance of the group's authority. Finally, at the post-conventional level, moral reasoning utilizes abstract reasoning based on universal ethical norms. At this level, morality is guided by conscience rather than the authority of the group. Kohlberg's theory is intuitively appealing; it makes sense that people gradually move from fear of punishment to moral decisions guided by conscience.

James Fowler based his own research in faith development on Piaget's model of cognitive development and Kohlberg's model of moral development. Both Kohlberg and Fowler found that people's thinking—about morality on the one hand, and about faith on the other hand—had three basic levels of complexity, namely, elementary, average, and advanced. Both

---

6. Statistics at: https://www.revolvy.com/page/Catholic-Charismatic-Renewal-in -Latin-America%252F?stype=topics&cmd=list.

named these three levels as pre-conventional, conventional, and post-conventional. Each level could be further divided into earlier and later stages, resulting in six stages of development in all. Although spatial images of "stages" and "levels" are used to describe their findings, what Kohlberg and Fowler are talking about are degrees of complexity. Pre-conventional thinking is fairly rudimentary and easily achievable by children, conventional thinking is more complex and achievable by most adults, and post-conventional thinking is still more complex and achievable only by adults who try to move beyond the ways of thinking of most people.

Here we will focus on the conventional level of faith, stage 3, which is where most adult believers find themselves. At stage 4 people tend to look reflexively at their faith, and at stage 5 they begin to move beyond conventional religiosity and accept religious diversity.

Adolescents thrive in peer groups. For them the locus of authority is external; it is located in the group, the friends, and the family. Stage 3 is the stage of adolescence, but also that of many adults who never go beyond it. According to Fowler, "a considerable number of the adults we have interviewed—both men and women—can be best described by the patterns of Stage 3."[7] "A lot of people do not function at a high level for a long time," said the pastor of Holy Family. "What they want is a Sunday mass of 40 to 50 minutes, a homily of ten minutes or less, little or no singing, and nothing more." This corresponds to stage 3.

> Stage 3 is conventional; it requires conformity to one's friends and environment. This makes it very difficult to move beyond, as one may lose one's friends or be rejected by them.

The values and principles of stage 3 are mostly tacit, meaning that people are for the most part unaware of them. Thus the parishioners of Holy Family are unaware that what they want—a short mass and a short homily—is what their upbringing and social environment lead them to want. They are like fish unaware of water. When questioned, they simply reaffirm the teachings of their external authority: The church (or the pastor) says such and such, and father knows best—no question asked.

Fowler labels stage 3 as synthetic-conventional,[8] signifying that it is a conglomeration of beliefs and practices that are common to those around them. "Much of the church and synagogue life in this country can be described as predominantly Synthetic-Conventional." Because

> Stage 4 requires moving out of conformity to the socially accepted norms, based on conscience and reason, not rebellion and individualism.

---

7. Fowler, *Stages of Faith*, 161.

8. Fowler, *Stages of Faith*, 164.

the meaning system is implicit and not thought out, change is difficult. As in the military and in business, obedience is paramount in stage 3 churches, with no one questioning the meaning of accepted teachings and practices.

Moving on to stage 4 requires two changes. First, one's reliance on external authority begins to be questioned, and things that were taken to be meaningful and sacred by themselves begin to be examined. Fowler calls this individuative-reflective faith because individuals begin to think for themselves and to reflect on their beliefs and practices. Scriptural narratives and religious rituals are discerned to be representations on the surface with deeper meanings underneath. This "demythologizing strategy" brings to an end the previously naïve acceptance of rituals and symbols. People in stage 4 can react negatively to the beliefs and practices that were previously unquestioned, or they can begin to theologize positively about them in an effort to develop an intellectually-defensible adult faith that can be rationally defended against other beliefs.

If people move on to stage 5 (and not many do, which is why it is considered post-conventional) they move beyond dogmatism to tolerance. Fowler calls it conjunctive faith because it "moves beyond the dichotomizing logic of Stage 4's 'either/or.' It sees both (or the many) sides of an issue simultaneously."[9] In this respect, it is dialectical and dialogical, not oppositional. People in stage 5 are most likely to engage in ecumenical dialogue, especially if they have been jolted out of their stage 4 dogmatism by encountering and listening to people of other faiths. Sometimes they experience a "second naiveté" that echoes at a higher level the first naiveté of childhood as they become open to learning from others.

Stage 6 in Fowler are those who have developed a universalizing faith that somehow embraces the deepest beliefs and ideals of all religions, yet also a faith that transcends any of them. Not many stage 6 people are likely to be found in a typical congregation. Fowler regards Mahatma Gandhi, Martin Luther King Jr., and Mother Teresa of Calcutta as examples of stage 6.

Identifying any individual's stage of faith would be complicated and lengthy. One would have to take many faith statements, analyze them, and generalize the results in order to reach a probable judgment about someone's faith development with any credibility. Since stages 3 and 4 comprise what Fowler calls the conventional level of faith, it would be safe to assume that most people in most congregations are somewhere at the conventional level. Moreover, it might be possible to discern whether and how people move from stage 3 to stage 4, thus growing developmentally while remaining at the conventional level.

9. Fowler, *Stages of Faith*, 185.

Each stage can be defined by its conception of authority, its principles of moral principles, and its understanding of symbols. The locus of authority at stage 3 is in socially approved figures and traditional forms of authority that are accepted on the basis on appearance, charisma, and group approval.[10] In contrast, someone in stage 4 tends to locate authority in ideas, systems, and institutions rather than persons. This authority is then accepted in accordance with ideological and rational principles. The locus of authority has moved from an outside power to a reflexive perspective centered on the self.[11]

The moral judgments of someone in stage 3 are based on the values of the group and the need for interpersonal harmony. Such a person's main values are role fulfillment and loyalty to the group, together with often stereotypical and critical attitudes towards outsiders. Moral decisions are made in reference to implicit collective norms.[12] In contrast, the moral judgments of someone in stage 4 are made in reference to laws, to the rights and duties of individuals, and to the maintenance of the social order. These judgments reflect the values of the self-selected class or ideology that the person has adopted.[13]

Symbols are part of any language but they are often understood differently. A person in stage 3 favors symbols that evoke feelings and values that reflect those of the group. Religious symbols are

> Symbols in stage 3 have a universal and uni-dimensional meaning like traffic signs. At a higher level they require poetic creativity.

powerful mediators of the divine when they are collectively accepted, but they can equally be dismissed by outsiders or when the social environment changes.[14] Someone in stage 4 tends to analyze socially accepted symbols and translate them into concepts and ideas. Such a person tends to view myths negatively and in need of demythologization. There can also be an attitude of debunking all truth claims unless a person at stage 4 can find an intellectually acceptable way of reflecting on and explaining long-held beliefs and practices. Dogmatic thinkers are often those who have found a way to systematically intellectualize their faith and defend it against others.

Although any evaluation of faith development needs to be thorough, Fowler recommends beginning with an "initial global stage code" to guide

10. Moseley et al., *Manual for Faith Development*, 124.

11. Fowler, *Stages of Faith*, 147.

12. Fowler, *Stages of Faith*, 116.

13. Fowler, *Stages of Faith*, 143.

14. Fowler, *Stages of Faith*, 130.

any concrete analysis.[15] It would therefore seem reasonable in our analysis of congregations to get an intuitive sense of where people are in their faith development. As mentioned earlier, I will focus on stages 3 and 4 as most common, and we will try to discern if and how people move from the third stage to the fourth.

4. Spiritual Growth, Intensity, and Social Factors

Fowler's theory deals with human development and the quest for meaning. It does not address spiritual growth within a given stage, but only the development from one stage to the next. In this analysis, therefore, we will have to find a way to incorporate growth (i.e., intensification) within Fowler's stages.

Because many adults retain conventional faith most of their lives, stage development theory would seem to be of little help. What is missing in Fowler's analysis is a distinction between high and low levels within a given stage, in other words, a measurement of within-stage growth. What is missing is intensity, that is, the degree of fervor and enthusiasm within a stage of faith development. Teachers easily notice the difference between highly and poorly motivated students in the same class. There may be millions of virtuous Catholics, but only those of heroic and extraordinary dedication can be considered for canonization. Fowler's theory, however, makes no distinction between the two. As mentioned above, great intensity in a given religious practice may lead to other practices, and possibly to a further stage of development. In some ways, then, religious intensity or fervor may provide the energy needed to move on to a further stage of faith development. It would be good, therefore, to incorporate intensity into our analysis of people's faith.

According to Fowler, people at the conventional level of faith accept what they have been taught; for Catholics, this means accepting what the church teaches. Those at stage 3 accept the teachings uncritically, whereas those at stage 4 have begun to think about, and to some extent to question, what they have been taught. In other words, they begin to examine it critically, with two possible results. Either they reject the doctrines as unworthy of intellectual acceptance, or they find ways to critically rethink the doctrines so that they become intellectually respectable and ideologically defensible.

> Conservative churches tend to grow, but is their growth due mainly to their conservative theology? Limited research suggests that social factors are more important.

15. Fowler, *Stages of Faith*, 43.

People at this conventional stage 3 level have a generally conservative attitude. Research has shown that Catholics who are more deeply involved in religious practices and devotions tend to be more deeply conservative, not only in religion but also in morality, politics, gender roles, dating, drinking, child-rearing, leisure activities, and cultural preferences.

Sociological research has also found that, in general, conservative churches are growing while liberal ones are declining. This finding suggests that stage 4 is a portent of decline. But is this always the case?

A comparison of 13 declining and nine growing Protestant churches in Canada found that the clergy and congregants in the growing churches (measured in terms of increased Sunday attendance) scored high on conservative theology. Thus 54 percent in growing churches, as opposed to zero percent in declining ones, endorsed the item "the Bible is the actual word of God and it has to be taken literally." Similarly 85 percent of the clergy in growing churches as opposed to 6 percent in declining ones agreed that "Those who die face a divine judgment where some will be punished eternally."[16]

A factor analysis of church growth can tell us the importance of individual versus social factors. When considering only individual factors in this study, the strongest determinant of church growth was clergy conservatism, followed by congregation conservatism. This would lead us to believe that conservatism is the only important variable in church growth.

But an apparent paradox appears when we consider styles of worship and music. It turns out that growing churches that are theologically conservative favor contemporary music and worship styles, which under other circumstances would be regarded as typical of liberal churches. Thus 78 percent of growing conservative congregations use drums often or always but only 8 percent declining conservative ones; 89 percent of growing conservative churches use electric guitars but only 8 percent of the declining conservative churches, and 100 percent of growing use visual projections and 77 percent use videos, but only 23 percent and zero percent of the declining churches. Traditional organ is used in only 44 percent of the growing conservative churches, in contrast to 77 percent in the declining churches.[17] These data raise the question of the relative importance of conservative theology versus modern styles of worship.

Doing additional analysis, the authors of this research added contemporary worship and youth ministry, which are both social factors, to the equation. What they found was that the social factors were statistically more

16. Haskell et al., "Theology Matters," 528.
17. Haskell et al., "Theology Matters," 530.

important than the individual factors of clergy and congregational conservatism—a very unexpected result![18] In a given church, the conservatism of the clergy is not likely to change over the years, but worship and ministries can easily be modernized. The result is not conflict but church growth.

Let us keep this in mind as we move next to discuss the Bayville church, focusing on two aspects of spiritual growth, namely, intensity of religiosity and stage development.

II. The Bayville Church

The evangelical movement in the United States has been widely studied. Among sociologists, Nancy Ammerman has dedicated much of her career to the study of evangelical churches. Christian Smith produced the classic, *American Evangelicalism: Embattled and Thriving*. With regard to the praise and worship movement, Robb Redman's *The Great Worship Awakening: Singing a New Song in the Postmodern Church*, is required reading in this area. A good overview of Pentecostalism in found in Steven Jack Land's *Pentecostal Spirituality: A Passion for the Kingdom*.

The evangelical/Pentecostal church, which I call the Bayville church, started in 1955 as a non-denominational house church. I have described its structure and spirituality elsewhere.[19] In 1978 the church purchased a vacant public school and created its own Christian school there. Having greatly expanded since then, the present compound is a maze of small rooms, used mostly for classes. In the middle is a sanctuary, which is a comfortable theater with a stage for the preacher and the orchestra but no religious images. The sound and video systems are state of the art. Video clips and the texts of songs are regularly projected on two large screens. All services, including the sermons, are recorded and made available on the Internet.

The Bayville church is part of the Fellowship of Christian Assemblies, which means that it belongs to the Pentecostal tradition, but the Pentecostal dimension in this church is muted in comparison to the Assemblies of God where it is more prominent. The main emphases are biblical and evangelical. Being an independent church, it has no denominational connection to any given tradition, so neither Luther, nor the Reformation, nor the origins of Pentecostalism are ever mentioned in sermons.

Sunday services attract around 3,000 people, but only about a third are registered members. The distinction between the two categories is not emphasized, and is not noticeable in any way. To become a member one

18. Haskell et al., "Theology Matters," 533.

19. Hegy, *Wake up Lazarus!*, vol. II, ch. 4, and *Lay Spirituality*, ch. 8.

has to attend this church for six months, take a thirteen-week course, and be water-baptized as the expression of one's public commitment. Members are expected to contribute ten percent of their income to the church, and most do.

The organizational structure of the church consists of ten full-time pastors, six elders to advise the senior pastor, about 20 deacons and nearly as many deaconesses, and a plethora of about 80 ministries. The general assembly of the registered members elects the elders, the deacons and deaconesses, and decides on administrative and doctrinal matters.

In my presentation and analysis of the Bayville church, I will use again Collins's eight variables.

1. Basic Information and Expectations

The website of the Bayville church is a rich source of information about the life and activities of the church. One can watch the sermons of the last three years. The senior pastor, Jim Orlando (not the real name) has been pastoring this church since 1991. He is a graduate of Oral Roberts University, founded in 1963 by the Pentecostal Methodist televangelist and faith healer of that name. Jim Orlando belongs to the first generation of graduates from that school. Students had to pledge not to drink, smoke, or engage in premarital sexual activities. The Bayville church similarly upholds strict moral principles and promotes spiritual healing. The time Orlando was a student was also the time when Rick Warren became nationally known for his purpose-driven church in the Saddleback Valley. The Bayville church drew much of its inspiration from his example; thus it has an "assimilation" program for church membership and offers numerous courses in Bible study and ministry preparation.

An internal survey about what attracts people to this church revealed that, "Number one, people enjoy the worship service. Number two, they enjoy the teaching of our senior pastor. Number three, they enjoy the activities, which involve the whole family, in our church." Because of its attractiveness, this church has been steadily growing.

On a different note, on the day of my first visit, someone pushed into my hand a book on intelligent design condemning evolution. Apparently there are people in this church with strong conservative views. In sum, the three basic characteristics of this church seem to be: the evangelical-Pentecostal tradition, the liveliness of its services, and a conservative worldview; they will be described as we move along.

2. Description of the Ritual Processes

This church has no lectionary, so every Sunday service is different. Every month there is a communion Sunday, a mission day, a family day, and a youth day. On the mission Sunday, there are likely to be four to six water baptisms in front of the congregation and a sermon by the pastor of missions. On family and youth Sundays, the sermon may be given by one of the family and youth ministers, but more often it is given by the senior pastor, Jim Orlando.

The Sunday service is planned by the senior pastor on Tuesday, so that at the Wednesday staff meeting, various responsibilities can be assigned to the various pastors. The choir meets on Thursday to rehearse the songs, together with the orchestra of about twenty members. Preaching is the main responsibility of the senior pastor, who takes Thursday off for sermon preparation.

I attended this church on and off for several years. I purchased the CD recordings of the Sunday services from October 16, 2016 to February 26, 2017. Some of the events that happened during this interval were several mission Sundays, Christmas celebrations, the yearly prayer week, and the pastor's prophecies for the New Year; I will mention them in passing.

The Sunday services consist of praise and worship songs, prayers by the pastor, usually a prophecy, a sermon, and a final prayer. Singing is the normal form of prayer here; there are no rote prayers, not even the Our Father. There are improvised prayers throughout the service, for example, after a few songs, after a prophecy, or after the sermon; this is always done by the senior pastor who acts as the prayer leader as well as the main preacher.

> The Sunday services are of a high religious quality. This is what attracts people at their first visit, and not the church's conservative theology.

Generally speaking, the singing is pious and fervent. Practically everyone participates. Many raise their hands, slowly swinging from side to side. The old saying that singing is praying twice applies here: people pray with their bodies as well as their hearts. Their faces express inner peace and fervor, and at times they sing in a low voice with tear-filled eyes. I have previously referred to paradise as an image evoked by singing in unison and polyphony. Here, as at Notre Dame in Paris, worship has a divine quality at times, although in a quite different modality.

On December 11, 2016, the first song was "How lovely is your dwelling place, Oh Lord Almighty," which is the text of Psalm 84. Lines in the next song, "My heart and flesh cry out for you, the Living God," were taken from Psalms 42, 73 and 84. Many songs are clearly of biblical inspiration although neither the Psalms nor the Lord's Prayer are ever recited. After this song, the pastor offered the following prayer without reference to the Psalms: "We offer this song to you, Oh Lord, with all our hearts. You alone are worthy. We adore you. We magnify you. We marvel at your mercy."

At a service during the Christmas season, people sang, "Noel, Noel, Noel, Born is the King of Israel." To me, this "First Noel" seemed more Catholic than Reform inspired. On that same day, another song was "Oh Come, All Ye Faithful," which is a translation of *Adeste fideles*, perhaps written by a medieval cleric. "Joy to the World," another Christmas carol, is taken from Psalm 98. Also used at Christmas time was: "Angels We Have Heard on High," an eighteenth-century chorus on the melody of *Les anges dans nos campagnes*. These examples show the tendency to use songs that are well-known, even if they are related to other Christian traditions: a sign of great open-mindedness.

In order to facilitate participation, the text of the songs is projected on three screens, two in front for the congregation to see, and one in the back for the choir facing the congregation. Most songs include a chorus that can be repeated endlessly. Thus, when the orchestra began playing and a soloist began singing, "Maker of heaven and earth, to you the glory," the congregation repeated over and over, "Maker of heaven and earth, every sunrise sings your praise." At the invitation of the song leader, the text of the chorus could be slightly changed, endlessly repeating, "Lord of heaven and earth, we sing forever your praise."

Praise and worship are the major theme of all songs and prayers. The pastor may begin with, "Let us give the Lord a shout of praise today" and the congregation may respond with shouts and clapping, while singing, "I sing praises to your name." People enthusiastically sang this song of praise. (Nearly all songs used at Bayville are on YouTube, which means that they are contemporary and popular.) The orchestra became louder and louder, the congregation wilder and wilder, and at one point the words of praise were totally overwhelmed by the sound of the instruments. Then, slowly, the sounds became softer and the human voices became audible again. The singing ended with wild applause for the glory of God.

There is usually a prophecy, and sometimes more than one. In the Pentecostal tradition, a prophecy is a message from God, spoken by someone with a special gift to proclaim what God wants people to hear. Here is an example. "I'm the one you're called to magnify, to glorify. I'm the one who brings life over death, and hope over despair. I the Lord am your hope and your purpose. Do not look to others. Only look to me, for I am pouring out my Spirit upon you. Don't hold back what you have received from me. Move towards me as I move towards you, for I am your Lord. I love you with an everlasting love." Prophecies are usually long and wordy. Here is shorter one. "My arms are wide open to you. My Son died for you. There is nothing that will keep us apart. Come to me, my children." Prophecies are usually shouted with great excitement, in a near-ecstatic state. When they are proclaimed, the congregation becomes totally silent, as in the presence of a divine manifestation. The pastor always offers a confirmation: "Thank you Lord for ministering strength and comfort through your prophecy (congregational applause). You are our source. We will pursue you and we'll receive your grace and your love, Lord. Alleluia!"

The pastor is a gifted orator, a pleasant preacher to listen to, and a judicious spiritual master. At the men's meeting on Wednesdays, it is common to refer to the pastor's Sunday sermons because they are not easily forgotten. He usually develops a major theme over several weeks. During the fall of 2016, he preached on "Wise Decision Making." Previously he had covered "A Pattern to Live By" and "Covenant with Almighty God." All sermons include numerous biblical quotations, but what comes first is the chosen topic or theme, not the biblical text. What comes first is a lesson supported by the Bible, not the exegesis of a given text.

> The pastor's sermons are admired for their mystagogical quality and their relaxed and imaginative performance, not their conservative theology.

Communion takes only a minute and a half, in the middle of a prayer or comment by the pastor. Here is an example: "I am going to read while they are preparing for communion." He reads from 1 Corinthians 11:23: "'On the night he was betrayed he took bread . . . This is my body . . . Do this in remembrance of me.' As we renew our covenant with God, let us remember to always please his Father. We now partake together (the pastor eats the bread). In the same way 'He lifted the cup'—you will now lift that cup of juice. The juice is a sacred symbol of the blood of Jesus. 'This cup is the new covenant in my blood . . . Do this in remembrance of me.' Let us renew our commitment and say 'God, I will be your servant. Let the motives of what I do be purified by your life blood.' Let us partake together." Here the text of the Bible comes with interpretations attached to it, for example when the pastor says, "The juice is a sacred symbol," but people in the audience may not be aware of the difference between the text and the added comments.

The Sunday service ends with a final prayer and an altar call, inviting people to come forward to be prayed over by deacons and deaconesses.

3. Attitudes and Emotions: Intensification

Fervor, dedication, and inner fire are major themes in all songs and prayers. Here is a prayer offered by the pastor: "We now ask the Lord that we would be set ablaze by the Holy Spirit. That a new fire would descend on all our lives, as you did in the book of Acts, with new tongues and new fire. For you are a consuming fire and the Holy Spirit will baptize us with fire from above. Let us ask for this fire as we sing, Alleluia! Alleluia! Alleluia!"

At the end of his sermons and again at the end of the final prayer, the senior pastor is often choking with emotions. He may then briefly pray or sing in tongues, then continue in a trembling voice. Thus, "Let every person young and old see what you have done (in trembling voice). You have sent your beloved Son. Simple and profound! So deep! (In a trembling voice) God so loved us, he gave us his only begotten Son. We thank you, Lord. We are no longer controlled by fear. There is no fear in me. No fear in us. Perfect love! We are no longer intimidated by demons, culture, society, thoughts and logic of this world. No, No, No, we will walk straight and courageously." Here the message is one of overcoming the fear of demons and society, with an appeal to courageous perseverance, in the "holy fire of obedience."

Speaking in tongues can be quite emotional, and emotions in turn may spark speaking in tongues. Here is a prayer over those who came forward at the end of a Sunday service with the purpose of being baptized in the Holy Spirit and begin speaking in tongues. It was a cacophony of individual prayers, choir voices, orchestra music, and words in tongues. "Wait on the Lord! Wait on the Lord, Wait on the Lord! Alleluia!" (Words in tongues) "We glorify you. Your name is worthy of praise." (Words in tongues) "Alleluia." (Some incomprehensible singing) "You're all I want." (Words in tongues) "We worship you, Lord. We are in your presence." (Words in tongues; more incomprehensible singing, now getting louder) "We praise you. Show us your glory." (repeated several times) "Alleluia, come! Alleluia, come! We wait on you, Lord." (Words in tongues; a new tune, but still incomprehensible; again prayer in tongues) "Holy Spirit, come!" At this point there was soft guitar music in the background, and the singing and speaking in tongues slowly faded away. Apparently, the cacophony of many voices speaking and singing different words and tunes at the same time is intended to lead to speaking in tongues. This culmination of the service lasted about 30 minutes. It was highly emotional, not only for the participants but also for the attenders. This fire of emotions was designed to set ablaze one's love of God and neighbors.

> The prophecies are impressive because of the force of their emotional expression, not their theological content.

4. Closeness to Others and to God

There is great closeness and warmth among members of this church. When one enters the church building, two or three greeters are there to welcome you. In the entrance hall, there is always an information desk to answer all kinds of questions. In one corner one finds news about missions. In the past, an enormous map of the world (about eight by ten feet) indicated the location of about one hundred missionaries from the congregation. It has now been replaced by a computer screen constantly showing the latest images. Many missionaries who come home for the yearly mission week are well known in the congregation. Moreover, many people know one another by their first name.

It is customary in this church to pray for one another. The pastor may say, "Would you pray for the person on your left and on your right, and pray a simple and sincere prayer for them, such as, 'Help this marriage, Lord. Bring reconciliation. Heal and touch this body which is sick. Remove confusion and bring clarity and direction, in Jesus's name we pray.'"

After that, the pastor may pray for the whole church. "We pray for the body of Christ at large, for the congregations to the North, South, East and West of us. May the church of God arise, be what you want it to be, Oh Lord! May she be obedient, surrender, and be fully submitted to you, in a whole new fire of obedience."

People not only pray for another in general, but they also pray over those asking to be prayed over. This is done during the altar call at the end of each Sunday service, and also in prayer groups when individuals are invited to sit in the middle of a circle while all extend their hands over them in fervent prayer.

> The emotional force of one's born-again experience is such that most people remember the day and even the hour of its occurrence.

Closeness to God is usually expressed in terms of a personal relationship with God, which for many people began when they were born again. "I usually say I am a born-again Christian. The big transition was that it became a personal relationship. When I was Catholic, I did not have that. God was out there, but there was a distance. I don't feel anything like that anymore." Some are very enthusiastic, like John: "The two most important days in my life were the day I married my wife and the day I accepted Jesus Christ." Even if expressed less enthusiastically, most people remember the day they were saved.

Personal encounters with God take place mainly during personal prayer and Bible reading. Many of the men that I interviewed spend about an hour in religious activity every day. This is justified in reference to Jesus saying in Gethsemane, "Can't you pray one hour with me?" The first person

I interviewed at Bayville was very open. "Every day when I rise, I have what I call devotional time: personal reading of the Word of God, prayer time, singing songs." This takes about an hour. "I also have devotions with my wife, and we pray and read the Bible together." This takes an additional 15 to 20 minutes. Personal prayer is strongly encouraged at Bayville, and every year there is a week dedicated to prayer, which is widely attended.

Bible reading is also a constant practice, but it happens without the help of historical, critical, and exegetic commentaries. One simply divides the Scriptures into manageable portions. One person divided the Bible into 365 readings. Another may read several chapters each day, which enables the whole Bible to be covered in 12 to 15 months. Many have read the Bible from cover to cover five, ten, or fifteen times. This practice would seem to lead to a fragmented view of the Bible. It would be like reading all of Shakespeare's works divided into so many lines—or perhaps one act—per day. This does not provide a global overview of the Bible, but the regular practice of Bible reading brings closeness to God, as attested by church member in interviews.

5. What We Learned

In the analysis of interaction outcomes, we can go beyond the mere description of facts and begin to raise questions. Now is the time to look more closely at the sermons and use of the Bible.

The Bayville senior pastor is fluent in biblical Greek and Hebrew. He avoids topics that have been historically controversial, preferring instead to concentrate on the meaning of a biblical word in Greek or Hebrew. His understanding of the Bible is similar to that of most evangelicals. According to liberal Scripture scholars, there should be a distance or "gap" between a biblical text and its interpretation, that is, between the meaning of a text in its literary and historical context on the one hand, and on the other, its implications in today's world. This distance is often missing among evangelicals.[20] Billy Graham commonly used the phrase, "as the Bible says," after which he expressed his own personal views. Evangelicals quote the Bible profusely, but the quotations are used to justify their theology; there is no critical exegesis of the texts upon which their theology is built. In a fundamentalist reading, the meaning of a text is one's understanding of it and one's understanding is said to be the meaning of the text.

When the senior pastor said "Hell is a horrible place, a real place, a place of torment, pain, and eternal judgment; Jesus warned us about its literal reality," was this an interpretation or the actual meaning of the

20. Olson, "Postconservative Evangelical Response," 65–66.

biblical text? "The Bible clearly teaches what comes after death: judgment, when there will be an assessment of everything you did and said throughout this life. Jesus went so far as to say, 'Every word you speak you have to account for.'" But where does Jesus say so? More importantly, the fear of God and hell seems to reflect more the God of vengeance of the Jewish Bible. Apparently, reading the whole Bible from cover to cover gives priority to the Hebrew texts which comprise 80 percent of the whole Bible, rather than to the New Testament.

This assistant pastor is probably more conservative and fundamentalist than his colleagues, yet he represents a major trend in the evangelical movement.

The following example illustrates some problems inherent in evangelical interpretations of the Bible. In a sermon on baptism in the Holy Spirit, an assistant pastor explained, "There are seven baptisms mentioned in the Bible." Here is the first one: "We read in First Corinthians, 12:13, 'We were all baptized into one body.' This happens when you give your heart to Jesus Christ." But how can giving one's heart to Jesus Christ be a baptism? No explanation was given. "Now we have three baptisms: by the Holy Spirit into the body of Jesus Christ, by John the Baptist, and by Jesus Christ who baptized into the Holy Spirit." The pastor did not mention the other four baptisms, but in the audience people were probably convinced that there must be seven baptisms in the Bible since the preacher said so. The pastor proceeded, without transition, to explain the consequences of accepting Jesus. "You either have the life of Jesus or you don't have it. If you got it, you got it for eternity. If you don't have it, you go to hell. That's the expression of the Bible. There is no way out of hell except through Jesus." Is this what the Bible says? Or is this a fundamentalist theology that is uncritically accepted by members of the Bayville church?

Prophecies raise another problem of interpretation. Every year on December 31, Pastor Orlando gives lengthy prophecies for the year to come. He explained the process in this way: "God would always allow me to see a prophetic picture. Then a Scripture would be downloaded into my spirit, and then the prophetic message." For 2017, he received six prophecies with six sets of pictures, scriptural passages, and prophetic messages. Here is an example: "I saw a set of new tools, and I heard the Lord saying, 'Now it is time to begin to build.'" The scriptural passage for this prophecy was from Isaiah 49; the message was, "This year I am going to invite you to do something you have never done before . . ." On the video of the prophecies which I am using, the text of prophecies and the biblical references were given at the bottom of the television screen. Each prophecy was related (as seen at the bottom of the screen) to perhaps 10 or 20 Scripture quotations. Not only could I not get the central idea of the six prophecies, but for each one I could not get the main idea of the many Scripture verses. Sometime later, when I inquired about the apparent wordiness of most prophecies, I was told, more or less clearly by one of the pastors, that, like the Bible, prophecies are inspired by God in all their words. But to me there were too many words to be able to get the general message.

This raises a question about the role of the individual in prophesying. In this church, there seems to be little sense of personal agency during a prophecy, either by church members during the church services or by the senior pastor at the end of the year. It seems to be taken for granted that the pious thoughts that come to one's mind all come from the Holy Spirit, and that one has little agency in the process. The reason many prophecies are very wordy is that in prophecy all of one's thoughts are seen as coming from God.

We now have enough information to analyze the data according to the criteria developed earlier in this chapter, namely, stages in faith development and growth in religious intensity.

Religious intensity at Bayville is high, even exceptional. This intensity inspires numerous ministries and foreign missions. But does this high intensity lead to higher levels of faith development? With regard to cognitive factors, however, stages 3 and 4 differ with respect to the locus of authority, moral judgment, and the use of symbols. In stage 3, authority is located in approved social leaders who are accepted without critical reflection. At Bayville, what the Bible says is usually identified with what the pastors say. Moreover, in the Bible, "All the words of God are equally inspired," which is a basic tenet of fundamentalism. As explained by an assistant pastor, "The words of Jesus are not more inspired than the book of Leviticus."

If all words of Scripture are equally inspired, there is no center in this infinity of equally inspired words. Thus, one can read the Bible in successive fragments, either a few chapters each day in devotional reading, or as an assortment of quotations in a sermon. The reason the Bible has no central message (Leviticus being as important as Jesus) is that the biblical texts spanning centuries from Moses to St. Paul are believed to have been written by the same hand, that of God. This unity in diversity inevitably leads to contradictions. Some biblical quotations can be used to justify slavery and others to condemn it. Because in many denominations there is no systematic theological and exegetical reflection, only a common training in denominational thinking, each denomination becomes a closed community admitting no superior authority other than itself. Even denominational traditions have no authority; Luther and the Reformers are seldom mentioned. *Sola scriptura* has produced intellectual fragmentation, as one interpretation is not better than another. There is little room for critical mindedness. This is faith of stage 3, where conformity is a major characteristic.

The interpretation of symbols at Bayville is also typical of stage 3. We have seen that communion is a one-and-a half minute ritual without special meaning. Baptism and the Lord's Supper are the only two ordinances accepted by evangelicals. In reference to both, the following ritualistic attitude expressed by one pastor is quite common: "Jesus ordered baptism. He also said 'Do this in memory of me.' So we just do it!" It sounds very much like mechanical acceptance without any critical awareness of purpose and meaning inside and outside the denomination.

Critical mindedness would inevitably lead one to ask how the 783,137 words of the King James Authorized Bible can be equally inspired. The same question can be asked about the year-end prophecies of Pastor Orlando.

At Bayville and in other evangelical churches, it is often said that the Lord's Supper is "just symbolic," and it is a matter of faith that is not open to questions or critical examination. Moving to stage 4 would lead some people to question commonly held symbols and ideas. As a result, they would either have to suppress their questions in order to stay in the church, or leave the church carrying their questions with them, or find an intellectual synthesis of a higher order which would benefit their church. All reformers have done so. This kind of questioning is common today and leads many people to leave their church or opt out of religion.

6. Moral Consensus

Godliness is often mentioned at Bayville as an ideal to pursue. It seems to have a very concrete content, as one can occasionally hear, "I would like to be as godly as some people here." Godliness conjures a mixture of biblical images, gender roles, sexual purity, and social conformity. The foul language of those who are unsaved is viewed as ungodly, as are cohabitation, tattoos, long hair, and punk hairstyles. More praiseworthy is attending church in one's Sunday best, volunteering in many church activities, showing zeal for the missions, and proficiency in God-talk and Scripture quotations. Godliness is different from holiness in the Catholic tradition, which is illustrated by the lives of many saints, canonized or not, who were nonconformists and who did things that were weird in the eyes of society—like St. Catherine of Siena telling the pope to move back to Rome, or like St. Frances giving up his family's wealth and dressing in the equivalent of a gunny sack. Because there are no saints in the evangelical tradition, there are no heroes to emulate, and what remains is conformity to social models of piety and behavior. There is, of course, also much conformity in Catholic churches in spite of saintly models to emulate.

A favorite topic of sermons in church, and also in small group discussion, is the story of one's born-again experience. I once went to interview a prominent evangelical pastor. Without me even asking a question, he told me his very exceptional life story from severe drug addiction to miraculous healing, but after that, he had nothing else to say. A few months later, this prominent pastor was the guest speaker in a major megachurch. He repeated again, in great detail, his life story from severe drug addiction to miraculous healing, and this was his whole sermon. Many evangelical men that I interviewed eagerly told me about their own conversion experiences, which in most cases were very intense and at time somewhat miraculous. Such storytelling creates social desirability—which is a psychological factor leading to social imitation.

Stories of born-again experiences often reinforce the dichotomy between "us," the saved, and "them," the unsaved. Sometimes this dichotomy is put very harshly. "There are some people in this church who come every week but who never accepted Jesus Christ as Lord and savior.

> Public testimonies about being born-again create and reinforce social models for all to emulate, especially when presented with some pious exaggerations about their supernatural nature.

Without Jesus you will be frustrated every day of your life, but when Jesus comes into your life, you will be changed every single day." This was a strong indictment of the church attenders by an assistant pastor. He continued in the same tone. "There are too many of us today who have no intimate time with God, ever! You don't open the word of God, ever! We wait for some preacher to give it to us on TV, or for the pastor to give it to us here, but we don't even know what the word of God is!" He ended with, "God is able. He will do things in the most intimate places of our lives!" The congregation showed its approval with applause. The "us" versus "them" is usually applied to outsiders, but in this instance the dichotomy was being applied to church insiders. From a sociological perspective, what was being called for was greater intensification, but at the same time, it was a call for greater submission to the church's collective models. The applause of the congregation expressed its approval of such dichotomous views. By presenting the social desirability of salvation in such a dualistic perspective, one offers no alternative other than, in simplistic terms, to submit or go to hell.

Conformity is present in most churches. When its leaders insist on the submission of intellect and will, Catholicism fosters levels of conformity that may be as great as, or may exceed those of evangelical churches. The TV masses described in chapter 2 are an example of clerical conformism. Holy Family parish of chapter 5 is another example of ecclesial conformism. Social conformity is what makes social life possible, at the most general level, even though it often impedes spiritual growth and it usually blocks faith development. What is of special interest to us is that, at the Bayville, the high religious intensity was not sufficient to break out of denominational conformity. Growth does not always lead to development.

Conclusion: Individual versus Social Factors and the Social Cost of Conformity

Evangelicals believe that it is individual transformation that will ultimately change the world, and they seem to be right because their churches are growing. But is this growth due to religious and theological factors, as it is commonly assumed? What is, then, the role of social factors? This question is a central one in sociology, and it leads us to turn to both Max Weber and Emile Durkheim to better understand what is going on.

A main issue for Weber was the routinization of charisma. For a social movement to survive, the special gifts and talents of its founder need to become routine among the followers, which is to say, they need to be institutionalized. In many cases, institutionalization is quasi-automatic. Exceptional personalities, for example, Princess Diana or Pope John Paul II, are imitated and become role models for their followers. This is, of course, a process of social conformity, and in most societies, conformity to social models is highly desirable. This is what evangelicals do: they tell their life stories as desirable models of spiritual fulfillment, and most people of good will are attracted by such desirable examples. If, besides individual examples of social desirability, there is also a strong push for social conformity in a particular group, one has little choice but to submit.

A society based on social conformity is likely to produce mechanical rather than organic solidarity. The more mechanical the social interactions are, the greater the conformity will be, and hence the more successful its social models will be. This is a recipe that was understood by all authoritarian regimes from Hitler to Stalin to Mao Zedong. The recipe is to impose your political agenda on the masses, make it desirable through state propaganda, and create social conformity by exterminating all opponents. This is also what all Machiavellian politicians have done through the ages. For Durkheim, however, mechanical solidarity will fall under its own weight under the onslaught of social evolution and technical progress. Moreover, as we have learned since the time of Durkheim, technology and specialization can lead to segmentation, and even to social fragmentation, which are the opposite of centralization and conformity.

At Bayville, social conformity works to the church's advantage. It is a megachurch that is still growing because its models of authority, Bible interpretation, and moral behavior are still highly desirable. Yet there is often a point when a conservative church becomes ultra-conservative and religious zeal becomes fanaticism. History is full of heroes and saints, but it is also full of fanatics. Can a liberal church be successful when it preaches personal commitment rather than social conformity, and critical mindedness rather than submission? This is the issue to be treated in the next chapter, which will also bring back the question of authority.

───── 8 ─────

The Liturgical Imagination

At St. Sabina

VERY OFTEN THE VALUE of a book is found more in the issues it raises than in the answers it provides. The following questions have been discussed thus far. In what sense can worship be understood in terms of interaction (chapter 1)? What happens when the mass is performed according to the minimum requirements (chapter 2)? How important is the relationship between faith and culture in worship (chapter 3)? Can leadership shine in mechanically produced liturgies (chapter 4)? What criteria are to be used to evaluate parish growth (chapters 5 and 6)? Finally, can social conformity be overcome by religious intensity (chapter 7)? What is left is to reflect on David Brown's emphasis on liturgical imagination, mentioned in chapter 1 along with Schillebeeckx and Chauvet. In this chapter and the next, our question will be: What are the permissible limits of creativity in worship? I hope to show that, in spite of the strict limitations that Catholicism imposes on ritual performance, creativity can overcome such limitations; it can also help people to develop beyond stage 3 of conventional faith—which again raises the issue of institutional authority.

This chapter will begin with a short introduction into the black Catholic liturgical movement, which promoted many of the innovations that can be found at St. Sabina today. When this liturgical vision faded away in the rest of the United States, it survived at St. Sabina, which probably is now the only black Catholic parish in America that uses a specifically African American style of worship.

I. The Black Catholic Liturgical Movement

The civil rights movement of the 1960s and the innovative spirit of Vatican II inspired liturgical renewal among African American Catholics that has

146

no equivalent in the white church.[1] Father Clarence Rivers was the inspiring voice through the 1970s and 1980s. Both a liturgist and a composer, he became the first director of the Office of Black Catholics in 1970, which saw the elevation of four black Catholic priests to the episcopate. This renewal movement found its forum in the journal, *Freeing the Spirit*, which supplied African American Catholics with a flow of new ideas. The first Black Catholic Theological Symposium took place in Baltimore in 1978. From that point on, there was an increasingly loud appeal for a specifically African American rite with a new Eucharistic Prayer. In the 1980s, eight more black priests were made bishops. In 1984, ten black bishops issued their first pastoral letter entitled *What We Have Seen and Heard*. The American bishops approved this movement by creating a Permanent Secretariat for Black Catholics within the National Conference of Catholic Bishops (NCCB) in 1988. The NCCB support for the movement became public a year later with the publication of *In Spirit and Truth: Back Catholic Reflections on the Order of Mass*.

Fr. Michael Pfleger, the future pastor of St. Sabina in Chicago, must have been aware of these developments. During his three years in a preparatory seminary, he was assigned to work in a black and Hispanic parish. He continued to work there throughout his years in the major seminary, spending actually more time in this parish than on the seminary campus. His first assignment after ordination in 1975 was to St. Sabina where the pastor had suffered a stroke and the assistant pastor was leaving. He was thus by default the captain of this ship. As an associate pastor just 26 years old, he had the ardor of youth and the imagination to innovate. Five years later when it was time to nominate a new pastor, the parish board unanimously requested that Fr. Pfleger be their new pastor. Cardinal Cody gave in reluctantly, and he nominated Pfleger as permanent administrator until he had time to find a suitable pastor. Pfleger wasted no time. On the advice of other priests, he had himself installed as the official pastor. He was only 31. He remained at the head of this parish for the next forty years. Pfleger transformed the parish liturgy from typically white Roman Catholic to black evangelical Catholic. In 1987, a documentary on black Catholic worship entitled *Fire in the Pews* documented black experiences in twelve parishes in eight cities around the United States. St. Sabina was one of them. With the release of that film, Fr. Pfleger achieved national recognition.

Even before the Vatican Council, Clarence Rivers had composed liturgical music in the black tradition, culminating in his *American Mass Program* of 1963. In this and other writings, he advocated the use of popular

1. McGann, *Let it Shine*.

black music, primarily jazz, the use of drums, and musical improvisation in liturgical music. He also wanted spontaneous participation of the people, as was the practice in the Protestant evangelical churches of the South. In 1974 he published *Soulful Worship*, which emphasized the importance of soulful spirituality through music, dance, drama, and a vibrant assembly. In *The Spirit of Worship* (1978), he further developed the African roots of religious worship. This was not lost on Fr. Pfleger, who adopted many of Rivers' recommendations.

In *The Spirit of Worship* Rivers included a Eucharistic Prayer in the Black tradition.[2] In it, the priest first praises God for having "breathed into our nostrils of clay the Spirit of Life . . . [so that we might] have the dynamism of your Spirit, have the power of Soul." Thanks be to God for having sent his Son so that "he might walk our walk and talk our talk, and grant to each of us a right to the tree of life." Praise to you, Oh God, "for having taken your seat among the downtrodden, the dehumanized, the dispossessed, and the denied people of the universe." New Eucharistic Prayers like this one were relatively common in those days, and Fr. Pfleger has used them creatively ever since.

In the 1980s as today, worship among Black Americans is characterized by traits of an oral rather than a written culture and the request for greater social justice.

Over the years, African American Catholics came to identify liturgical traits that were special to the black community. For example,

a. Black culture is prominently oral because for centuries slaves were deprived of formal education and today economic deprivation hinders the education of black children. White culture, in contrast, is very book-oriented, especially in its formal education.

b. An important aspiration of the black community is liberation from the social and economic consequences of slavery and its aftermath. Modern forms of oppression are unemployment, food uncertainty, depression, and drug addiction. Worship needs to acknowledge this central dimension of black life.

The request for a separate black rite within the church seemed natural at a time when the Black Panthers were promoting a separate cultural identity. Black Catholics wanted to be more than just another ethnic group in the church like the Italians, the Poles, or the Irish, with the prospect of seeing their cultural identity progressively obliterated by Catholic uniformity.

2. McGann, *Let it Shine*, 82–85.

Insisting on black Catholic cultural identity, Fr. George Stallings founded Imani (Faith) Temple in Washington, D.C. as an independent black church in 1989. One year later he broke all ties to the Catholic Church and was excommunicated.

Fr. Pfleger moved along these same lines, insisting on primacy of oral culture in worship, liberation spirituality in education and preaching, and independence, but not separation from centralized authority.

In 1990, the American bishops published a second document, *Plenty Good Room: The Spirit and Truth of African American Catholic Worship*. The bishops recognized the legitimate aspirations of blacks but insisted on "adaptation" and "accommodation" rather than "inculturation." The current Roman rite was to be taken as normative with only minor adaptations. In 1994, a survey of African American Catholics (which later was found to be unrepresentative) indicated that 72 percent rejected the idea of an autonomous black rite, and that 79 percent felt comfortable in their parish. The inescapable conclusion was that there was "very little support for, and a great deal of opposition to, the creation of a full canonical rite." Shortly after the survey, the NCCB subcommittee on the Liturgy in the African American Community was disbanded. In 1994, the Vatican issued an instruction entitled "Inculturation and the Roman Liturgy," which reasserted that the national conferences of bishops were the only legitimate authorities on local "inculturation." Black Catholics no longer had a voice in the NCCB. The dream of a specifically black American Catholicism was dead.

Nonetheless, the dream endured and gained energy at St. Sabina.

II. The St. Sabina Inculturated Liturgy

Until the 1960s, St. Sabina was an all-white—mainly Irish and German—parish of about 3,000 families. Seven priests celebrated 11 masses on Sundays, and 20 Dominican sisters staffed the grammar school that enrolled about 800 children. White flight began suddenly when, in August 1965, an altercation between black and white teenagers ended with a white girl being shot in the leg and a white boy being shot and killed in front of the parish community center. Six months later there were only 1908 registered parishioners left, and two years later, this number had dropped to 530. When Fr. Pfleger arrived, the parish had turned black, with only a few white families left.

How could this parish survive financially with only about 15 percent of its original population? The writing was on the wall: the parish would be closed, especially since it owed about $100,000 to the archdiocese. Pfleger could do little as an assistant pastor, but as soon as he became permanent administrator, in effect the pastor of the parish, he proposed tithing—a 10 percent contribution from each family—as a challenge to the people and a gamble for his teaching. The Sunday collections rose steadily, doubled and tripled, and by 1990 the parish had paid back the totality of its debt to the archdiocese. Now the parish was financially independent and ready to venture into expansion.

Let us take a tour of the parish campus. One block from the church is the Resource Employment Center. It is funded in part by the city of Chicago, and its purpose is to help the whole person, psychologically, spiritually, and economically. The center is staffed by three specialists: one with experience in management who empowers people to have a vision of their future, a financial counselor with experience in corporate accounting who helps clients to manage their finances, and a technician who manages the computer lab where people can write résumés and find jobs through the internet. The center also provides hundreds of summer jobs to teenagers through city and government programs.

Another block away from the church is the local office of Chicago Catholic Charities that provides food, clothing, and financial assistance. People in need can get a basket of groceries on a regular basis from the food pantry there, as well as nutrition guidance for families.

On the same city block as the church is Elders Village, an 80-unit apartment building for seniors who had previously lived in poor and isolated apartments. It is a pleasant building with an African style façade, financed by Catholic Charities and the US Department of Housing and Urban Development (HUD). Seniors pay no more than 30 percent of their income for rent, and in addition, Elders Village offers facilities such as a library, computer space, an exercise room, a beauty salon, a barbershop, and monthly activities. "It's a ministry, not just a job," said the director.

Behind the church is the youth center called The Ark, which is a safe haven for at-risk youth. It houses a gymnasium and offers after-school activities for about a hundred students from neighborhood high schools. At three in the afternoon, there is an hour of recreational activities, after which everything stops, and all students go to designated places for homework with help and tutoring available. After an hour of study, activities begin again in a great variety of areas including art, music, dance, boxing, and even cooking. Weekends offer basketball tournaments to promote peace and cooperation in the neighborhood. In the past, teams of gang members played against one another, and teenagers played against police officers.

Adjacent to the church is St. Sabina Academy, a grade school serving children from pre-kindergarten to eighth grade. All classes begin the day with five minutes of prayer and meditation. The school is strongly committed to both Christian and black values, with the sense that "God has a purpose for every child's life." This perspective is obviously appreciated by parents in the neighborhood since four out of ten children in the school are not Catholic, and seven out of ten receive financial assistance from the government.

One institution for which St. Sabina is well-known are the Friday night marches that take place from the last day of school in beginning of summer until the beginning of the next school year. This is a peaceful walk rather than a protest march and it begins at the church to make it clear that its non-violence is inspired by the gospel. On their way from one block to the next, the marchers engage people who are walking in the streets, sitting on front porches, or waiting at bus stops. They may hand out flyers about the activities at St. Sabina, offering help whenever possible, for employment, housing, food, or youth activities. The march may also go to a hotspot after a gang shoot-out to bring peace and reconciliation through communication, prayer, and singing. At other times the march may stage protests in front of stores that do not hire blacks, or who sell alcohol, cigarettes, and possibly drugs to minors. In all these marches, Fr. Pfleger is always in the vanguard.

Looking back over the past five decades, it can be said that all of these accomplishments were achieved under Pfleger's leadership.

A. Interaction Processes

The church building is a neo-Gothic structure that has not changed much since its construction, but the inside, especially the sanctuary, has been completely renovated to reflect black sensitivities. What is striking as one enters the church is a mesmerizing gigantic picture of a black Jesus stretching out his hands within the hands of the Father. The colors are brown, white, gold, and black. Jesus is smiling at the visitors. The size and location of the painting make this black Jesus the background image of every liturgy. All the furnishing and statues are carved in black walnut and reflect African art. There is a massive altar in black walnut facing the assembly. On one side of the church, a sculpture of the Holy Family depicts an African Joseph raising his hands to give praise. The liturgical vestments and the fabric covering the altar are local creations in the colors and style of African art.

1. Basic information and Expectations

In order to understand the liturgical interactions in this church we need some basic information about the pastor and the music. Father Mike, as Pfleger is commonly called, is at the same time an activist, a warm friend, an evangelical convert, an improviser, a friend of power elites, and a skillful planner.

A social activist.

Fr. Pfleger spent high school summers working for social justice in an Indian reservation in Oklahoma. While still in high school, he attended a march organized by Martin Luther King Jr. that changed his life. King had been struck in the head, yet he continued preaching love. "I saw Martin Luther using faith as a transitional agent for building community. I decided then I wanted to be a priest because the church can be an element of change."[3] One of his first acts as pastor of St. Sabina was to put a bronze bust of King at a prominent place in the sanctuary. Over the last 30 or 40 years, he has made the headlines in the local press as the social activist priest of Chicago.

Personal warmth.

His public image is that of a warrior always on the attack, but in private he emanates great warmth. All the people I interviewed described him as a friend and mentor, never as a Catholic Malcolm X. It is this warmth that allowed him to be a successful father to his three adopted children. According to his biographer, Fr. Pfleger made breakfast every day for his eight-year-old adopted son, Lamar, went bicycling and had picnics on the beach with him, and watched Superman cartoons with him on Saturday mornings. "I think I am a better person and a better priest for it."[4] He extends this family warmth to all visitors and acquaintances.

An evangelical convert.

While serving in a black and Hispanic church during his seminary years, he regularly attended evangelical churches. He sat in the back and carefully observed the preaching and worship styles that he later adopted in his own ministry. It was in one of these churches that he personally came to "confess Jesus as Lord and Savior." As he recollected in one of his sermons, "I learned about sin and guilt in the Catholic Church, but at Hopewell Baptist, I learned about Jesus."[5] Hanging from the ceiling of St. Sabina church is the monogram "Jesus"

3. McClory, *Radical Disciple*, 21.
4. McClory, *Radical Disciple*, 43–44.
5. McClory, *Radical Disciple*, 22.

in neon letters, something that cannot be seen in any Catholic church; they all have a crucifix instead. The motto of St. Sabina in front of the presbytery reads "Turning believers into disciples." It is also the motto of Saddleback, the megachurch of Rick Warren.

An improviser.

In all things Fr. Pfleger is committed to going his own way, yet he can unexpectedly change direction and compromise. In his conflicts with the archbishops of Chicago, he always took an uncompromising position, only to recant at the last minute to avoid a catastrophe. His prayers and exhortations are central in the praise and worship part of the Sunday service, but they are mostly improvisations. His homilies are written out, but he may ignore his text and improvise. The altar calls are often improvisations—as happened once at the end of the funeral mass for a prominent gang leader. Praying and singing at St. Sabina is mainly improvised. Pfleger was offered to have his Sunday mass broadcast live on a commercial channel, but he refused, saying that the ways of the Spirit are unpredictable and his Sunday services of two to three hours cannot be scheduled into 50 minute time-slots like TV masses.

A friend of the power elites.

Fr. Pfleger has contacts with many local and national people of power. First of all, he is friendly with the mayors of Chicago whose support he needs for his social justice programs. His connections extend to the whole state of Illinois and to the federal government in Washington, DC. He has friends among black politicians, artists, writers, and film-makers, whom he invites to speak in his church, and he has corporate donors like Coca-Cola and Amazon, who responded generously to his requests. A good planner, he has prominent personalities speak or perform in his church on a regular basis. After the shocking killing of a thirteen-year-old boy of the neighborhood, he invited—again—the mayor of Chicago, Rahm Emanuel, to address the assembly. A few weeks earlier, he had invited Arne Duncan, the US Secretary of Education, to join the Friday night march and to preach on Sunday. During Black History Month, he might have a black evangelical preacher or a prominent black professor preach, to the delight of the crowd. The director of *Chi-Raq* (Chicago-Iraq, a critique of Chicago violence) was invited to speak several times.

Music at St. Sabina.

Muic is an essential part of worship. Thomas Andrew Dorsey, considered the father of black gospel music, was the music director of the Pilgrim Baptist Church in Chicago from 1932 to the late 1970s. He created a new genre of gospel songs that combined praise lyrics with the rhythms of jazz and blues. He defined black religious music for his generation. In 1981, Dr. Walt Whitman created the Soul Children of Chicago Choir at the St. John de La Salle Catholic Academy. For the last thirty years they have performed around the world, including at the White House. To this day the bi-weekly rehearsals begin with praise and worship, and the singing of "I am in love with Jesus." For ten years, Dr. Whitman was the music director of St. Sabina, bringing with him his love for contemporary black gospel music as well as members of his choir. The current lead singer and choir director of St. Sabina, Samuel Williams, was a member of the Soul Children who came to St. Sabina with Whitman.

> The flow is the learned coordination between the music leader, the choir, and the participating assembly. It is common in black but also in white evangelical churches.

An important aspect of gospel singing is what is called the flow. At St. Sabina as in other black churches, the choir director receives his instructions from the music director at the keyboard, who himself follows the lead of the pastor. The flow is the coordination between all three, especially when the same song or the same chorus or even the same line is repeated many times.

For spectators and the people in the pews, this coordination seems totally natural, but it is actually a learned process. The Second City Training Center of Chicago offers classes to actors to improve their skills in improvisation. Samuel Williams has attended some of these classes. The leitmotif of the teaching was, "Always agree, agree, agree. If something is thrown out, it is your job to agree and add on top of that." This is the tradition of jazz, where every member of an ensemble agrees and adds something new. It is the basic principle at work in the flow, not only in singing but also in improvised dances and choreography.

2. Description of the Ritual Processes

The Sunday service usually lasts between two and three hours, divided into about ten parts: the welcome and introduction (5 to 10 minutes), the call to worship by Fr. Pfleger (10 to 15 minutes), praise and worship (about 30 minutes), the readings, the homily (30 to 40 minutes), the altar call (20 to

30 minutes), the presentation of gifts (15 to 20 minutes), the Eucharistic Prayer, the Our Father and communion (30 minutes), and the announcements followed by the final prayer. Here is their description and their liturgical significance.

a. Welcome and Introduction

Sunday services are usually quite informal, so they may not begin on time. They start when the commentator welcomes people in the audience, reads announcements, and invites all to prayer by praying aloud. Meanwhile, the choir members walk to their seats, the dancers take position in the sanctuary, and the musicians test their instruments. The pews slowly fill up.

The minister of music is seated on the right side of the sanctuary, in front of the choir. While playing on the keyboard, he may lead the assembly into singing. "Praise the Lord, everybody!" (There is a tepid response.) "Come on, we can do better than that! Praise the Lord everybody!" (There is a stronger response.) "Now jump to your feet and greet your neighbors. Alleluia! Greet the people on your left and on your right." (He plays a few notes.) "Come let us give praise! (More piano music.) "From sunrise to sunset the Lord is worthy of praise!" (Louder piano music; several instruments join in.) People begin clapping and the dancers begin dancing. Within a short time the whole sanctuary is filled with the Spirit of David dancers (the name of the choreography group), clapping and dancing. The whole church follows in rhythmic motions, singing, "I need you . . . I praise you . . . Forever."

This beginning is very different from the traditional entrance of the priest from the back of the church. Here Sunday worship is thought of as a celebration, perhaps even a party. From the time of the Byzantine emperors to the absolute monarchs in modern Europe, the entrance of dignitaries—in church and society—was an occasion for pomp and ceremony. So it is also at pontifical and papal masses when the procession proceeds according to the participants' ecclesiastical rank. At St. Sabina, there is no official entrance or exit of the priest. At the end of the mass, for example, Fr. Pfleger walks down the center aisle greeting people right and left amidst the liturgical ministers dancing and singing.

b. Fr. Pfleger's Call for Praise and Worship

After a song or two, Fr. Pfleger appears in front of the assembly, having come unobtrusively from the side. People sing "Nobody's like you, Lord" and over their voices, Pfleger adds his own invocation, somewhat in this manner:

People: Nobody's like you, Lord."

    Priest: "This is the day the Lord has made."

"Nobody's like you, Lord."

    Priest; "We are glad and rejoice in it."

"Oh-oh-oh, Lord."

    Priest: "Bless the Lord, oh my soul!"

"Oh-oh-oh, Lord."

    "And all that is within me, praise him!"

"Oh-oh-oh, Lord."

    "Nobody's like you, Lord."

"Oh-oh-oh, Lord."

    "The Lord is good, and his mercy endures forever."

"Nobody's like you, Lord."

    "Open your mouth and give God a scream!"

People shout praises. When there is silence in the assembly, Fr. Pfleger exhorts:

Turn to your neighbor and say:

Neighbor, if you knew everything God has done for me

Neighbor, you sit next to a miracle!

Come-on, and give him some praise! Alleluia! Come on,

I know you're a miracle, open your mouth, and say, Thank you God!

People wave and shout. There is loud saxophone music. Fr Pfleger continues when there is silence in the assembly.

We now come to that part of the service that is only for God. Everything else—the prayer, the music—is for us, but worship is just about him. Just say,

God, I love you.

Not just because of anything you have done,

But just because of who you are.

If you never do anything for me, I worship you because you are worthy.

Just raise your hands and worship God with your mouth,

God, you're awesome. How wonderful you are!

Come on! Let your worship rise like incense.

After a moment of silence people sing again:

Nobody's like you, Lord . . .

Nobody's like you, etc."

c. Praise, worship, and dances

At times, attention is drawn to the choir, at times to Fr. Pfleger, but most of the time it is drawn to the dancers who express the meaning of a given song. Thus when the choir sang the words on the left, the dancers performed movements described on the right:

"Hallelujah!"	Standing and waving right and left in large motions
"You have won the victory"	Raising both arms in victory sign
"Hallelujah!"	Bowing down in reverential movement
"You have won it all for me"	All raise their hands on high

A different song:

"Death could not hold you down"	(Camera shows image of burning candles
"You are the risen king"	superimposed on images of dancers)
"Seated in Majesty"	Strong music with drums. All dancers bow deeply
"You are the risen king"	and raise hands on high

A different song:

"Worthy is the Lamb"	Taking one step to the left, waving to the left
"Worthy is the Lamb"	Taking one step to the right, waving to the right
"Holy! Holy!"	Taking one step forward, bowing down
"You, Lord God almighty"	Taking one step backwards, raising hands on high
"Worthy is the Lamb"	Large motion of victory
"Holy! Holy!"	Bowing down reverentially several times

A song on Pentecost Sunday:

"Let it rain. Let it rain."	The dancers, all in red, enter in a whirlwind
"Open the floodgates of heaven"	in a choreography of movement and jumps
"Let it rain. Let it rain"	Dancers close together in one group
"Open the floodgates of heaven and rain down from heaven."	Vivid motions of petition

The importance of dancing in an oral culture has been studied by Walter J. Ong. According to him, a basic characteristic of orality is that it evolves in the present in the ongoing sounds and movements of speech that cannot be stopped and looked at like a text on a page. Any sentence calls for a response. Without a response, the conversation stops, and silence is perceived as social emptiness. Motions and rhythm are everything. "Thought must come into

> Social events in the oral culture evolve in the ongoing flow of their happening. They require intense participation rather than silent reflection.

being in heavily rhythmic, balanced patterns, in repetitions or antitheses."[6] Rhythmic dancing combined with rhythmic music in the sanctuary invites to rhythmic dancing and singing in the assembly. To impose five minutes of silence like at St. Benedict would be deadly here. "Redundancy characterizes oral thought and speech."[7] Many songs at St. Sabina endlessly repeat the same line, such as "Nobody's like you, Lord! Nobody's like you!" Oral culture thrives in the profusion of sounds and motions, in an aesthetic of improvisation and flow, rather an aesthetic of parsimony based on a written script. Oral culture wants to achieve "close, empathetic, communal identification with the known," while "writing separates the knower from the known" in order to achieve emotionless objectivity.[8] Worship at St. Sabina is, indeed, communal and emotional, because emotions are the motions that bring people out of themselves. The printing press and the Internet have not totally replaced the oral culture that still prevails in childhood and everyday conversations. It is likely that many believers would like to find a "close, empathetic and communal" relationship with God in their parishes. If this is so, St. Sabina is a model, rather than an exception.

It should be noted that there is no Kyrie, no Gloria and no Credo. This will be discussed below.

d. The Readings

Lectors are supposed to *proclaim* the Word of God. Examples of proclamation can be seen at pontifical and papal masses where the lectors may sing the readings according to a Gregorian melody. The most famous of these proclamations is the *Exultet*, which is sung in all Catholic parishes during the Easter Vigil. It is a very difficult piece, with very high and very low notes, and only the best cantors can perform it well. When well performed, the *Exultet* is often remembered more for its melody than for its

> In the oral culture, liturgical readings are proclamations of a living tradition rather than references to a written text.

text. In sum, a proclamation is usually a scripted performance, which is common in a writing culture.

6. Ong, *Orality and Literacy*, 34.

7. Ong, *Orality and Literacy*, 40.

8. Ong, *Orality and Literacy*, 45.

Quite different are the readings at St. Sabina. Oral cultures always evolve in the present, which means that every single word is important. Here are several examples. When reading the story of Abraham from the book of Genesis, one lector emphasized nearly every word: "The Lord—appeared to Abraham—by the terebinth of Mamre." Here the evocation of "the Lord" was as important as the evocation of Abraham and the terebinth of Mamre. Another reader added body language, gestures, and great conviction to her reading of Colossians 2:13: "God—brought us to life.—I say that again! God!—brought *us* (pointing to herself)—to life—(waving finger as sign of importance) along with Jesus!—(waving finger) having forgiven—us (pointing to herself)—of *all*—not some!—*all* transgressions!" In contrast with this, an elderly woman read in a soft voice as if talking to children, making sure they were paying attention to every single word. In an oral culture every word is pronounced as if it is being said or heard for the first time ever.

A male commentator introduced the responsorial Psalm of the day with the words, "The church does not have to fear, because the response today is, 'He who does justice—will live—in presence—of the Lord!'" At that point he broke into in tears, sobbing uncontrollably, and had to leave the lectern to wipe off his tears. The assembly applauded in support. When he came back he had to contain himself but his voice choked each time he read, "He who does justice—will live—in presence—of the Lord!" It was as if he had had heard these words for the first time in his life. It was an awesome experience for him (and the audience). As to Fr. Pfleger, he usually invites the assembly to open the Bible and read the text with him, as is the custom in many evangelical churches.

John's Gospel opens with the words, "In the beginning was the *Logos*." This Greek word has many meanings, such as word, story, plot, logic, and reason. John's opening sentence is an implicit reference of the first verses of the book of Genesis: "In the beginning . . . God said 'Let there be light!' So there was light." At the beginning of time there was God's spoken and creative word. The English language has only one term for both spoken and written pronouncements. Now, in English, "the word of God" is often taken as a reference to the written Bible, while in French "*la parole de Dieu*" may refer to the spoken creative word that reverberates through both written and spoken traditions. Throughout Catholic history, however, the church's hierarchy has promoted liturgies that follow a written script because it can be monitored and controlled. Such scripted liturgies can be very effective among the cultural elite, as is the case at Notre Dame in Paris. Scripted liturgies, however, are not very functional in oral cultures where God is perceived as the spoken word of interactions, not as the *logos* of books and of those who know how to read.

e. *The Homily*

Because an altar call is the normal continuation of a given homily at St. Sabina, I will present such a homily with an altar call. This example will also give us a glimpse into Fr. Pfleger's own spiritual life. Here are some excerpts from his sermon.

> A sermon is supposed to be a message from God. In a few cases this is literally true.

"I was going to preach from the first book of Samuel but God woke me up at five this morning and told me to put aside what I had prepared and speak about today's Gospel of Luke 11:1–13, on teaching the Our Father. I read the Our Father and thought God wanted me to preach about prayer. I read this passage over and over, but God said, 'Keep reading.' Then I read the next part where Jesus said that God will answer you because of persistence. That was to be my topic.

"God brought me to different parts of the Bible. Bartimaeus had been blind his whole life but never gave up. When pushed back by the disciples, his faith out-shouted their condemnation. Then God brought me to the hemorrhaging woman to whom every doctor had said, 'There is nothing that can be done.' When the doctors said, 'No,' something inside her said, 'Yes.' So she pushed beyond the naysayers, pushed beyond those who say, 'That's the way it's going to be 'round here.' She pushed beyond being a mule to violence and racism and hatred. She pushed beyond giving up. (Shouts of approval.) You have to learn to say 'I can' when the world says, 'You can't!'

"God is looking for some folks whose Yes is greater than men's No. Bartimaeus had to shout louder than the disciples. The hemorrhaging woman had to shout louder than the doctors' No. Zacchaeus was not a believer, but something inside him said, 'You have to see that man Jesus.' Sometimes your faith is weak, but inside you something says, 'You got to see Jesus.' Sometimes your flesh says, 'I can't do that no more' but something says, 'Get to Jesus.' Zaccheus had no faith, but he ran ahead of the crowd and climbed a tree. Do you hear me? Jesus wants to say to you, 'Come, I want to dine with you tonight. I want to turn your life upside down, tonight!'"

> When a speaker shows his vulnerabilities, he or she gives others the strength to accept their own vulnerable self.

"Yesterday afternoon I had to go to my room and weep because I was hurting. Yesterday I got a call about someone having been shot where we had just passed by the night before. I had to go my room and sit down (he sits down on the floor leaning against the altar). I said, 'God, I'm tired of violence, I am tired of things happening. God, your son is tired!' God said, 'Get up! Walk around your room like Joshua around Jericho. Walk around until a spirit of determination rises up and gets louder than the spirit of doubt and discouragement. Just think that I am the Almighty God.' And as I was thinking about who God is, I felt something rising in me: God is still our hope." (Shouts of approval.)

"Maybe there are people here who find themselves in a place of pain and discouragement. Sometimes we need a new touch. If that's you, I invite you to come forward right now. If you need a new touch, just move out of your seat." (People move forward in droves.)

Fr. Pfleger had improvised for half an hour. There was still an hour-and-a half to go before the end of this three-hour service.

f. The Altar Call

At St. Sabina there is an altar call about once a month but it has little to do with the common Protestant practice. At St. Sabina, when people are moved, they clap in approval and sometimes stand up and shout. Something similar can be seen in Congress during the State of the Union address. Sometimes things can get wild there, too. The altar calls at St. Sabina go one step beyond the clapping and shouting in the assembly because people come forward to where the action is, around Fr. Pfleger and around the altar. It is a collective expression of faith, not mainly an individualistic commitment. It is a collective revival, and a commitment to spiritual renewal.

After the improvised homily on persistence in prayer came a twenty-minute improvised call for spiritual renewal that went through various stages. At first, while the choir sang the Pentecost song, "Let it rain, let it rain. Open the floodgates of heaven," Fr. Pfleger covered the song with his strong voice inviting to pray, "'Lord, I need you to rain down your anointing. I need you to rain down your power against everything the devil throws up against me.' Just lift your hands and say, 'Lord, touch me. Yes God, touch me! Touch me! Touch me!'" (The choir sings, "Shower down!") "Breathe!" (The choir sings, "Breath on us!") "Rain!" (The choir sings, "Rain on us! Shower down! Shower down!")

"If you are hungry and thirsty for the things of God you can say, 'I am not letting go until I get what God has in store for me.' For the thirsty people, I want you to shout,

> The altar call is a public expression of a community's spiritual and social drama—as is any worship.

on the count of three. I want you to name your need and bring it to the throne of God. I want you to shout, so that every demon in hell has to shut up. To all the thirsty people: One. Two. Three! (Strong shouting.) 'God, I need you to answer my call. I need you to answer my finances. I need you to answer my relationship. I need you to answer right now!'" (Strong calling out; strong saxophone music, for a long while.)

"God is loosening his storehouse. He is loosening finances. He is loosening healing. He is loosening breakthroughs. Right now." (After a while, the choir and the orchestra become silent.) "God has dispatched angels. To the thirsty ones, what you have been waiting for, God says, 'It's on the way.' Now listen to me. You got to have the kind of faith that says, 'I believe it's on the way. I have enough faith to wait for it, and understand he keeps me safe till it gets here.' The righteous have never been forsaken."

"You have to have enough faith to know it's already done. Raise your hand with me and declare with all your voice, 'I believe—God has already—handled my situation.—I believe—God has already—worked it out. And I believe—God will keep me—until then—in Jesus' name.' Now if you believe it, give a shout to let the devil know it." (People shout and wave.) "Yes! Yes! Yes! Yes!" (Shouting.)

The altar call ends with singing softly, "Thank you, Lord" and other songs, for ten more minutes before people retake their seats.

g. The Presentation of Gifts

What is special here is that everyone in the pews comes to the altar through the central aisle and returns by way of the side aisles to deposit their offerings, as they do for communion. This takes over fifteen minutes.

One may argue that this practice is meant to increase donations. This may be true the first or second time, but not when it has become a routine, since nobody at the altar will be able to see what is in a person's envelope.

One may argue that this is a waste of time. In most churches the offerings are collected in a short time by many ushers. More efficiently, the offerings could be dropped in a box at the entrance, or even more efficiently, mailed to the rectory. More efficiently still, one could mail a check for the whole year. But why come to church then? Efficiency cannot be the main rationale for spiritual fruitfulness.

The rubrics require a short moment of silence after the homily. This is not done at St. Sabina. Instead there is the opportunity during the offering of gifts for a 15-minute reflection about the emotional homily that just ended. This reflection is likely to be fostered by the repeated singing of a chorus, such as the following:

"And we'll sing songs to the Glory of the Lamb

Let us sing songs to the Glory of the Lamb

And we'll sing songs to the Glory of the Lamb

Hallelujah! Glory to the Lamb."

One may also, then, follow the advice of St. Paul, "I urge you, brothers and sisters, to offer your bodies as a living sacrifice, holy and pleasing to God; this is your true and proper worship" (Rom 12:1).

h. The Eucharistic Celebration

The eucharistic celebration consists of four basic parts: the invocation of the Holy Spirit, the institution narrative, the recitation of Our Father, and communion. There was no Preface and no Sanctus at the liturgies I attended. The Eucharistic Prayer begins when a jug of wine and an elongated basket of bread are brought to the altar. The leader of the Spirit of David dancers stands next to the priest. He will be the only acolyte at the altar.

The invocation of the Holy Spirit (which corresponds to the epiclesis or invocation in the Eucharistic Prayer) usually summarizes the main themes of the homily, so it is always an improvisation. Here is the invocation summarizing the homily presented above:

"Holy Spirit, stir up in us boldness and tenacity. Stir in us the kind of faith that out-shouts all the other voices, even the voice of our own flesh that tries to tell us what we can't be, can't do, and can't have. Holy Spirit, set up a kind of crazy faith in us that looks at the devil in the face and laughs, and calls us to have the kind of boldness and courage that call things that are not but makes them become." Then, with both hands held over the bread and wine, Fr. Pfleger said, "Holy Spirit, bless our gifts and let them become the body and blood of our Lord Jesus Christ."

> The epiclesis or invocation of the Holy Spirit is more implicit than explicit in the four official Catholic Eucharistic Prayers. Here it is explicit.

"For we remember how, before he went to Calvary to pay the price for our salvation, he invited us at the table, and there took bread, and broke and blessed it, and (raising high the basket of bread) gave thanks to you God, our Father, and gave the bread to us and said (turning around to the right, holding the basket of bread) 'Take this all of you and eat it, (turning around to the left) for this is my body which is given up for you.' Then he took the cup of wine, and again, Father, (raising high the cup with one hand) he gave you thanks and praise, and blessed the cup, and gave it to us and said (turning to the right and left with the cup), 'Take this, all of you and drink from it, for this is the cup of my blood, the cup of the new and lasting covenant. And it is shed for you and for all people so that sins may be forgiven. Do this, and remember me.'" (The priest and his acolyte bow reverently.)

Then there is another improvised prayer, which corresponds to the part of the Eucharistic Prayers after the consecration. Here is an example. "We remember, Holy Father, the love Jesus has especially for the poor and the disfranchised. May we follow his example, and most of all, may we follow Jesus who said, 'If you love me, follow me, and do what I do.' This is our prayer, Lord. We make it, not in our own name; we make it in the name of him who can do all things." Giving the chalice to the acolyte, the priest continues, "For it is through him, (raising the bread basket with both hands while the acolyte raises the cup) with him, in him, in the unity of the Holy Spirit, that the glory and honor are yours, Almighty Father, forever and ever." In response the assembly sings enthusiastically the Great Amen.

> The recitation of Our Father, together with the kiss of peace, is one of the most memorable images—among many others—of the Sunday liturgies.

At this point the whole assembly converges to form a single chain of hands around the altar. "So now we pray as Jesus taught us, and we proclaim, "Our Father . . ." The scene of the assembly holding hands and praying in unison, followed by the warm embraces of the sign of peace, is one of the most memorable images of these Sunday celebrations. The priest says, "May peace, who is Jesus, be with you!" All turn around, move around, and exchange peace.

It must be remembered that African American Catholics wanted to have not only their own Eucharistic Prayer but also their own liturgical rite. Quite a few Eucharistic Prayers were written in the 1980s and 1990s. The next chapter will describe the one of the Zairean rite. The above eucharistic celebration must be seen in the context of this liturgical creativity.

Communion is distributed in only two lines by eucharistic ministers (in both bread and wine), so it takes ten to fifteen minutes. There will be inspirational music of harp, flute, and soft trumpet for personal meditation. The melodies repeat the major songs of the day. The priest and his acolyte are seated on one side of the sanctuary. The celebration finds is conclusion in silent and peaceful prayer facilitated by inspirational soft music. Then there are ten more minutes of songs, announcements, and a joyful exit.

3. & 4. Emotions and Attitudes & Closeness to God and to Others

The above descriptions have provided ample information about people's attitudes and emotions. For the altar call, nearly all people moved up to the sanctuary; the few left were probably old and unable to walk. In the previous chapters it was relatively easy to point to the time of the greatest devotion, at the recitation of the Our Father in most churches, the kiss of peace at the church of the Resurrection, or at prophetic utterances at the Bayville church. Here, devotion was high at most times: at the Bible readings as if they were divine revelations, during the homilies meant to fire up the spirit, at the memorial of the Last Supper with its sober institutional narrative, during the visual unity of the church during the Our Father and the exchange of peace, and at communion and its inspirational background music. Only in a few evangelical, Pentecostal, or Catholic charismatic churches can one find such highly engaged religiosity.

The desire for closeness to God is depicted in vivid images by loud singing, waving, and prayers of praise. Particularly fervent was the part of the service that was only for God when people pray "not just because of anything you have done, but just because of who you are. If you never do anything for me, I worship you because you are worthy." Equally inspiring was Fr. Pfleger's sharing of having been awakened by God at five in the morning, and that the day before, he had been weeping, depressed by bad news. It was comforting (and revealing) to learn that God said to him "Get up! Walk around your room like Joshua around Jericho so that a spirit of determination will overcome the spirit of doubt and discouragement." And so it happened. It is known that Fr. Pfleger prays for about an hour every morning. It is what keeps him going, and this is what he transmits to others.

B. Interaction outcomes

Here I will cover in reverse order the four outcome items, namely, what we learned, patterns of relationship, moral consensus, and emotional energy. I will spend most of the time on what we learned, which was mainly about violating liturgical rules.

Spiritual and Emotional Energy.

The energy generated by an interaction is, according to Collins, the sum of the energy produced by each of his seven processes and outcomes. In the case of St. Sabina, these levels are remarkably high. There is constant interaction during the service, people clapping and shouting spontaneously or when invited to do so. On many occasions Pfleger said, "Turn to your neighbor and say . . ." and people did. At altar calls, people came forward in droves—even in the extreme case of a funeral when many of friends of the murdered gang leader came forward. All Sunday services lead to action: there are announcements for action at the beginning and again at the end when Fr. Pfleger has additional things to say about parish activities.

For Collins this energy is emotional, and so it is at St. Sabina, but all along I have argued that in parishes this energy is also spiritual and religious. The over-arching goal of St. Sabina is discipleship, namely to "turn believers into disciples" as stated in big letters on the billboard in front of the church. Evangelism is as much a priority as social justice. When one enters the church from the back, one is confronted by the fluorescent monogram "Jesus" hanging above the sanctuary and the oversized painting of a black Jesus. And when one leaves the church, there is again an evangelistic sign, "Discipleship will cost. Are you willing?" Those willing will find here spiritual—not just emotional—energy for social action and everyday living.

Moral Consensus

In all my interviews I never heard any criticisms about the church. Strong personalities usually create dissent, but not when relationships are egalitarian. There are two occasions when the parish moral consensus appeared in all its force. Some months after the death of the pastor of St. Sabina in 1981, the archdiocesan personnel board called for a parish town hall meeting to inquire about the desired characteristics for the new pastor. Obviously Cardinal Cody would make the decision. Pfleger had no chance since he had been in conflict with the cardinal on several occasions. When the personnel board members arrived, "they faced a standing-room-only phalanx of determined people [who] did not want to talk about 'characteristics.' Young, old, rich, and poor, everybody was unanimous. It had to be Mike."[9] Not wanting to antagonize the black community, the cardinal gave in, reluctantly.

In 2001, Cardinal George urged Fr. Pfleger to make plans for a new assignment, because after his three six-terms as pastor, there would be no fourth one. The conflict turned bitter; it was widely discussed in the local press. Then twenty-one members of the St. Sabina leadership team requested a meeting with the cardinal. As the end of the meeting the cardinal supposedly said that "he would continue to seek input from St. Sabina members," and that "he was in no hurry to replace Pfleger."[10] The replacement was deferred indefinitely. It is likely that the unanimous consensus of the parishioners had an impact, in this case as in many others. Moral consensus is one of the strengths of St. Sabina.

Patterns of Relationship

We noticed that there is no entrance procession, which usually is a display of clerical importance. At St. Sabina the relationships are egalitarian. The choir,

9. McClory, *Radical Disciple*, 37–38.
10. McClory, *Radical Disciple*, 100.

the dancers, the assembly, and the pastor each make their contribution to the Sunday services. Moreover in the flow, each party joins and contributes to all others. There is a head dancer and a head singer, but they are not "stars." A few times a year, dancing and singing is performed by children, and their contribution is seen as valuable as that of adults. In my interviews, people described Fr. Pfleger as a friend and mentor. These are the terms used, for instance, by a young evangelical pastor in charge of youth ministry at St. Sabina; he was a third of Fr. Pfleger's age, so his reference to the older man as a friend and mentor is very significant. When Fr. Pfleger invited many of his collaborators to the positions they now hold, long before they thought of applying for them, they appreciated his mentorship, as he guided their first steps in these jobs.

The ideal relationship at St. Sabina is discipleship; and this mentoring is for discipleship. Besides the homilies, Fr. Pfleger is influential through his well-attended Bible classes. Private Bible reading is a common practice in this parish, which leads to discipleship and egalitarian social relations, as the Bible is seen as open to all, not just to the clergy.

Fr. Pfleger seldom mentions the pope or the American bishops' conference. St. Sabina is seen as a local church with local ties in the neighborhood and the city of Chicago. To the extent that discipleship is companionship with other local churches, it fosters an ecclesiology of local church identity, with its possibilities and limitations.

What We Learned: Church Authority versus Creativity

Fr. Pfleger has violated many liturgical regulations, but these did not create open conflict. When Joseph Bernardin became archbishop of Chicago in 1982, he made Fr. Pfleger the official pastor of St. Sabina and all seemed well then. The situation became conflictive when he learned that Fr. Pfleger invited non-Catholic speakers to preach during mass. By church law, only priests and deacons are allowed to do so. The cardinal became incensed when he heard that the next speaker would be none other than Louis Farrakhan, the leader of the Nation of Islam. He ordered the speaking engagement to be cancelled at once. Fr. Pfleger replied that it was too late, and that the parish council had voted unanimously in favor of Farrakhan. Interestingly, the conflict was about church rules, not the liturgy as such. Sometime later, Bernardin came to attend privately a mass at St. Sabina. Afterwards, he confided to Fr. Pfleger that "the mass had been one of the most spiritual experiences of his life."[11] He approved a second and third term for Pfleger at St. Sabina. There was no conflict about the liturgy.

11. McClory, *Radical Disciple*, 93.

The Vatican instruction, *Redemptionis Sacramentum* of 2004, makes perfectly clear what is permitted in the liturgy, and what is not. "Only those Eucharistic Prayers are to be used which are found in the Roman Missal." More specifically, quoting Pope John Paul II, "It is not to be tolerated that some Priests take upon themselves the right to compose their own Eucharistic Prayers."[12] This norm requires "conformity of thought and of word, of external action, and of the application of the heart."[13] In order to close any loophole, the instruction began with the general statement that, "As early as the year 1970, the Apostolic See announced the cessation of all experimentation as regards the celebration of Holy Mass." Even bishops and conferences of bishops were not allowed to permit liturgical experimentations.

What is, then, the relationship between church authority and creativity? There are two extreme options, either total submission or innovation by breaking the rules. Neither is satisfactory. Fr. Pfleger justified his position by an appeal to conscience. "My allegiance is to God. I don't believe in blind obedience to a pope, bishop, or pastor is healthy. Though I respect authority, when my moral beliefs contradict that authority, I will challenge an order."[14] Let us review his conflict with authority and his appeal to conscience.

In his zeal for protecting his flock from alcoholism, Fr. Pfleger found himself in conflict with civil law. For about six months in 1980, a team of two or three went out a few times a week with Pfleger to deface billboards advocating alcohol and tobacco in their black neighborhood. Pfleger had decided on this course of action only after all attempts of settlement had failed. He was finally arrested and faced up to five years in jail and hefty fines for property damage. In court a year later, Pfleger developed the so-called necessary defense argument, that is, a course of action necessary in conscience in order to avoid a greater evil. His action was the necessary response to the presence of five times more alcohol billboards in black than in white neighborhoods, and also three times more billboards for tobacco geared toward blacks. The jury consisted of eight white and four black people. "After just ninety minutes the jurors returned with a unanimous verdict of not guilty. Someone in the courtroom shouted, 'Thank you, Jesus!' Pfleger shouted back, 'Thank you, jury!'"[15] The great victory for Pfleger was that he had convinced all twelve jurors that the demands of conscience can be greater than blind obedience to human laws. Pfleger also learned an important lesson, namely that the necessary defense argument cannot be

---

12. Congregation for Divine Worship, "*Redemptionis Sacramentum*," 51.

13. Congregation for Divine Worship, "*Redemptionis Sacramentum*,"5.

14. McClory, *Radical Disciple*, 93.

15. McClory, *Radical Disciple*, 73.

repeated very often. In ordinary times, that is, most of the time, creativity must work within the limits of the law.

Pfleger found himself in conflict with Cardinal Bernardin over the clerical rule that only clerics can preach during mass. The purpose of this rule is to avoid

> Fr. Pfleger's conflict with authority was about ecclesiastical rules rather than liturgical violations.

abuses. In response, Pfleger could have pointed out, first, that the guest speakers at St. Sabina do not preach, which technically means explaining the Scripture readings of the day; they only give a talk, an address, or a reflection, not a sermon. Secondly, in reference to the addresses given by Arne Duncan, the US Secretary of Education in September 2015, and the address three months later by Rham Emanuel, the mayor of Chicago (as well as others that I have not recorded), the spiritual and moral benefit of these exceptional talks outweighed by far the legal need to prevent abuses. This too is an argument of conscience versus legalism. Pfleger had good reason to hold his ground.

The conflict between Pfleger and Cardinal George was more acrimonious because it quickly became a power struggle; it was related to the canonical rule that pastors must be rotated every six years. This rule serves the needs of the institution rather than needs of pastors and parishioners and it has been questioned many times. Again Pfleger pleaded for the good of his parish in the name of conscience. The Chicago conservatives had long petitioned the removal of Pfleger from St. Sabina. When the cardinal took a stand publicly, it became a power struggle because Pfleger was an exceptional public debater, eminently popular in the liberal press. The conflict was ultimately defused by circumstances that allowed the conflict to drag on and allowed Pfleger to remain indefinitely. Conscience seemed to have won the day, but the fundamental tension between authority and creativity had not been addressed.

The emphasis on conscience is a clear sign that Pfleger encourages moving out of social conformity, which dominates stage 3 in Fowler's theory of faith development. In stage 3, authority is seen as outside the self, as residing in the authority figures of the group, which in the Catholic Church is the hierarchy. Typically, Fr. Pfleger does not teach church doctrine to be accepted in obedience according to the laws of the church; instead he promotes Bible studies that invite believers to turn inward and listen to the spirit within them. In stage 3, moral judgments are made with reference to group norms, while stage 4 invokes moral laws and the maintenance of the social order. The Friday night marches at St. Sabina call for universal justice, not for ethnic interests. A just social order is what Pfleger argues for in most of his sermons. Finally, in stage 3, symbols have a quasi-magical quality that turns off reflection and leads to ritualistic performances, but they can also in some cases open people up to mystical dimensions. Someone at stage 3 would say routinely, "Peace be with you," but someone at a more advanced stage of faith might crack open the symbol and say, "May peace, who is Jesus, be with you!" Clearly there is little social conformity at St. Sabina.

In the Catholic Church, an appeal to conscience ordinarily has little weight because the rights of conscience and of loyal dissent have no clear legal status in canon law. The issue of authority and dissent will be discussed more fully in the next chapter. It will be addressed within the sociological framework of the individual versus society, rather than within the framework of theology and canon law, where it has little place—in sharp contrast with the civil laws of most Western nations.

Conclusion: From Conformism to Creativity and the Issue of Succession

Creativity implies moving beyond conformity in order to be able to think "outside the box." We have seen in the previous chapter that at the Bayville church there is great intensity of faith, private devotions and outreach, but all endeavors usually remain within the limits of social conformity. I now want to show that even within the limits of conformity to church rules the field is wide open to creativity. I will develop two points. First, at St. Sabina only that part of the liturgy related to the Eucharistic Prayer breaks church rules. Second, in all areas of life, and also in the liturgy, what is not prohibited may be permissible. Therefore, the field is wide open to innovation.

The content of *Redemptionis Sacramentum* can be summarized in one rule, "Only those Eucharistic Prayers are to be used which are found in the Roman Missal." At St. Sabina, the Eucharistic Prayer is only one of the many parts of its liturgy. I have described above ten parts of the liturgy: the welcome and introduction, the call to worship by Fr. Pfleger, followed by praise, worship and dance, the readings, the homily, the altar call, the presentation of gifts, the Eucharistic Prayer, the Our Father and communion, the announcements, and the final prayer. Only one of these, Pfleger's improvised Eucharistic Prayer, falls under church condemnation. All criticisms would be muted if Pfleger were to use the prayers from the Roman Missal, that is, include a traditional mass at the end of his two to three hour service. Actually, every Sunday morning at 9:30 there is such a mass at St. Sabina for those who want a traditional worship. Moreover, Fr. Pfleger

> Opposition to innovation comes more often from conservatism and conformism than from responsible authority.

is willing to compromise. During an official parish visit by the archbishop of Chicago, the liturgy included the traditional Kyrie, Gloria, Credo, Preface, Sanctus, and all the rest. Thus the archbishop was satisfied.

I now want to show that in Catholicism and elsewhere, the opposition is not between authority and creativity, but between conformism and innovation. In short, creativity is hindered by clerical conformism, that is, by the attitude that innovations are expected to come from above. I will argue, on the contrary, that creativity is wide open if one considers that what is not prohibited may be permissible and open to change. Let us review the various aspects of St. Sabina's liturgy.

At the Latino and Anglo masses at Holy Family, the introduction is usually in the form, "Today is the xth Sunday in Ordinary Time. The celebrant is Fr. Pat. There will be a second collection." How unimaginative in comparison to: "Praise the Lord, everybody!" (Tepid response.) "Come on, we can do better than that! Praise the Lord everybody!" (Stronger response.)

All parishes begin with an entrance procession according to clerical rank. The assembly usually sings a stanza or two, that is, only until the priest reaches the first steps of the altar. At St. Sabina, Pfleger avoids this ceremonial display of power. He appears unobtrusively in front of the assembly to loudly encourage singing songs of praise for an extended period of time.

At St. Sabina, all songs are popular and nearly all of them are posted on YouTube. In most parishes, the hymns may have been modern fifty years ago, and they are forgotten as soon as one leaves the church. It is true that some church documents frown upon dancing in the church, associating it with eroticism. There is no such thing as St. Sabina, where choreography is a form of art of professional quality, in stark contrast to the religious kitsch of the TV masses on Catholic television networks.

The readings at St. Sabina are expressive and moving. At the Latino masses at Holy Family, the readers and even the priest stumbled over words, as if unprepared. Fr. Pfleger preaches for half an hour. I enjoyed listening to his homilies several times on videos, but I would not say the same about most homilies at the other parishes. Only at St. Sabina, maybe in the whole Catholic world, are there altar calls on a regular basis. These are one of the most powerful aspects of Pfleger's liturgies. More could be said about the other aspects of the St. Sabina liturgies to show their imaginative power in comparison to the other parishes.

In short, it is not authority that impedes creativity but conformism. We have seen in the previous chapter that the pastors of the Bayville church are as conformist in their literal understanding of the Bible as their flock in their practices. The conformism of stage 3 is essentially the inability of the clergy to think "outside the box," continuing a submissive attitude ingrained by seminary training. Obedience is also the most praised virtue in the Catholic Church, where the clergy are expected to shine by their submissiveness. Such an attitude impedes creativity. An appeal to conscience makes one move out of conformity.

To follow one's conscience is the guiding principle of all prophets, but authentic prophets are often lone voices in the desert and in the biblical tradition most prophets are killed. Undeniably Fr. Pfleger is a prophet, but what will happen when he will retire? Max Weber has described the prophet and the priest as too opposite forces at work in most religions. Prophets make the headlines for a few days but priests occupy the seats of power at all times. The social drama of prophecy is the difficulty of succession after the prophet retires. Clearly some kind of compromise between the prophet and the priests seems desirable, which raises the issue of authority, to which we now turn.

9

The Zairean Rite and Usage

Creativity versus Authority

IN THIS CHAPTER WE will look at the basic question of the relationship between the individual and society, and more specifically, between creativity and submission to rules. I will use the Zairean rite in the Democratic Republic of Congo to illustrate the ideas that will be discussed.

Before presenting the interaction processes found in the Zairean liturgy, we need to define the nature of the problem. In theory, in the United States there is no ambiguity about individual rights *vis-à-vis* the government because the issue was resolved in principle by the Bill of Rights. There are, however, potential conflicts in the Catholic Church between the laity and the hierarchy because the laity has few rights and the hierarchy has many. In the view of Prosper of Aquitaine (390–455), prayer should inform belief, while in fact bishops decide the contents of liturgical prayers. The liturgy therefore provides a unique opportunity to explore the relationship between creativity and authority.

According to the Declaration of Independence, the power of government is derived from "the consent of the governed." In addition, the Bill of Rights safeguards important rights, which can be upheld by an independent judiciary. The principle of the separation of church and state guarantees religious freedom and prevents the state from imposing a religion on the citizenry. Only elected representatives can make laws. Members of society are called citizens (not subjects); society cannot function without their active participation.

The situation in the Catholic Church is very different. There are no elected officials. There is no separation of power into different branches of government. There are few individual rights to be upheld by independent courts. Members of the church are the "subjects" of the hierarchy, as is stated explicitly in the 1917 code of canon law and as is still implicit in the 1983 code. The relationship between the local churches and the Vatican is best exemplified by the situation of bishops who are selected by the pope and supervised by the Roman Curia. They are accountable to the papacy and not to the faithful. In all cases, the relationship between inferiors and superiors is supposed to be one of submission. According to rules of obedience defined in canon law, submission is expected to solve all conflicts.

In summary, there is no conflict between the individual and society in the United States because citizens can find redress for injustices through the courts, at least in theory. One could say that there is no conflict in the Catholic Church either, because the duties of obedience are clearly spelled out for all according to their rank. Yet this solution is increasingly unsatisfactory to many Catholics, especially in the area of liturgical practices and their relation to personal faith.

Opposite Conceptions of Church and Worship

What is the relationship between religious beliefs and liturgical practices? The principle, *lex orandi lex credendi*, is said to have originated with Prosper of Aquitaine (390–455) and it is often translated as "the law of prayer is the law of faith." This is inaccurate and misleading. Prosper's statement is part of a sentence stating that in the sacraments, "supplication determines belief" (*legem credenda lex statuat supplicandi*). In this sentence, *supplicandi* refers to more than supplication since it may include other parts of worship, so it is better thought of as referring to liturgical prayer. This general principle has been given two opposite interpretations: the official Catholic position defended by Pope Pius XII, which rejected Prosper's position, and that of Aidan Kavanagh, who defended it.

Does the prayer life of the church define its collective beliefs (as during the first millennium), or should the magisterium define both the prayers and the beliefs (as in modern times)?

According to Pope Pius XII, it is an error to claim that the law of prayer is the law of faith. "This is not what the Church teaches."[1] But it is "perfectly correct" to state, according to him, that *lex credenda legem statuat supplicandi*, in other words, that the rule of belief determines the rule of prayer, or more loosely, what the church believes determines how we pray. This is so because, according to official doctrine, it is the hierarchy that determines both the beliefs and the liturgy. In fact, "From time immemorial the ecclesiastical hierarchy has exercised this right in matters liturgical." It is clear that for Pius XII, belief should determine prayer, in opposition to Prosper's position that prayer should determine belief. This official position is consonant with the Tridentine perception

---

1. Pius XII, *Mediator Dei*, 46–49.

that the hierarchy whose duty it is to regulate the liturgy is actually the whole church. This view interprets prayer and sacraments as rituals to be performed according to church prescriptions, not as liturgical practices in which people find and express their personal faith. In other words, it interprets prayer as liturgical things (rituals), and beliefs as official church doctrines and not as people's lived faith in their daily lives. In short, the official position only considers the institutional dimension of both prayer (in the liturgy) and faith (in church doctrines). In this perspective, there is little room for liturgical creativity unless it comes from above.

In his book, *On Liturgical Theology*, Aidan Kavanagh's reflections on how public worship centers on the subjective experience of prayer and faith, rather than on the official theology of the liturgy as ecclesial ritual. He describes liturgical practices as interactions forming an endless chain (although not using these terms), in three steps. First, in its encounter with God, "the liturgical act precipitates change in the liturgical assembly." Because of these inner changes, "the assembly adjusts through critical reflection upon its own stance in faith before God." Thus beliefs and practices are transformed by the experience of prayer. Finally, "The faithful assembly brings all this with it to its next act of worship, an act which then precipitates further change and adjustment."[2] All adjustments form a chain of transformations in both prayer and faith. "The *lex credendi* is thus subordinated to the *lex supplicandi*," he wrote.[3] Since the time of the Council of Trent, however, academic theology has separated itself from the experience of prayer. In this Tridentine trend, according to Kavanagh, Prosper's maxim "is effectively reversed, with the law of belief founding and constituting the law of worship."[4] Church doctrine has come to control worship. There is no room for local worship creativity.

Kavanagh calls the beliefs inspired by the experience of prayer *theologia prima*, or primary theology, and calls academic theology secondary theology. There is a great difference between the two. The primary theology is rooted in prayer experiences. To the extent that prayer is a personal encounter with God, it is the private domain of conscience, and so it is free of outside impositions. Primary theology is the expression of people's prayer experiences; it is the *sensus fidei*, the sense of faith guiding daily living. Vatican II calls this sense of faith "supernatural discernment" which, to a certain extent, shares in the infallibility of the church.[5] We will find examples of

2. Kavanagh, *On Liturgical Theology*, 93.

3. Kavanagh, *On Liturgical Theology*, 91.

4. Kavanagh, *On Liturgical Theology*, 83.

5. *Lumen Gentium*, 12, in Abbott, *Documents of Vatican II*.

theologia prima in people's voices in prayer groups and in the interviews presented below. This primary theology is often poor in academic content but rich in spiritual experience. In the secondary theology of academia, on the other hand, "the rule of belief determine[s] the rule of prayer." In such a theology, reason is primary and spirituality secondary, and so it is less likely to be spiritually creative.

It is only at the end of his book that Kavanagh defines his position on worship as being a subjective experience. He did not elaborate on how individual religious practices are related to church structures. Kavanagh's alternative conception of church and worship is incomplete, but even so, Pius XII and Kavanagh stand at opposite poles. Perhaps we can find a middle ground between the two.

The Individual and Society: a Framework for Analysis

In a graduate sociology course on the individual and society, it is common to discuss various theories on the subject, particularly Marx, Weber, Durkheim, and Foucault. Instead of these, we will turn to Tocqueville's theory of self-interest properly understood, which is more appropriate for our topic.

In *Democracy in America*, Alexis de Tocqueville described the young republic as he saw it in the 1830s. One of his defining concepts was "self-interest properly understood." In a few words, it is the belief that "by serving his fellows, man serves himself, and that doing good is to his private advantage." This enlightened self-interest "continuously leads them to help one another and disposes them freely to give part of their time and wealth for the good of the state."[6] In sum, there is no conflict between perceived self-interest and the common good, but why is this so?

Tocqueville began his analysis with the study of American institutions and only in his second volume did he discuss individual self-interest, suggesting that enlightened self-interest should be viewed as a consequence of certain institutions. Tocqueville showed great admiration for local associations. "Local institutions are to liberty what primary schools are to science; they put it within people's reach."[7] It is in local government that individuals can see the need for the common good and participation in it. Small towns engage in discussions about both common good and private interest, to the point that the former becomes the latter and the latter the former. "American legislation appeals mainly to private interest; that is the great principle

---

6. Tocqueville, *Democracy in America*, 525–26.

7. Tocqueville, *Democracy in America*, 63.

which one finds again and again."[8] In legislation, private interest is understood in reference to the common good.

For Tocqueville, there is a great difference between aristocratic and democratic societies. In aristocracies (and hierarchical societies like Catholicism), the elites "entertain a sublime conception of the duties of man," encouraging people to do "glorious things . . . without self-

> According to Tocqueville, in aristocratic societies and churches the collective good is defined from above, while in democracies the common good depends on the participation of all.

interest, as God himself does." These sublime models coming from the top often stand in opposition to the self-interest of the masses. In democratic societies, on the other hand, "there is hardly any talk about the beauty of virtue."[9] Instead, there is discussion about the common good in which self-interest properly understood finds its place.

We now have a framework to address the conflict between individual and society and between creativity and central authority. There must be a general agreement about the common good. Social leaders must define it and followers must accept it, so that the enlightened self-interest of all will promote the shared common good of society.

In hierarchical societies, the common good is defined from above and must be accepted in the name of obedience. This model was very successful at the time of Pius XII, which was also the time of global dictators like Stalin, Hitler, Mussolini, and global democrats like Churchill, Roosevelt, and de Gaulle. Today, however, there is need for a more democratic understanding of the common good. In this study, any model will be seen as democratic if it reflects the *sensus fidei*, the inner sense of faith, what Kavanagh called the "primary theology" of the people. These two models—democratic processes as outlined by Tocqueville and prayer defining beliefs as outlined by Kavanagh—can be seen at work in the Zairean rite.

I. Interaction Processes

Before we begin the analysis of the interaction processes, we need information about two major aspects of the Zairean liturgy, namely its history and development, and also the structure of the Zairean church. Both are quite different from the rest of Roman Catholicism. Zaire is the only country that has a special national ritual for the Sunday liturgy, and the archdiocese of Kinshasa, the capital of Democratic Republic of Congo (formerly

8. Tocqueville, *Democracy in America*, 79.

9. Tocqueville, *Democracy in America*, 525.

the Republic of Zaire from 1971 to 1979) is the only diocese where the basic church unit is not the parish but the lay communities within each parish. About both the national ritual and the diocesan structure we must ask whether there is a common good acceptable to all in the name of self-interest properly understood.

1. Basic Information: Zairean Rite and Zairean Usage

In 1969, the conference of Catholic bishops of the Congo petitioned the Congregation for Divine Worship for permission to elaborate a project for a truly Zairean liturgy. One year later, an indult was granted to do so. After three years of discussions, a proposal for a Zairean rite for the eucharistic celebration was submitted to the Congregation for Worship which then granted permission for "experimentation." Negotiations took place between 1974 and 1988, when finally *le Missel Romain pour les dioceses du Zaire* was approved. The word "rite" is not used in this document. In his master's thesis on this missal, Nathan Chase translated the title of this document as "Missal for the Zaire Usage of the Roman Rite."[10] The bishops wanted a Zairean rite; what they got was a special usage of the Roman rite.

> There is a difference between a liturgical script and its implementation. In this work I concentrate on liturgical practices, on the Zairean rite rather than its special usage of the Roman rite.

From the beginning of the negotiations, the Congregation for Divine Worship had requested that the *Ordo* of the Roman Mass be taken as a point of departure for discussions. It will be remembered that the request of African American Catholics for a black rite was met with the same response: the Roman rite must be taken as normative with the possibility of only minor adaptations. For the bishops of Congo to accept the *Ordo* as a point of departure was probably a fatal "flaw."[11] From that point on, the die seemed cast: there would only be adaptations. In 1974 the African bishops had already rejected as "completely out-of-date the so-called theology of adaptation. In its stead, they adopt[ed] the theology of incarnation."[12] When the Congregation for Divine Worship insisted on "adaptation" rather than "inculturation," structural changes in the liturgy were out of the question.

Before considering what was agreed upon through negotiations, let us consider the role of the papacy in defining the common good. In theory, the pope is the most powerful man on earth. He is head of state, prime minister, supreme legislator, and ultimate judge in the church, which may

---

10. Chase, "History and Analysis," 5.

11. Egbulem, *Power of Africentric Celebrations*, 39.

12. Egbulem, *Power of Africentric Celebrations*, 26.

be too much for a single person to handle efficiently. Moreover he is also the grand theologian of the church (the preferred role of John Paul II), and the grand master of the liturgy worldwide. This may well be an impossible assignment because a pope is likely to concentrate on his primary interests (for example, works of charity) and neglect secondary ones (for example, the liturgy, doctrine, administration, theological innovation, and so on). The pope is assisted by the curia, but the curia has only administrative power, not executive power like the cabinet members of modern governments. The curia can only grant favors, not rights. The favor of the Zairean usage was granted to only one of the five countries of the Congo basin, the Congo-Kinshasa called Zaire at that time. It is not a right to be claimed by countries like the Congo-Brazzaville, which lies just across the Congo River from the Congo-Kinshasa. According to Chase, granting the Zaire usage was "an anomaly" as no other similar favor has ever been granted; the chances that such a favor will be granted again are "extremely unlikely."[13] It is not that the papacy cannot deal with the common good; it is only that papal authority is too vast to allow popes to deal with issues that are not important to them, for example, the decline in worship attendance or the role of women in the church. The curia has little or no independent power. It can only grant permission for experimentation and a special usage of the official rite. Much more is needed if the good of the worldwide church is going to be addressed.

The bishops' commission for a Zairean rite wanted to incorporate three Zairean traditions into the liturgy: the role of the tribal chief, the palaver,[14] and the invocation of ancestors. In colonial Africa, the arrival of the tribal chief was publicly and loudly announced before the chief

> In the 1960s the bishops of the Congo wanted to integrate into the liturgy the Zairean traditions of the tribal chief, the invocation of the ancestors, and the palaver or public forum. Today only the latter seems relevant.

appeared in full regalia, surrounded by warriors in arms. Similarly in the Zairean usage today, the priest is preceded by an announcer or commentator, he is surrounded by two guards carrying spears, and originally he wore a hat of goatskin with a horse tail, symbols of royalty and power. (The use of this hat has been abandoned since.) It is noteworthy that the Zairean clergy wanted to be seen as tribal chiefs, men of power and wealth, who sometimes had several wives, in contradiction to gospel ideals. The second tradition to be incorporated was the African custom of the palaver, a public forum

---

13. Chase, "History and Analysis," 5.

14. The French word "palabre" refers since colonial times to endless talks in Africa between traders and the natives, and among the natives themselves. Since then the custom of the palaver has been accepted in Africa as an authentic African tradition.

or village meeting, often lasting several hours, where everyone can speak up. The Zairean rite wanted popular participation by constant interaction between the priest and the assembly. This is achieved today by having the priest interjecting on numerous occasions "Boboto!" (an African equivalent of "The Lord be with you!") to which the assembly responds enthusiastically, "Bondeco!" ("And with you too!") This controlled spontaneity gives the Zairean mass the oral characteristic of improvisation.

"Most tribes of black Africa would not begin a public ceremony without invoking the ancestors who are believed to exercise control over the living."[15] The traditional African pantheon was populated not by gods but by good and evil spirits, the ancestors, who continuously intervened in human affairs. Sickness, disease, drought, a village rift, and sterility were usually blamed on evil spirits and required the help of healers, medicine men, and magicians. This pantheon could not be included into the mass. As a compromise, the "invocation of saints" was substituted for the invocation of ancestors. It constitutes the central prayer of the introductory part of the liturgy, but in fact it takes only a couple of minutes to recite. At the end of the invocation of saints, the following invocation was added: "*Vous, nos ancêtres au coeur droit*" ("You, our righteous ancestors") with the response, "Be with us." It is doubtful that today this five-second mention of anonymous ancestors will bring to mind the memory of the village invocation of ancestors. The colonial days of public invocation of ancestors by the tribal chiefs surrounded by bodyguards are already three generations behind us. Today, the Zairean usage appears to some as folklore from a bygone era. To others, like an archbishop from Chad, it is "A Latin rite with local changes in dress and song."[16]

An Alternative Vision of Parish and Church

When the situation of the Catholic Church in Zaire seemed desperate, the archbishop of Kinshasa, Cardinal Joseph Malula, offered a new vision of the common good to which all Catholics could rally in self-interest.

The independence of the Congo from Belgium in 1960 was followed by several years of violent unrest. About 200 priests and 10,000 catechists were killed. Consequently, the majority of Belgian and foreign priests left. In 1965, Mobutu Sese Seko took control of the country in a military coup and instituted a one-party dictatorship that lasted until 1997 when he was overturned by another dictator. Mobutu renamed the Congo as Zaire, and instituted a policy of Zairization, which brought him in conflict with the

15. Egbulem, *Power of Africentric Celebrations*, 59.
16. Egbulem, *Power of Africentric Celebrations*, 95.

Catholic Church. In progressive escalations, he expropriated the Catholic University of Kinshasa, nationalized all Catholic schools and hospitals, instituted the de-Christianization of first names by requesting the replacement of Christian names by African ones, expelled the archbishop from his residence, which he made the headquarters of his Revolutionary Party, wanted some members of his revolutionary youth party to live in the seminary (and after being refused, he closed the seminary), and forced the archbishop into exile after an attempt on his life.

Throughout his ministry and in the midst of the greatest tensions, Cardinal Malula stood for an alternate model of the church. First, he stood up against the excesses of the Mobutu dictatorship. In response to the de-Christianization of names, he refused to drop Joseph as his first name, which encouraged others to do the same, leading to the failure of Mobutu's campaign. In response to the one-party youth movement, he created the Youth of Light, which is still active today. When he came back from exile, he demanded a new episcopal residence in place of the one that had been confiscated. Instead of Mobutu's "return" to mythic African traditions, he recommended the "recourse" to tradition in the light of the gospel in the Africanization of the church.

An excellent orator, Malula found the words that stirred up the imagination. "A Congolese church in a Congolese state" was a key phrase in his homily at his episcopal ordination in 1959, one year before the independence of the Congo from Belgium.[17] At the height of the Mobutu's Zairization, he proclaimed, "Yesterday, foreign missionaries have Christianized Africa; today Negro Africans will Africanize Christianity."[18] At the time of feverish nationalism, the Africanization of the church was a social program that spoke to the imagination of most Catholics. One of the cardinal's priorities was the promotion of laypeople who were to be the main actors and beneficiaries of this Africanization. Malula proposed a program for the common good of the church that the laity was eager to promote in enlightened self-interest.

A careful administrator, Malula put in place the mechanisms of lay involvement in the church. He created the first lay parish administrators at a time when such a concept did not exist in canon law. Next he promoted neighborhood communities as the basic church units in replacement of parishes, and in 1977 he made them mandatory throughout the archdiocese. Over the years, the parish councils were assigned new functions. Finally in 1981, he created the archdiocesan pastoral center to foster the development

17. Moerschbacher, *Les laics dans une Église d'Afrique,* 51.
18. Moerschbacher, *Les laics dans une Église d'Afrique,* 102.

of parishes and small communities. These various organizations are best illustrated by the following chart:

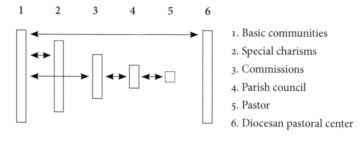

1. Basic communities
2. Special charisms
3. Commissions
4. Parish council
5. Pastor
6. Diocesan pastoral center

In each parish there are about ten to twenty basic communities ("1" on the chart) that are each assigned a geographical area. They consist of 20 to 60 members who meet every Thursday evening for prayer and reflection. They are the front line of evangelization since they are expected to befriend most people in their area. They handle requests for baptisms, marriages, and funerals, and therefore are truly and officially the basic units of church life. In each parish there are also ten to fifteen "groups with special charisms" ("2" on the chart), such as the charismatic renewal, the rosary society, the Holy Name society, the Sacred Heart association, and so on. These are devotional groups that meet one evening during the week. Their members are necessarily part of basic communities, so they may even attend two meetings during the week. The parish is called the community of communities. This is where all people come together for sacramental life.

At the parish level there are about ten to fifteen specialized commissions ("3" on the chart) to support the various aspects of parish life. Thus there will be a commission to support the basic communities, another for the groups with special charisms, another for adult education, one more for the liturgy, one for religious education, and a few more for family life, intellectual life, social justice, and so on, depending on the needs of the parish. The leaders of all groups are elected for three years. The members of the parish commissions are elected representatives from the various groups. The presidents of all specialized commissions form the parish council ("4" on the chart), which meets once a month with the pastor ("5" on the chart). There is constant interaction from the bottom up and from the top down.

The most effective tool for active church life is the archdiocesan pastoral center ("6" on the chart) consisting of 17 specialized commissions replicating the parish commissions. The presidents of these commissions are nominated by the cardinal but most members are lay representatives from the parishes. Most useful for the basic communities is the publication by the pastoral center of a bulletin suggesting the readings and the topics of reflection for the weekly meetings.

In all groups and units from top to bottom there is an elected secretary whose tasks it is to serve as liaison officer between the various organizations. Thus each unit may know what happened and what will happen in other groups. This nearly perfect organizational chart was the creation of Cardinal Malula. Strangely enough, it required no curial permission, only imagination. We will see below how it works in the few parishes I visited.

2. Description of Interaction Processes: Script versus Process

I spent five weekends observing the Sunday liturgies and interviewing key members during the week. St. Alphonse of Kinshasa, one of the parishes I visited, is the one where the experimentations about the Zairean rite took place after permission was granted in 1973, and it is still the flagship of the Zairean liturgy. There and in other parishes I found vibrant and enthusiastic celebrations that seemed true creations, not just mechanical productions of the ritual. Hence I will write about the "Zairean rite" when describing these creative practices, and "Zairean usage" when referring to the liturgical text which was the product of 17 years of negotiations and power struggles.

The Zairean mass consists of three parts. First, the Opening Celebration takes about half an hour; it consists of the entrance procession, the veneration of the altar, the invocation of the saints, and the singing of the Gloria. Next follows the Liturgy of the Word (readings, homily, Creed, and penitential rite), which takes an hour and a half, and finally there is the Liturgy of the Eucharist (offering of the gifts, Eucharistic Prayer, and communion), which takes another hour.

A description of the ritual processes of the Zairean rite is very difficult because it mainly consists of music and rhythmic participation. The TV masses and the Sunday masses at the Holy Family and St. Benedict parishes follow the ritual script faithfully, and so they can easily be summarized. In the Zairean rite, the script is the basis for endless melodic variations, as in jazz or in evangelical churches. How do you summarize a 10-minute entrance procession and a 25-minute offering of the gifts when the action is in the music, the rhythm, and the clapping of hands? The video recording of the St. Sabina liturgies could be watched repeatedly for better analysis but none was available here. In Kinshasa, the Zairean rite is celebrated in Linguala, and most of the songs are local creations unknown to outsiders. Rhythm and music cannot easily be described in words.

Opening Celebration

The first part of the liturgy that displays the pageantry of the priest as village chief and the invocation of the saints has little connection with the rest of the liturgy. The service begins at the sound of the gong or drum with an upbeat dialogue between the announcer and the assembly:

> The Announcer: "Boboto-o-o-o!"
>> The assembly: "Bondeco-o-o-o!"
> Again, "Boboto-o-o-o!" (Peace!)
>> "Bondeco-o-o-o!" (Peace with you too!)
> "Who is our Lord?"
>> "Jesus!"
> "Who is our Savior?"
>> "Jesus!"
> "Let's all give a loud shout to the Lord!"
>> The people respond with shouts and applause.

Before the appearance of the entrance procession, about ten little dancers, five to eight years old, perform choreographed movements in front of the assembly. They wear white dresses, white shoes, and white gloves. Their perfectly coordinated movements indicate dedication and practice. They give a somewhat angelic dimension to the liturgy. They perform at the key moments of the liturgy, most visibly during the Eucharistic Prayer.

The grand opening of the liturgy is the processional entrance of the priest and his retinue. There are two ways a procession can attract attention: by the number of participants, and by the way it proceeds. The priestly cohort includes all the ministers and their insignia: the cross bearer, the incense bearer, the candle-bearers, the acolytes, the guards with spears (but what is their ministry?), the deacon carrying the missal, and the priest. A military procession proceeds swiftly to inspire power and discipline. The Zairean procession proceeds, on the contrary, at a turtle speed, advancing only a few inches at each step, to the music of the choir and the drums. It is not exactly a dance, and this word is not used in the official text of the Zairean usage; it is a rhythmic march which consists of moving two steps forward and one step backwards, with swinging motions of the whole body. It is expected to take a long time to emphasize its importance.

The veneration and incensing of the altar is the next important moment. The *Supplement to the Missal for the Zaire Usage* reminds us that, in villages, people dance in a circle around a center. "To dance in circle means participating in the irradiating force that comes from the center. To dance around the altar expresses the will to communicate with the vital force that radiates from the altar."[19] At a bishop's mass in the Roman rite, at the offering of the gifts, the bread and wine are incensed, and also the altar, the celebrant and the assembly, but there is no mention of a vital force emanating from the altar. In the Zairean rite, the importance of the altar is communicated by being incensed a second time during the invocation of the saints and a long processional march around it. All the ministers, including the guards, participate in this procession, which also proceeds at turtle speed, not just once, but three times around the altar. This slow rhythmic march is expected to take a long time—again in order to emphasize its importance. It is doubtful that the 10 million slum dwellers of Kinshasa know the irradiating force of village dances around a circle. In church, however, they eagerly participate in the rhythmic dancing that spreads to the whole assembly. This is no dance properly speaking, only "rhythmic movements in place,"[20] which consist of swinging to the left and to the right, with bodily movements of head and limbs.

The invocation of the saints and righteous ancestors are explained in two pages in the *Supplement*, longer than any other aspect of the Zairean usage. In the actual performance, however, it only takes a couple of minutes. Here are the words spoken at St. Alphonse translated from Linguala by a seminarian:

> Mary, pray for us.
> You, the mother of God, be with us.
> St. Matthew, pray for us.
> You, the apostle of Jesus Christ, be with us.
> All the saints, pray for us.

The translator did not mention "Righteous ancestors, be with us." Apparently this twenty-year-old seminarian did not know the significance of righteous ancestors, having probably never experienced circle dancing and ancestor invocation in a traditional village. This detail suggests that some African aspects of the Zairean rite are already fading away; the liturgy cannot be written on stones.

Songs of praise follow the invocation of saints, usually by singing the Gloria, not just in a translation of its Latin text but in choral variations that can take a long time. Altogether, the Opening Celebration takes from 20 to 40 minutes.

19. Anonymous, *Supplément au Missel Romain*, 15.
20. Anonymous, *Supplément au Missel Romain*, 10.

The Liturgy of the Word

In two places, the *Supplément* mentions the importance of the palaver. Generally speaking, "the structure of the African palaver" should be integrated into the liturgy using the "African oral styles" of communication. More specifically, the liturgy of the Word should be "inspired by the structure of the African palaver" as a "dialogue leading to communion."[21] The various moments of this dialogue are the singing, the readings, the homily, the penitential act, the kiss of peace, and the universal prayers.

> The palaver is a public forum like a town hall meeting or an assembly in schools or universities where everybody is given a chance to speak up. Dialogue in any form should be part of any participatory liturgy.

Singing is the most basic form of liturgical dialogue, between the choir and the assembly, and within the choir between the male and the female voices. Litanies are dialogues. In the invocation of the saints, the name of a saint is followed by the incantation, "Pray for us" or "Be with us." This incantation of voices, supplemented by the incantation of drums, may lead the whole assembly into quasi-mystical state of mind.

The African drum is called *tam-tam*, a two-syllable word that evokes repetition and rhythm. There is usually a bass drum similar in sound to the gong that supplies the basic beat, and two or three smaller ones that provide the rhythm. Together they induce clapping in the form of "word! clap-clap-clap" or "word! word! clap-clap-clap". Thus at the beginning or middle of a song one may hear "Boboto! [clap-clap-clap]" "Bondeco! [clap-clap-clap]" "Alle! [clap-clap-clap]" "Alle—luia! [clap-clap-clap]" repeated many times. Clapping continues during the rest of the song as naturally as the beating of the tam-tam. When there is no clapping, people follow the rhythm through body movements, facial expressions, and inspirational motions of the hands. Singing is rhythm, and rhythm is prayer. This is at the core of the Zairean rite.

The readings are preceded and followed by singing. Thus on October 22, 2017, the reading of Isaiah 45:1–6 on Mission Sunday (the Lord calling Cyrus into his service) was followed by:

> Who can I send? Says the Lord.
>> Response: Send me, Lord Jesus. Send me at your service.
> You who have accepted my service, you must do it to the end of your life.
>> Send me, Lord Jesus. Send me at your service.
> Who can I send? Says the Lord.
>> Send me, Lord Jesus. Send me at your service.
> (Many repetitions of "Who can I send? Says the Lord" and the response.)

21. Anonymous, *Supplément au Missel Romain*, 16.

The multiple melodic variations of the above "Who can I send?" were of incomparable beauty, similar in power and inspiration to Russian choirs in the Orthodox sacred mysteries.

All readings are usually introduced by an explanation by the announcer, and followed by a choral response such as, "This is the word of the Lord. We accept it. We accept it." On this special Sunday, the Alleluia included the multi-part singing of, "Make us apostles, Lord. Make us your disciples!" The introduction of the gospel reading was sung, for example, "Reading of the Gospel of Matthew 22:15–21." This reading was followed by singing again, "Who can I send? Says the Lord." Response: "Send me, Lord Jesus. Send me at your service."

The homily, which usually lasts half an hour, is expected to be in the form of a dialogue. Here is an example of what the priest said one Sunday:

"Today on this Sunday of Missions, the Lord asks us this question: Who will I send? Each of us must ask these questions: Where does the Lord want to send me? What for? To do what? In his letter, St. Paul recommends that we listen at all times to the voice of the Lord. Alleluia! Amen!"

"Shalom! Shalom! The word of the Lord is our life. It is what helps us live our daily lives. Let us listen to the word of the Lord in order to be able to recognize that we are children of God."

"Pay attention! God sends us like lambs in the midst of wolves. Pay attention! Pay attention! The Lord recommends us to be attentive and wise."

The homily ended with, "Alleluia! Amen! We at the parish of St. Mary Magdalene must contribute to the mission of the church. Alleluia!" The assembly applauded.

People's attention might understandably slacken during long homilies early in the morning. Hence it is the duty of ushers and greeters at St. Alphonse to patrol the aisles and tap the shoulders of those whose heads tend to drop slightly. Only in Catholic and Buddhist monasteries does one find such zeal for everyone's active participation!

The readings and the homily can lead to a sense of sinfulness and a need for conversion. For this reason, the penitential rite is placed here, and not at the beginning of the mass as in the Roman rite. The Zairean usage sometimes employs images from the past, such as, "We are attached to sin the way animals are attached to trees in the forest," an image reminiscent of forest life in ages gone by. In the masses I have recorded, the choir repeated numerous times, "Lord, have mercy on us, have mercy," in response to the priest's invocation, "Lord, have mercy. Christ, have mercy." This refrain, repeated many times without drum, was a tantalizingly humble petition, most appropriate for a penitential admission of sin.

The visual aspect of the penitential rite is the sprinkling of holy water on the assembly by the priest. Like other Zairean rituals, this gesture is performed in grand fashion. The priest sprinkles holy water in great qualities throughout the church, and the acolytes have to bring additional buckets of water—four in all, at St. Alphonse. The profusion of water on one's face and clothes clearly brings to mind the experience of washing, cleaning, purifying, and drying—from dirt and sin—rather than the abstract doctrine of baptism received in infancy. At St. Alphonse, this penitential rite took fifteen minutes, long enough to induce reflection at the sound of continuous rhythmic singing.

The kiss of peace follows naturally as a sign of reconciliation. It finds its place here rather than after the Our Father in the Roman rite where it has no special meaning.

The Liturgy of the Eucharist

At the heart of the mass there are two important rituals, the processional offering of gifts and the Eucharistic Prayer, each lasting about half-an-hour.

At the offering of the gifts, the assembly becomes more alive. In a parish where the church was two-thirds empty during the Opening Celebration, it was now full and most people participated. The drums began to beat without music or singing, making people and the walls vibrate with rhythm. It is during the offering of gifts that programmed spontaneity may turn into unrestrained self-expression.

There is usually an offering of both money and food. At St. Alphonse, all the faithful come forward, pew after pew, to put their donation into a basket. In that church of 2,000 seats, this takes a long time, but it is filled with rhythmic singing and dancing. I had asked before coming how much I should put into the basket. My respondent, who knew I was not poor, suggested between 1,000 and 2,000 Congolese francs (between $0.75 and $1.50). Since most people are poor, the offerings are small. In the Congo as in Europe, there is a yearly church collection. The proposed offering is the value of a bottle of beer per person (less than $1.00), but I was told that this amount is often not reached.

The offering of food for the priests and the poor is a gesture of great psychological significance, besides being useful work of charity.

The offering in money goes to the diocese to pay priests, starting with the poorest parishes; those in the richer parishes may get little to nothing. Hence it is the custom to also have every Sunday a collection of food for the priests in the parish. At one mass, I saw the following items being brought forward: a bag of rice, cans of sardines, bottled water, a case of beer, coffee, and other goods. Each week it is a different basic community that is responsible for the weekly offering, each family bringing what it can afford, which can be a bunch of bananas or a sack of onions.

At this point in the liturgy, the singing and swinging become more excited. The ministers with the candle-bearers and the spear-carrying guards have moved to the back of the church to lead the procession of the gifts. At the rhythm of the tam-tam, the procession proceeds at turtle speed, each step advancing only a few inches. The choir may sing, "Receive the gifts of your children. We offer you our money: receive our gifts. You, who created heaven and earth, receive our offerings." As the procession moves forward, people start dancing more enthusiastically, moving body and limbs in wider motions. From time to time, there is an eruption of spontaneity: women make their famous sound of "o-o-o-o-o" by rapidly covering and uncovering their mouths with the hand to produce this typical sound, a custom practiced throughout Africa. As the procession reaches the sanctuary, the priest receives the bread and wine. Then a roaring applause, accompanied by an explosion of drum sounds, fills the church.

The dialogue introducing the Preface is sung by the priest in a melody that is very different from Gregorian tunes. The choir and the assembly respond in African harmony and clapping, at times with applause from the crowd. The singing of the Preface may take five minutes in melodic variations, which can be very inspirational, especially when the priest has a good singing voice. The Holy, Holy, Holy, can be particularly enthusiastic, with the women's "o-o-o-o-o" interjected several times in prolonged explosions, with some rhythmic clapping of the crowd in great excitement, in the spirit of praise and acclamation—the whole lasting over ten minutes.

The Eucharistic Prayer was sung in its entirety at St. Alphonse. It requires good preparation and voice control to be inspirational—which was the case when I visited. A pageantry of adoration suggested the importance of this sacred moment. From the time of the Holy, Holy, Holy, to the Our Father, all the ministers, acolytes, candle-holders, spear-holders, and the little ballerinas gathered in front of the altar for adoration. At the elevation, the sanctuary was silent except for the sound of a percussion instrument made from a gourd, and the tinkling of a small bell rung by an acolyte. At the proclamation of the mystery of faith, the assembly sang in one voice, "We proclaim your death and we celebrate your resurrection. Amen!" The rest of the Liturgy of the Eucharist is similar to that of the Roman rite, but the Zairean rite takes about three hours.

3. Attitudes and Emotions: Commitment and Participation

Active participation in singing, swinging, and clapping was a common characteristic of all the parishes I visited. In one mass in the Roman Rite, celebrated in French, the assembly was rather subdued, yet people applauded for three minutes after a vibrant song by the choir, and no one left church during the 12 minutes of announcements at the end of the mass. At the other extreme, when I arrived at exactly at 6:30 am at St. Alphonse for the Sunday Zairean mass, there was no seat left in the whole church, but because I was a white visitor (the only white man in the church), a greeter found me a seat in one of the front rows.

The choir sings during most of the mass, which is to say, at all times except during the readings. All singing is done from memory, which implies intense preparation because the Sunday liturgy changes every week; different choirs out the six or seven are assigned to the various Sunday masses. The choir members sing in total confidence, looking at the choirmaster only at key moments, usually facing the assembly. They rhythmically moved their hands and feet, clapping as did most people in the assembly. Their faces betrayed emotions of assurance, openness, excitement, and praise and worship. This was no routine participation out of custom or obligation.

The Zairean rite is the preferred rite in Kinshasa. Although there are masses in the Roman rite that only last about one hour, the majority of the parishioners prefer the three-hour mass at 6:30 am. At St. Alphonse, two more Zairean masses had to be scheduled by public demand, one on Saturday evening and one on Sunday evening. These are clear signs of strong commitment and participation.

4. Closeness to Others and to God

One of the goals of the Zairean rite was to promote active participation, resulting in closeness to others and to God. This goal is usually largely achieved. Individual voices of the choir may be crude, women may scream and men may blast, but together their voices create harmony. More generally, the singing and swinging brings people together into prayer. All pews fill up when people are entering, so there was no tendency as in US parishes to sit as far as possible from one another.

> Closeness to God by closing one's eyes for silent meditation is a monastic apophatic tradition. Most people prefer singing with body and soul not just the mind, as in the Zairean rite

Closeness to God in the Roman rite is often symbolized by closing one's eyes for inner prayer, alone with the Holy One, often disconnecting oneself from others. This is not the case in the Zairean rite. While the monastic tradition of the Roman rite may favor introversion in silent personal prayer, the collective dancing in place and the long processions in the central aisle and around the altar favor extraversion in loud public prayer.

Throughout the service, the announcer, the choir, and the priest exhort the faithful to seek closeness to God. A Sunday mass may typically begin interactively with: "Boboto!" Response: "Bondeco!" "Who is the Lord? Response: "Jesus!" "Who is the Savior?" Response: "Jesus!" The invocation of saints is a short repetition of "Pray for us!" and "Be with us!" On a specific Sunday, after the first reading the choir sang in the name of all, "Who can I send? says the Lord." Response: "Send me, Lord Jesus. Send me at your service." This hymn was repeated after the reading of the gospel. The homily repeated the same invitation several times, "Where does the Lord want to send me? What for? To do what?" To a certain extent, the Sunday assembly represents quite well on earth the communion of saints in the life to come.

II. Interaction Outcomes

As a document defined by the Roman decree of 1988, the Zairean usage may not seem much more than "a Latin rite with local changes in dress and song." As a liturgical practice, however, the Zairean rite is an active form of worship well superior to many Roman rite services. The preference for the three-hour mass is symbolic of people's active participation. Moreover, the choirs need to rehearse for six to eight hours every week to be able to sing local creations of lyrics and music, usually in African harmonies. How is such massive participation achieved? Interviews and field research provide some answers.

5. What We Learned about the Sense of the Faithful

The concept of *theologia prima*, the voice of the faithful inspired by faith, can explain the people's full participation in the liturgy. One major characteristic of the interviews here was their transparency and openness, which I also found among Catholic charismatics and Protestant evangelicals. By contrast, when I asked a US priest about his prayer life, he interjected. "How dare you! This is private!"

On the first day when I wanted to interview parishioners after mass, not knowing how to proceed, I turned to the first person I saw. Here are some of his answers to my questions.

"Yes I read the Bible every day, mornings and evenings. No, I am not an exception.

"Yes I belong to a basic community, to the group called the Sacred Heart of Jesus.

"Today we have just started a novena in preparation for Christmas, 'Nothing is impossible to God.'

"Yes there are several such novenas during the year. They are organized by the commission on adult education."

He then introduced me to Felix, the president of the commission on basic communities. Here are some of Felix's responses:

"We read the Bible every Thursday at our basic community meetings, and we share the Word of God. After that, we deal with social problems like health, epidemics, or family issues. This should lead us to action because we are the church in our neighborhoods.

"Yes we have read Vatican II, a lot actually. In this neighborhood you can meet people who say, 'Yesterday we did not eat.' Or, 'We haven't eaten for two days.' In my small community I may realize that the little I have, I must share it with those who have nothing.

"I come to mass every morning. For us, mass is the only time we feel joyful. When one comes back home, there may be no bread, but here everybody is happy."

For Felix, active participation in the liturgy is the extension of his active participation in the life in his neighborhood.

Let us visit a weekly community meeting. The president of this basic community has been a member for 15 years and its leader for 12. She sits in front of the small group of 15 to 20 members behind a small table with a candle and a crucifix. After an introductory prayer, she introduces the first song. One member grabs maracas for rhythm and all sing. The secretary then summarizes the content of the previous week for those who were absent. The president introduces the two themes of the day, in preparation for Christmas, "What in the heart of Jesus gives you joy? And "What in the celebration of Christmas gives you happiness?" These two themes were treated separately, each taking 20 to 30 minutes. A few people replied within seconds, without hesitation. Everybody contributed freely, without shyness, with implicit or explicit biblical references. A few times, the president invited those who had not spoken to participate, and all found something to say. She then summarized all the contributions in a spirit of unity.

Towards the end of the meeting, everyone was invited to pick up from a basket a slip of paper with a Scripture verse on it. Everyone was to read it aloud and reflect on it during the week. These verses would form the basis of the following week's meeting.

In every community there is a *balendi* whose assignment is to get to know all the families in the neighborhood and learn about their problems so that the basic community might help. At each weekly meeting, a collection is taken and the money recorded by the treasurer. Each week, a decision of social action may be taken, for instance about a mother with a newborn baby, a recent marriage, the sickness or death of a member, etc. Each time the community may make a small financial contribution. The treasurer must account for the money spent, and the secretary of the group must report on the action decided the previous week. Each basic community functions like a small parish, with a president, a secretary, and a treasurer, all united in prayer and social action.

I left the meeting with the feeling of wanting to come back because of the warm family spirit where everyone felt comfortable and accepted. There was great love of God expressed during sharing and prayer. All expressed a deep personal relationship with Jesus Christ and familiarity with Scripture. Truly these neighborhood communities are the basic units of the church, and the parish is a community of communities, making the Sunday liturgy an expression of their life in faith.

6. Patterns of Relationship and Church Structures

The church model that prevails here is one of discipleship. Such a description, however, is incomplete. Ecclesiology describes theoretical models for theological reflection rather than church practices. The Vatican II ecclesiology of "people of God" and "communion" had little practical effect because only the pope can change church structures. This is not the case at the diocesan and parish levels where bishops and pastors can change some structures. We must therefore look at church polity rather than ecclesiology, which is also the way things work in Protestant churches.

The polity of the Bayville church is denominationalism since this church recognizes no authority beyond itself. At the church of the Resurrection, the social relations are based on consensus and equality, but there is no central authority to offer guidance for growth and conflict resolution. Its church structure is a form of denominationalism. The parishes of Holy Family and St. Benedict, by contrast, follow the prevailing structure of hierarchical organization. The parishes of the Congo follow neither; they have an original structure that is found nowhere else in the Catholic Church.

Here the top and bottom are linked, as shown in the chart on page 182. At one end, the meetings of basic communities must follow the guidelines coming from

> Neither hierarchical nor denominational, the Zairean parishes link the top to the bottom and vice versa.

above because they are the official cells of the church, not independent devotional groups. At the other end, the archdiocesan pastoral center is not just a clerical structure since most of its members are laypeople and there is constant dialogue between top and bottom. Conflict may arise between these two poles, especially between the pastor and parish council, but there are norms for conflict resolution.

"This is our parish," a new pastor creating conflict was told. "The food you eat, it is we who give it to you. The parish house you live in, it is we who built it. If you want to impose your ideas, there will be no more offerings." The speaker then reminded me that smartphones can go into quick action for nearly immediate effect. Moreover, the parish council can write to the archbishop who will act as mediator and not as the ultimate power. Conflict resolution must lead to peace. In this parish, a previous conflict led to the removal of the pastor, and then peace returned. This is a new polity, one based neither on ideology nor power but on dialogue and mutual listening.

7. & 8. Moral Consensus & Spiritual and Emotional Energy

In any society, consensus depends on the common values created by the similarity of education, wealth, and social class, but in religion, the consensus should also be built on closeness to God, that is, on spirituality. This is the case in the parishes described above.

Biblical texts can be explained historically, critically, and theologically, as is done in many homilies. These explanations tend to be general and impersonal, and they are often unsatisfactory because ultimately Scripture must be appropriated, that is, understood in a personal way as in a personal relationship. Appropriated biblical texts can only be shared in personal testimonies, not in discussions or lectures. It is this understanding of Scripture that I found in small groups and in interviews—but often not in homilies.

> Scripture must be appropriated by believers in a personal encounter with the texts. Liturgical scripts must similarly be appropriated by the local communities.

The liturgical ritual can also be appropriated and not merely executed literally and faithfully. The church of Congo-Kinshasa has appropriated the Zairean usage. Although the conference of Catholic bishops of Congo mandated the adoption of the Zairean usage in the whole country, only three bishops in the 48 dioceses have appropriated it. The reason seems obvious. The demands on the choirs are enormous: in two parishes of about 1,500 members there are seven choirs rehearsing for two and a half hours on Mondays, Wednesdays, and Fridays. The demands on the celebrant are also great: he must create active participation through numerous calls for dialogue, and not every priest is ready for such a task. The archbishop of Kinshasa does not celebrate mass in the Zairean rite; the Roman rite takes a third of the time.

The conference of Catholic bishops in Congo has also mandated the adoption of neighborhood communities, but only in the archdiocese of Kinshasa are the basic communities the official smallest units of the church. To be effective, the whole diocesan structure must be reorganized and the clergy reeducated for it, so that top and bottom can be in constant mutual communication. The 47 other dioceses may have neighborhood devotional groups, but if left to themselves, these tend to wither away over time.

Not only Scripture but also the official liturgy must be appropriated. This is the message of the church in Kinshasa. When Scripture and the liturgical text are appropriated, they become a source of creativity.

Conclusion: From Appropriation
to Creative Imagination

This chapter wanted to address the tension between creativity and authority. At one end of this continuum, in the case of literal performances of rituals, there is no tension because there is no creativity. When a community truly appropriates the spirit of its rituals, the tension will be resolved creatively. This is actually the case with numerous mass celebrations in vibrant parishes, in the semi-private masses of intentional communities, and the official and sometimes grandiose masses in Paris, Rome, Bethlehem on Christmas Day, and Nazareth on the Feast of the Annunciation. Yes, there is worship creativity in vibrant parishes all over the world, but they are a small minority.

Over time, weekly performance of the liturgy may lead to routinization, boredom, and even a feeling of estrangement on the part of the public. Then, for lack of continued creativity, attendance declines, sometimes on a massive scale. This is the situation of many, and perhaps even most, parishes in the West today.

Prosper of Aquitaine, writing around the time of Augustine, was the first to sense a tension between public prayer and official beliefs. For him, the spiritual practices of Scripture reading and liturgical worship were at the heart of faith. This position is not very practical for church administrators. For them, it is more efficient to have church authorities define the norms for both beliefs and rituals. This was the position of Pius XII in his statement, "Let the rule of belief determine the rule of prayer," in which case it is Rome that defines both rules. This policy has come to a dead end today.

Kavanagh saw that the language of faith, the *theologia prima* of the *fides fidelium*, is different from the academic theology that has prevailed since the time of scholastic theology in the Middle Ages. The popular piety of South

America and elsewhere is an example of the *theologia prima*, and it is valued
as such in the Latin American bishops' document of *Aparecida* (2007), and in
Pope Francis's *Joy of the Gospel* (2013), but this has not been the case in the
past. It is still a common mistake today to interpret people's faith through the
categories of church doctrine. When finding not much agreement between
the two, theologians adopt the position of Pius XII. They allow doctrine to
dictate faith, that is, to define and impose what people ought to believe. When
this happens, faith is muted in the hearts of many.

Tocqueville made an important contribution to this debate. In aristocratic societies, the elites "entertain a sublime conception of the duties of
man," encouraging people to do "glorious things . . . without self-interest, as
God himself does." The Catholic Church as an aristocratic clerical society
emphasizes the sublime conception of submission for the harmony of the
institution. This model, still viable at the time of Pius XII, is obsolete today.
In democratic societies, there must be some idea of a common good that
can appeal to the majority. The Second Vatican Council operated according
to this second model, which was also followed in the years immediately
after the council. Then the magisterium, tentatively under Pope Paul VI and
aggressively under John Paul II and Benedict VI, turned the clock back to
the pre-Vatican II era.

In the economic language commonly used in the sociology of religion,
there must be a balance between the supply and the demand. Such a balance
is achieved in both the Zairean rite and the church structures of the archdiocese of Kinshasa. But how can such a balance be reached more generally?

This chapter and the previous one suggest three routes, all requiring
creative imagination.

First, one may take alone the road of reform, as Fr. Pfleger of St. Sabina
has done. He violates numerous church rules, but he has never been told to
return to standard practices the way audacious theologians are told when
they supposedly exceeded the limits of orthodoxy. But a lonely prophet has
seldom a successor. When Fr. Pfleger retires, his achievements may fade
away for lack of institutionalization.

Alternatively, one can seek change through the proper channels, as
did the Congolese bishops for the Zairean rite. This road is long, tortuous,
and usually leads to paltry results, but it has the outstanding advantage of
being available to future generations. Innovations that are not institutionalized ultimately fade away, which is often what happens to the work of
lone innovators.

Another option is to be creative in areas that are not subject to canon
law. This is the achievement of Cardinal Malula in his redesigning of the
diocesan structure. He had the wisdom to propose a common good that

was attractive to the majority of his contemporaries, and to institutionalize his model into a multi-layered structure linking top to bottom and bottom to top.

This latter option holds the most promise for Catholicism today. Most of the innovations in the Zairean liturgy could have been introduced without permission because, to a certain extent, none was needed. Some church documents frown on dancing, but there is no dancing in this liturgy, only rhythmic processional marches and rhythmic movement in place. Nothing prohibits the recitation of a local litany to which would be added the unthreatening words, "Holy forefathers and righteous ancestors, pray for us." Nothing prohibits singing songs of praise that paraphrase the liturgical Gloria. It can be said, therefore, that the Zairean Opening Celebration required no special permission, even if Rome would have been displeased by such innovations. Nothing prohibits the processional presentation of gifts, or the sprinkling of the assembly with buckets of holy water. As to the moving of the Our Father from one place in the mass to another, one might have asked for permission *ex post facto*—which then could hardly have been denied. In short, the great achievement of the Zairean reform is not so much the liturgical innovations but the innovative spirit that pervades its appropriation of Scripture and ritual.

Taken as an example of what can be done and how to do it, the Zairean rite is a model that any local church can follow by adapting it to its own culture. In this sense, it is also a gift to the entire Catholic community.

10

Method and Vision in Worship Analysis

From Social Drama to Mystagogy

MANY INSTITUTIONS AND ORGANIZATIONS undergo periodic self-evaluation. Schools and universities are evaluated in order to certify their educational quality. Many business and non-profits use self-evaluations in order to improve efficiency, profitability, and quality of services. Isn't it time for congregations and parishes to examine their worship services, and by implication, other services as well? Neither people nor the churches benefit from public prayers that do not bring them closer to God and to one another year after year.

Parish self-evaluation could be a three-step process. The first would engage staff members and key parishioners in a process of reflection, for example about the positives and the negatives of parish life. The second step might concentrate on worship, following the eight points of the Collins's model, raising questions about the issues of closeness to others and to God, people's attitudes and emotions, the relationships between church leaders and members, the ecclesiology of the parish, the prevailing spirituality, and community consensus. The third step might entail a review of parish life in its various functions: worship, education, outreach, etc. in order to improve worship. These various functions are interrelated, and all affect worship. In order to bring the evaluation to a closure, an outsider could be invited to synthesize the findings. At the end, decisions will need to be made and plans for improvement implemented.

Returning to the main focus of this book, the social drama of the worshiping community, let us look in greater detail at two issues that are basic for worship analysis, namely, the methodology of observations and the importance of theory in the analysis. Methodology and theory should lead to uncovering the social dynamics at work in a given church.

I. The Methodology of Worship Analysis

In 2017 the magazine *Commonweal* commissioned twelve individuals, mostly members of its staff and academics, to report on one parish mass of their choice on an ordinary Sunday. The results were published in the issue of September 22, 1017. They will enable us to raise questions of methodology.

Any quantitative analysis needs to face two basic methodological issues, namely reliability and validity. An observation is considered reliable when repeated observations yield the same results. In this regard, the Sunday mass observations made for *Commonweal* failed because only one Sunday mass was observed by each reporter; it is likely that a second observation at a different time would have yielded different results. How often should one attend a liturgy for the purpose of worship analysis? I would suggest attending until one finds nothing new of importance. In this study I usually attended around ten times because I wanted to make sure that I did not miss an important observation.

Descriptions need to be reliable which can be achieved through repeated observations. In addition, analyses need to be valid, which is more difficult to prove. Observations are often open to various interpretations, and all are somewhat subjective. A valid interpretation is one that makes a significant contribution to our understanding of the observed data, that is, one based on solid sociological, philosophical, theological, or ritual theories which shed light on the findings. There was no theory of any kind behind the observations of the Sunday masses published by *Commonweal*. They were merely descriptive, but then what was the point of their research?

With regard to the method used to analyze worship, I selected Collins's eight-point model, but other models could be as good or even better in certain cases. Without a methodological model, there can be no consistent way to describe and interpret worship in different churches and religions. Moreover, a standardized methodological model allows other researchers to verify, critique, and support one's findings. Then research becomes cumulative.

A clear methodology allows one to observe rituals in a consistent manner. In the case of liturgies, the analysis should include observations about the presider or celebrant, the assembly, the choir, and the homilist. In *Commonweal* some articles mentioned the singing but not the homily, and others emphasized the role of the priest but gave little attention to the assembly. In the Collins model, physical closeness among participants, and spiritual closeness to others and to God (as evidenced by body language, facial expressions, and

> A methodology must be reliable through multiple observations. It must also be valid in light of well-known theories.

ritual gestures) are very important, as are the participants' attitudes and emotions such as enthusiasm or boredom, engagement or estrangement. Observations about closeness and emotions are significant components in the analysis of community relations, ecclesiology, and moral consensus. A good ritual analysis must also include interviews with the pastor and key parishioners. In short, worship analysis requires a methodology leading to reliable observations and valid interpretations, but much more is needed.

The purpose of a good methodology is to serve the goals of a study, in our case, to uncover the dynamics at work in the congregation and its worship. The ideal finding would be the discovery of very few or even a single factor (e.g., ritualism, low expectations, internal conflicts, conformism, etc.) that explains much of the limitations of the worship experience. But more should be expected: worship is not only a social gathering; it is also expected to be a mystagogical experience.

II. The Importance of Mystagogy and Vision

There is a qualitative difference between TV masses recorded in the Boston studios of CatholicTV and the three-hour Zairean masses in Congo. The difference is not just in the length of worship, the quality of the singing, and the enthusiastic participation of the assembly. There seems to be a difference in mystagogy. To suggest this difference I have used the term "mass" in my analysis of the TV masses, the pontifical masses, the papal masses, and the traditional Catholic worship at Holy Family Parish and St. Benedict parish. In contrast, I have used the term "eucharistic celebration" when referring to Sunday worship at the church of the Resurrection, in the St. Sabina Community, and in the Zairean rite. There these services were more elaborate, the participants more engaged, and the rituals more celebratory. Most importantly, there are theological differences between the two and a different attitude towards the sacred.

Sacredness at TV masses seems limited to the very performance of the rituals, as little or no effort is made to evoke sacredness through sound and vision. Their sacredness is in the institution, in what Bonhoeffer called "religion." Sacredness is expected to be the automatic result of the ritual performance, which may lead to ritualism, that is, the attitude that sacredness resides in the performance. Quite different is mystagogy, which tries to evoke mystery beyond the mere performance. The prophet Elijah found that God is not in earthquakes and fire, and not even in the gentle breeze of the Sinai (1 Kings 19:11). For very few people, however, can exceptional circumstances like earthquakes and stormy fires be mystagogical experiences, as was the case for young Luther frightened by a sudden storm. For the majority it is art, music, rhythm, dance, motions, chanting, expressive readings, evocative rituals, and enlightening homilies that can invoke and evoke mystery. The high points of worship were the consecration in traditional masses, the recitation of Our Father in many parishes, the kiss of peace at Resurrection, and the prophetic utterances at the Bayville church. Of course, "mystagogy" in early Christianity referred to the catechetical teachings about the mysteries of faith, but today much more than catechism is expected. In this work I have used "mystagogy" in reference to the subjective experience of mystery in worship. For our contemporaries the experience of the divine is the very purpose of religion and worship. Hence special attention must be given to it in worship analysis.

Mystagogy is different in the apophatic and the kataphatic forms of worship. Judaism and Islam prohibit images of the divine (the apophatic tradition) while Hinduism and baroque Catholicism exult in forms and colors in the kataphatic tradition of worship. The two traditions cohabit within Catholicism: the monastic orders like the Trappist order reject all ornaments, while pontifical and papal liturgies favor courtly pomp. The pre-Vatican II liturgy combined the two traditions every Sunday, scheduling an early morning low mass in silence and a high mass with incense and music later in the morning. Reverential silence during mass may still be the favorite attitude among old-timers, while the smartphone generation expects rhythm and drama.

> A liturgy must be mystagogical, if not it may appear as a mechanical production. Yet there are many forms of mystagogy, even in simple rituals.

Mystagogy can also be found in the material aspects of worship: the architecture, interior design, ornaments, statues, music, singing, and processions. I have mentioned some of these in the course of my presentations of the various liturgies. Let us turn to the role of various participants to suggest how their performance may evoke sacredness. I will review the role of the presider as mystagogue, the choir as inspirational and festive, the assembly as mystical, and the homilist as visionary.

The Presider as Mystagogue

Ordination to the priesthood requires at least six years of seminary training, but the celebration of the mass only requires the ability to recite the liturgical prayers from the missal. Any professional actor could do that. There is no visible difference between a TV mass celebrated in front of cameras in a chapel-studio in Boston and a fake mass recorded in Hollywood as part of a movie. There are, however, two possible differences; one is based on faith and the other on performance. For believers, the priest is more than an actor; and at mass the consecrated bread is more than its appearance. Secondly, while an actor playing the role of a priest is merely roleplaying, a priest may try to convey, through words, demeanor, and tone of voice something more than roleplaying, namely mystagogy. An actor only plays a role before a camera, while a minister should endeavor to lead his or her congregation into prayer and the experience of sacredness. The actor performs a drama, but the priest evokes mystery.

In the Zairean rite, the presider can accurately be called the celebrant because one of his main functions is to help the faithful become more aware of the mysteries that are being celebrated in the ritual. He does so through controlled improvisation, interjecting known phrases calling for equally known responses. In the examples cited in the previous chapter, some of the mysteries celebrated were God's peace, the Lordship of Christ, the vocation of responding to God's call, and doing God's will. Controlled improvisation can easily be learned, but in practice it requires effort and imagination. If too controlled, it can turn into ritualism, and if too uncontrolled it may generate uncontrolled emotionalism. Most importantly, it requires the appropriation of the meaning of the liturgical prayers and the scriptural readings, because the priest can only share the enthusiasm he has personally found in his understanding of God's mysteries.

According to the official *Supplément*, the "full and active participation" of the faithful in the liturgy will be achieved through "the integration of cultural elements inspired by . . . local traditions."[1] In the Zairean rite, these cultural elements are the arrival of the tribal leader, the palaver, and the spiritual force that emanates from the altar. These elements can have significant mystagogical value for the celebrant and the participants, but its value depends on availability and active participation. Thus, Congolese Catholics outside the archdiocese of Kinshasa where the Zairean rite is not practiced can see these celebrations as primitive and tribal, perhaps even as folklore. For the participants in the liturgical practices in Kinshasa, however, this is not the case when they actively participate in the singing as will be seen below.

The Choir as Inspirational, Supportive, and Festive

As described in the first chapter, there are three primary functions of music in Christian worship. It can be celebratory, as on feast days and weddings. The music can also be inspirational when it elevates the mind and arouses a transcendent sense of beauty. Finally, instrumental music and choir singing

1. Anonymous, *Supplément au Missel Romain*, 9.

can be supportive when they foster the participation of the assembly. In TV masses, the music, like the stained glass windows of the chapel, is extraneous to the liturgy. There the singing is off-screen and the organ music is equivalent to the background music played in department stores: it fills the pervading silence. At the Cathedral of Notre Dame of Paris, on the other hand, there is a near perfect integration of music, choir singing, song leadership, and participation of the faithful. This integration is the result of an effort to integrate faith and culture by the archbishop, the school of sacred music, the rector of the cathedral, and the choir director.

In the Zairean rite, this integration goes even further because most of the pieces sung by the choir are original Linguala creations set to Congolese melodies and African harmonies. In addition, there is an obvious integration of art and spirituality. "I joined the choir six years ago," said one member, "because I promised the Lord to work for him. This is the only way I can give him my life, by singing. For me singing is my prayer; it is my offering." There is also an integration of individual and community life. In one parish of 1,500 members there are seven choirs with about 40 members each, and they rehearse three times each week. Having memorized the lyrics and the music, members of the choir are able to sing from the heart, as a prayer rather than a performance.

The Assembly in Mystical Participation

What prompts people to participate in worship is a complex question. In many places, the choir director or a song leader is responsible for getting the people to participate, and in some places, this is the song leader's main function. The Cathedral of Notre Dame has excellent song leaders who actively engage the assembly. In most American parishes, on the other hand, these leaders perform rather poorly, for they simply raise both arms as an encouragement for parishioners to sing. In the papal masses at St. Peter's, there is no song leader, so it is not surprising that nobody sings. In Paris, the cathedral rector seems to have an advisory role in the coordination of the various functions of the liturgy. In the Zairean rite, most people participate, but strangely there is no song leader. In Kinshasa as in Rome, the choir director only directs the choir, not the assembly, and yet in Kinshasa the assembly participates, if not by singing, then by clapping and swinging.

There is no song leader at St. Sabina, either, but there is "flow" in both music and inspiration. Flow is necessary in any jazz performance because all instruments must at all times follow the lead musician. At St. Sabina, the choir follows the lead of the music director, who himself follows the lead of the pastor. There, flow refers to the coordination between all participants, which is necessary when the same phrase is repeated many times, depending on the inspiration of the music director. At St. Sabina, Fr. Pfleger has a somewhat advisory role, bringing all of the participants into harmony.

Rhythm seems an inborn quality in some people, especially in the global South. In the Congo, even in small groups at weekly meetings, someone may reach for maracas or beat the rhythm when they are singing together. Thus, although rhythm plays a strong role in the Zairean rite, it is a cultural phenomenon found in many parts of sub-Saharan Africa.

The Zairean rite lasts three hours, which is not a deterrent for most parishioners. Indeed, other Congolese Christians also meet and sing for three hours at a time, and often several times a week. Hence the success of the Zairean rite cannot be attributed mainly to the quality of the choir or to the religiosity of the parishioners. As Tocqueville might have put it, there must be a social contract between a leader and the people in the name of a common good. Cardinal Malula defined the common good as Africanization—both the Africanization of Catholic worship and the Africanization of the local church into a community of communities. It is in this collective contract that the choir and the assembly find both their active role, and all are eager to participate. A collective contract can be something mystical that is implicitly shared by all.

The Homily as Dream and Vision

Churches where preaching is the central focus of worship grow or decline depending on the talent of their preachers. The megachurches of Willow Creek and Saddleback have grown to their present levels thanks mainly to effective preaching. Politicians and preachers are seen as outstanding when they have a vision, not just oratory talent. They need to propose, in Tocqueville's terms, a vision of the common good that is acceptable to their followers.

Few world leaders have been more outstanding on a world scale than Mahatma Gandhi, Nelson Mandela, and Martin Luther King Jr., whose "I Have a Dream" speech still reverberates in many people's hearts today. Arguably every Sunday sermon or homily should create a vision in the mind of those who hear it, as it is God's dream to reconcile all things in Christ, or Jesus's dream to bring forth the kingdom of God on earth.

Fr. Pfleger's homilies describe his dream for social justice in the parish neighborhood. They are emotional processes that may take up to an hour in order to communicate to the audience this inner vision. Fr. Pfleger has appropriated both the language of his black audience, with their special grammar and pronunciation, and the language of Scripture, which he paraphrases freely. He likes to tell biblical stories, especially the stories of Jesus healing the sick. His prepared improvisations are in the oral style of interactions with the audience, and he uses body language to dramatize his message. He may sit or lie on the floor of the sanctuary, or walk to individuals in the pews and address them personally. Although a man of great talent, he learned to preach by listening to black preachers in their churches, and he learned about biblical interpretation by having a black Protestant minister teach Bible classes in his parish. Although he can easily improvise, he spends an hour every morning listening to God's dream for humanity while reading the Scriptures. Fr. Pfleger seems charismatic, but he has learned and cultivated his charisma for a lifetime.

The size of the Bayville church is that of an average Catholic parish, but it has ten full-time paid ministers, about 40 unpaid deacons, and about 80 lay ministries. In this well-organized community, Pastor Orlando has created the structure he needed to be a successful preacher. He takes off a day in order to prepare his Sunday sermon. The following day, in a meeting with the assistant pastors, his sermon is taken as the basis for the Sunday worship. Nothing is left to improvisation. Technicians will project on a screen at the appropriate time the biblical quotations of the sermon and the lyrics of the songs. Sermons may develop a theme over several weeks or months. All Sunday services are recorded, and they are available on CDs only minutes after the recording. All of the pastor's sermons are available on the Internet.

Pastor Orlando's sermons are so well prepared that they seem effortless conversations with the audience. He walks around the pulpit, using body language, hand movements, and props to make a point. He is relaxed and friendly, which makes the audience all the more receptive. His sermons are called messages, which in a Pentecostal environment is tantamount to divine oracles or prophecies. They usually develop a single point that can easily be remembered throughout the week and beyond. Like Pfleger, Orlando has a dream for his church, although it is a different one, namely, God's salvation through Jesus as revealed in the Bible.

In conclusion, we can say that visionary preaching leads to spiritual development and church growth. This is not something that is found in most Catholic parishes, including the ones visited for this study. Their homilies are too short to develop a vision and have an emotional impact on the listeners. There is no evidence of the intense preparation that is needed if preaching is to make a difference in people's lives. What can God communicate in a three-and-a half-minute (or even a ten-minute) homily that seems more improvisation than preparation? Preaching must be mystagogical which requires both preparation and improvisation.

Conclusion: Mystagogy for Spiritual Growth

We have now moved way beyond the level of observation and analysis for the purpose of understanding the social drama of a given church. Such an undertaking was necessary but ultimately what is needed is mystagogy and spiritual growth.

All churches wish for the spiritual growth of their members, but most do little to foster it. They are like parents wishing for the intellectual and moral growth of their children but who do not know how to provide it. Catholic parishes seem to rely on the traditional theology according to which the sacraments are automatically effective, and few bother to check if this is actually the case. Some Catholic pastors consider personal devotions to be private affairs, like at the parishes of Holy Family and St. Benedict. The Notre Dame Cathedral in Paris has no devotional groups. Resurrection has no Bible study program, although it encourages people to get involved in many of its ministries. St. Sabina has a weekly Scripture class that is well attended and offers many opportunities for social action. The Bayville church offers five to ten Bible classes every semester, each thirteen weeks long, which allows for in-depth study. The classes on the Bible and on family life attract over hundred people each, and personal Bible reading is emphasized, as it is in all evangelical churches.

In Kinshasa, faith development involves both basic communities and devotional groups. Committed parishioners are invited to participate in both. The program of reflections in the basic communities encourages constant dialogue between the top and the bottom of the archdiocesan structure. At Bayville, the volunteers who teach courses are chosen from among the 3,000 members of the church, but in Kinshasa, the members of the archdiocesan pastoral center are chosen from among millions in the diocese. The themes for reflection in the basic communities vary, sometimes focusing on the liturgical calendar, at other times on a special biblical reading, and at other times on political, social, economic, or family problems. One reason the basic communities are attractive is because they deal with everyday issues. They promote not only spiritual growth but also development from one stage of faith to the next, for example, by helping people grow out of biblical literalism and overcome the close-mindedness of social tribalism.

A relatively new term has found its way into chanceries and parishes, that of pastoral planning. Most parishes do not seem to have any plan, except on paper. Pastoral planning should embody a vision, a dream that reflects God's grand design for humankind. Worship analysis offers one opportunity to review the pastoral plan of a parish.

To do worship analysis properly, a good theoretical model is needed. In this study, we used the eight-step model proposed by Collins. There are other ways to examine social interactions in worship and parish ministries, but worship analysis must include mystagogy if it is to promote growth. This was the purpose of this book.

Bibliography

Abbott, Walter M., ed. *The documents of Vatican II*. New York: Guild, 1966.

Anonymous. *Catechism of the Catholic Church*. San Francisco: Ignatius, 1994.

―――. *Supplément au Missel Romain pour les dioceses du Zaire*. Kinshasa: Editions du Secrétariat Général, 1989.

Blumer, Herbert. *Symbolic Interactionism: Perspective and Method*. Englewood Cliffs, NJ: Prentice-Hall, 1969.

Bradshaw, Paul, and John Melloh. *Foundations in Ritual Studies. A Reader for Students of Christian Worship*. Grand Rapids, MI: Baker Academic, 2007.

Brown, David. *God and Enchantment of Place: Reclaiming Human Experience*. Oxford: Oxford University Press, 2006.

―――. *Tradition and Imagination: Revelation and Change*. Oxford: Oxford University Press, 1999.

Brown, Keith. "Interaction Ritual Chains and the Mobilization of Conscientious Consumers." *Qualitative Sociology* 34.1 (2011) 121–41.

Castelli, Jim, and Joseph Gremillion. *The Emerging Parish: The Notre Dame Study of Catholic Life Since Vatican II*. San Francisco: Harper & Row, 1987.

Chase, Nathan Peter. "A History and Analysis of the Missel Romain pour les Diocese du Zaire." School of Theology and Seminary Graduate Papers/Theses 1376 (2013). http://digitalcommons.csbsju.edu/sot_papers/1376.

Chauvet, Louis-Marie. *The Sacraments: The Word of God at the Mercy of the Body*. Collegeville, MN: Liturgical, 2001.

Collins, Randall. *Interaction Ritual Chains*. Princeton: Princeton University Press, 2004.

Congregation for Divine Worship and the Discipline of the Sacraments. "*Redemptionis Sacramentu:* On certain matters to be observed or to be avoided regarding the Most Holy Eucharist." http://www.vatican.va/roman_curia/congregations/ccdds/documents/rc_con_ccdds_doc_20040423_redemptionis-sacramentum_en.html.

Draper, Scott. "Effervescence and Solidarity in Religious Organizations." *Journal for the Scientific Study of Religion* 53.2 (2014) 229–48.

Dulles, Avery. *Models of the Church*. Garden City, NY: Doubleday, 1978.

Durkheim, Emile. *Elementary Forms of Religious Life*. Translated by Ward Swain. Mineola, NY: Dover, 2008.

Egbulem, Nwaka Chris. *The Power of Africentric Celebrations: Inspirations from the Zairean Liturgy*. New York: Crossroad, 1996.

Erickson, Rebecca J. "Review Essays on Randall Collins's Interaction Ritual Chains." *Contemporary Sociology: A Journal of Reviews* 36.3 (2007) 215–8.

Fowler, James W. *Stages of Faith: The Psychology of Human Development and the Quest for Meaning*. San Francisco: Harper & Row, 1981.

Francis. *The Joy of the Gospel*. https://w2.vatican.va/content/francesco/en/apost_ exhortations/documents/papa-francesco_esortazione-ap_20131124_evangelii-gaudium.html.

Francis, Leslie J., et al. "What Helps Christians Grow? An Exploratory Study Distinguishing Among Four Distinctive Pathways." Paper presented at the annual conference of the Society for the Scientific Study of Religion. Atlanta, 2016.

Gerhards, Albert, and Benedikt Kranemann. *Introduction to the Study of Liturgy*. Collegeville, MN: Liturgical, 2017.

Glock, Charles Y., and Rodney Stark. *Religion and Society in Tension*. Chicago: Rand McNally, 1965.

Goffman, Erving. *Asylums: Essays on the social situation of mental patients and other inmates*. Garden City, NY: Doubleday, 1962.

———. *The Presentation of Self in Everyday Life*. Garden City, NY: Doubleday, 1959.

Haskell, David Millard, et al. "Theology Matters: Comparing the Traits of Growing and Declining Mainline Protestant Church Attendees and Clergy." *Review of Religious Research* 58.4 (2016) 515–41.

Hawkins, Greg L., and Cally Parkinson. *Reveal: Where are you?* Barrington, IL: Willow Creek Resources, 2007.

———. *Move: What 1,000 Churches Reveal About Spiritual Growth*. Grand Rapids, MI: Zondervan, 2011.

Hegy, Pierre. *Lay Spirituality: From Traditional to Postmodern*. Eugene, OR: Wipf & Stock, 2017.

———. *Wake Up, Lazarus!: Paths to Catholic Renewal, Volume 2*. Bloomington, IN: iUniverse, 2013.

Kavanagh, Aidan. *On Liturgical Theology*. New York: Pueblo, 1984.

King, Morton B., and Richard A. Hunt. "Measuring the Religious Variable: Replication." *Journal for the Scientific Study of Religion* 14.1 (1972) 240–51.

Lubac, Henri de. *Catholicism: a Study of Dogma in Relation to the Corporate Destiny of Mankind*. London: Darton, Longman & Todd, 1950.

McClory, Robert. *Radical Disciple: Father Pfleger, St. Sabina Church, and the Fight for Social Justice*. Chicago: Lawrence Hill, 2010.

McGann, Mary E. *Let it Shine: The Emergence of African American Catholic Worship*. New York: Fordham University Press, 2008.

Mead, George H. *Mind, Self, and Society from the Standpoint of a Social Behaviorist*. Chicago: University of Chicago Press, 1969.

Moerschbacher, Marco. *Les laics dans une Eglise d'Afrique: L'oeuvre du Cardinal Malula (1917–1989)*. Paris: Karthala, 2012.

Moseley, Romney M., et al. *Manual for Faith Development Research*. Atlanta, GA: Emory University Press, 1986.

Niebuhr, Richard. *Christ and Culture*. New York: Harper & Row, 1951.

Olson, Roger E. "A Postconservative Evangelical Response." In *Four Views on the Spectrum of Evangelicalism*, edited by Kevin Bauder, R. Albert Mohler Jr., John G. Stackhouse Jr., and Roger E. Olson. Grand Rapids, MI: Zondervan, 2011.

Ong, Walter J. *Orality and Literacy*. New York: Routledge. 2002.

Parkinson, Cally, and Nancy Scammacca Lewis. *Rise: Bold Strategies to Reform Your Church*. Colorado Springs, CO: NavPress, 2015.

Pius XII. *Mediator Dei. Encyclical of Pope Pius XII on the Sacred Liturgy.* http://w2.vatican.va/content/pius-xii/en/encyclicals/documents/hf_pii_enc_20111947_mediator-dei.html.

Schillebeeckx, Edward. *Christ the Sacrament of the Encounter with God.* New York: Sheed and Ward, 1963.

Schutz, Alfred. *On Phenomenology and Social Relations.* Edited by Helmut R. Wagner. Chicago: University of Chicago Press, 1973.

Stark, Rodney, and Charles Glock. *American Piety: The Nature of Religious Commitment.* Berkeley, CA: University of California Press, 1968.

Stringer, Martin D. *A Sociological History of Christian Worship.* Cambridge, UK: Cambridge University Press, 2005.

Tocqueville, Alexis de. *Democracy in America.* Translated by George Lawrence. Edited by J. P. Mayer. Garden City, NY: Doubleday, 1969.

Turner, Victor. *The Ritual Process: Structure and Anti-Structure.* Chicago: Aldine, 1969.

US Conference of Catholic Bishops. "Built of Living Stones: Art, Architecture, and Worship." http://www.sfdslg.org/Church/Documents/ChurchReno/Built%20of%20Living%20Stones.pdf.

Wainwright Geoffrey, and Karen H. Westerfield Tucker, eds. *Oxford History of Christian Worship.* Oxford University Press, 2006.

Warner, Stephen. "2007 Presidential Address: Singing and Solidarity." *Journal for the Scientific Study of Religion.* 47.2 (2008) 175–90.

Warren, Rick. *The Purpose-Driven Church: Growth without Compromising Your Message & Mission.* Grand Rapids, MI: Zondervan, 1995.

White, James. *Roman Catholic Worship since Trent.* Collegeville, MN: Liturgical, 2003.

Winseman, Albert L. "Congregational Engagement Ascends: Percentage of Engaged Members Highest since 2001." *Religion and Social Trends.* https://news.gallup.com/poll/14950/congregational-engagement-ascends.aspx.

Wollschleger, Jason. "Interaction Ritual Chains and Religious Participation." *Sociological Forum* 27.4 (2012) 896–912.

Zech, Charles E., et al. *Catholic Parishes of the 21st Century.* New York: Oxford University Press, 2017.

Index by Chapter

Index of Subjects